Liars! Cheaters! Evildoers!

Liars! Cheaters! Evildoers!

*Demonization and the End of
Civil Debate in American Politics*

Tom De Luca and John Buell

NEW YORK UNIVERSITY PRESS
New York and London

NEW YORK UNIVERSITY PRESS
New York and London
www.nyupress.org

© 2005 by New York University

Library of Congress Cataloging-in-Publication Data
DeLuca, Tom, 1946-
Liars! cheaters! evildoers! : demonization and the end
of civil debate in American politics / Tom De Luca and John Buell.
p. cm.
Includes bibliographical references and index.
ISBN-10: 0-8147-1974-0 (cloth : alk. paper)
ISBN-13: 978-0-8147-1974-9 (cloth : alk. paper)
ISBN-10: 0-8147-1975-9 (pbk. : alk. paper)
ISBN-13: 978-0-8147-1975-6 (pbk. : alk. paper)
1. Communication in politics—United States.
2. Political culture—United States. 3. Rhetoric—Political aspects—
United States. 4. United States—Politics and government—Moral
and ethical aspects. 5. Social ethics—United States.
I. Buell, John. II. Title.
JA85.2.U6D45   2005
306.2'0973—dc22   2005007344

New York University Press books are printed on acid-free paper,
and their binding materials are chosen for strength and durability.

Manufactured in the United States of America
c 10 9 8 7 6 5 4 3 2 1
p 10 9 8 7 6 5 4 3 2 1

To my mother Katherine J. De Luca,
the fairest person I have ever known.

To the Victims of September 11, 2001,
we write in your memory.

Contents

Acknowledgments

We began our book on the politics of demonization in the midst of the media frenzy over the Clinton scandals. As political vitriol became more toxic, culminating in the Clinton impeachment, we had to think and rethink our ideas. A year spent by De Luca teaching in China, from 1999 to 2000, U.S.-Chinese confrontation shortly thereafter in 2001, the absolute horror of 9/11 in De Luca's beloved New York, the threat of further terrorism and our war against it, and the war in Iraq as an illicit extension of our legitimate response in Afghanistan to the real terrorist threat both delayed the book's completion and deepened our ability to go below the surface. Our ideas are still challenged by each passing day, but our wonderful editor at New York University Press, Ilene Kalish, and her fine assistant, Salwa Jabado, and NYU's excellent managing editor, Despina Papazoglou Gimbel, have given us a deadline and made us stick to it. All we can guarantee our readers is that we were revising and fixing right through Election Day, when they for the last time plucked our manuscript from our hands. So if we missed something, rather than demonize our editors, we say it's all our fault.

As with all of our intellectual collaboration, the ideas in this manuscript go back to the rolling hills of Amherst, Massachusetts, and the early 1970s when we first met each other, and engaged in a thirty-year discussion of the simultaneous needs in politics and society for both individuality and community, for liberty and justice. Our main interest has always been how can democratic theory and practice respond to the tensions between these ideals, in ways that preserve what is best in each of them, and bring out what is best in America. Each of us owes the other a debt of gratitude: De Luca to Buell for reminding him that all that is practical is not gold, and especially for pressing him to be fearless in bringing to light problems of demonization against groups that are truly without political support, such as prisoners and nonviolent drug offenders; Buell to De Luca for, on occasion, pulling him back from the edge of political correctness and reflex criticism. Both of us will always owe a great debt to the man who mentored our dissertations, who remains our great teacher, and who has become our good friend, Bill Connolly.

In the course of the long journey of this manuscript, over the years we have accumulated a number of personal and intellectual debts to friends and colleagues. Dave Wagner shared with us early work on the limit of charity in U.S. life and its role in shaping its limited welfare state. His careful reading of two earlier drafts was especially helpful. Bill Corlett also read our early drafts and called to our attention a range of critical feminist and postcolonial scholarship. Conversations with Bill Connolly over the years have shaped our understanding of the multiple sources of political universals and the limits such universals encounter. Jane Bennett's work has helped shape our understanding of the connections among our picture of nature, the consumer culture, and our democratic commitments. Her careful criticisms and generous support have been essential to the work. Conversations with Juliet Schor about consumption, work, and the role of the corporate media have deepened our considerable appreciation for her work. Conversations with Theda Skocpol and her scholarly work on the evolution of domestic politics and changes in the goals and organization of interest groups have given us an invaluable historical perspective on our theme. So too has the work of Bonnie Honig on foreignness and immigration. Lectures by Stanley Greenberg and writing by James A. Morone have, unbeknownst to them, also played an important role.

Individually we have accumulated debts as well.

For John Buell: former College of the Atlantic colleague John Anderson helped clarify my understanding of schools of ecology and their implications for concepts of community. His irreverent skepticism about both the war and some of its opponents stimulated several fruitful discussions. My oldest son helped with sources, footnoting, and, sometimes as a sparring partner regarding the themes of the work. Susan Covino Buell read drafts of early renditions of major themes in the book and offered both editorial suggestions and further examples in support of major themes. Elisabeth Buell was patient enough to listen to earlier versions of several talks emanating from the book. Her comments helped both improve the style and clarify the arguments. Conversations with Timothy Buell about the culture wars over homework, drugs, and sex in public

schools deepened my sense of the breadth of these wars and their deleterious effects on teenagers. Discussions after presentations at the Belfast
Unitarian Universalist Church, College of the Atlantic, and the Midcoast
Foreign Policy Association helped clarify themes in the chapter on terror
and culture wars.

For Tom De Luca: my political discussions with those closest to me,
most especially my mother and father, Katherine and Thomas De Luca
Sr., have in themselves been an education in the politics of differences,
and the love that transcends all contingent boundaries. They will always
be my teachers in many things about life but most especially in the hope
for greater generosity of spirit among people. We are *all* in this together.

Some of my very best friends have been with me along what is by now
a long journey. My brother Robert De Luca is my constant companion in
everything I do, and every day I do it. My good friend Alan Bridges has
taught me how to see beyond polished or ragged surfaces of people (or
myself), to see what's really inside. His family is mine away from home.
Kathy Waters, my eternal friend, has found a path different than mine,
but it is her path, and she always uses it to do good. Cookie Herbert Tex-
idor keeps her raised eyebrow on me wherever I am, and whatever I'm
doing. She demonstrates with her life, not just words, how important ed-
ucating our young really is. Michael Immerso and I devise together grand
games of political strategy, then he goes back to his books, and I to mine.
If only the coach would put us in. My very good friend Jack Adler is always there for me, and has the added virtues of short e mails and even
shorter phone messages. Bill and Rose Vitale are my friends, allies, and
paisani and there is no couple quite like them. Jill Kirschenbaum is both
my friend and my toughest editor: both my life and writing are better for
her good work. I have been lucky enough to find (and be found) by two
old friends. Peter Mulhall from Brooklyn College days has again become
a main pal and he's in my corner no matter the round or points on the
scorecard. My old 84th Street, Lafayette High, and swimming buddy Bob
Schulman is back to remind me that the real world has a say too, and he
can scuba dive to boot. Two newer friends, Lilian and Don Di Marzio,
have made their home my family's own. It's a warm home, and we're
grateful. And from grade school till tomorrow, Jeff Bromberg always reminds me: "take chances."

Peter Matson, a fine literary agent and even finer person, gave us important insight into the craft of book writing and equally vital encour-
agement, early on when it was most needed. Three other friends, Bob

Higgins, Michelle Lin, and Peter Cocks, made contributions to this work, Bob and Michelle on voting inequality, Peter on "free trade." My secretary Linza Mostert-Tirado always lends a hand just at the right moment. My graduate assistants Ben Taylor and Alexandra Cervenka also pitched in to provide last-minute assistance.

I also want to acknowledge and sincerely thank Fordham University and its president, Rev. Joseph M. McShane, SJ, academic vice president, John Hollwitz, and my own Dean, Rev. Robert R. Grimes, SJ, for the support they have given me, enabling me to take my computer and views to other parts of the world, and aiding my small efforts to broaden democratic dialogue, especially in China. Finally, to the public relations people at Fordham, particularly Libby Schmalz and Michele Snipe, a heartfelt thanks for helping me get my ideas, baked or not, out to a broader public.

We both believe that it is our *American* political heritage that has allowed and enabled us to come up with our views. It is a heritage that is far from perfect, but one that is still the envy of much of the world. Our goal is to strengthen it, build on its most generous moments, and struggle always and mightily against those moments that are far less proud. As Americans, to our own political culture we owe our final debt.

Introduction
Holy War by Other Means

September 11 seemed to change the face of American politics. It made many Americans feel that regardless of differences of party, ideology, ethnicity, race, or gender, they were united *as* Americans. Post-9/11 unity seemed so moving because pre-9/11 partisanship had felt so petty, ugly, and intense.

How quickly that moment passed.[1] By December 1, 2003, *Time* magazine captured the change in its cover story entitled, "Our Polarizing President: Why do Americans either adore Bush or loathe him—and what does it mean for 2004?"

By September 2004, the meaning was clear. The thousandth U.S. soldier had died in Iraq and peace was not on the horizon. Fears of an imminent nuclear threat from North Korea increased. The economy still was not producing enough jobs to keep up with increases in population, inequality was widening, and the percentage of Americans losing their health care each year was increasing. Instead of these, the issue that dominated the convention-laden summer of 2004 was the actions of navy lieutenant John Kerry on a "swiftboat" in a Vietnam river over thirty-five years ago. Incredibly, medals he won under fire became the venue for a renewed Republican attack on the purported military and moral weakness of Democrats. Meanwhile, without a hint of irony, some Democrats attacked Bush for finding a way to avoid combat in a war many of them loathed, and themselves avoided, at the time.

Why attack Kerry for his war record (and later repudiation of the war) and Bush for his choice to avoid combat? Why, indeed, did Kerry need to bring up his war record in the first place, and would the attacks have really been less likely had he not brought it up? Instead of tit-for-tat retribution, we think these occurrences are emblematic of the use and abuse

1

of personal character as strategic moves in a complex and sophisticated game of political chess. It is a game that too often works because of the distinctive, if not unique, way in which personal character and characteristics become surrogates for policy disputes and even leadership contests in American politics, and why many in the public can be successfully enrolled in such contests.

To attack an opponent's policies as being wrong-headed, of course, is the stuff of democratic politics. Why is it, however, that we often see the opponents' character as germane to the moral bona fides of the political and policy agendas they advance? Might not a bad man and a good woman agree on the same platform? Might not a bad woman be a better political leader than a good man?

In the case of Kerry and Bush, the political motivations were clear. Kerry was attractive to Democrats precisely because he was decorated in Vietnam and therefore able, it was thought, to withstand the "weak on defense" attacks sure to come from Republicans. Kerry's effort at self-sanctification was partly an effort to inoculate himself from demonizing attacks on his "liberal" voting record. Bush was attacked on his National Guard Service in order to raise questions in the public's mind, not only of privilege, but more importantly, as to whether he really had the character of leadership necessary in the trying times of our post-9/11 world. Each move in this character battle was attuned to the Republican effort to deploy its "strong on the military" trump card, and the Democratic effort to win a draw on that hand and move the game to the domestic agenda.

Cathy Young, a thoughtful and provocative conservative columnist for the *Boston Globe,* reminds us that tendencies toward demonization have been bipartisan. We differ with her in our belief that it matters which party or person initiates particular rounds of illicit attacks and, more importantly, the kind of attack is also important. To demonize someone as stupid, however harsh, for example, is not equivalent to demonizing someone as un-American. All demonization is not equal.

Nevertheless, her larger point has much merit and it was reflected during the "debate" over President Clinton's character and impeachment. Some right-wing media, for example, suggested that Clinton had engineered the murder of presidential counsel Vincent Foster.[2] George Will, a respected columnist and commentator on ABC TV, called the Clintons "vulgarians." He also went so far as to imply that they were both a cause and symptom of a general demoralization of public life. Mocking European puzzlement at the Clinton impeachment, he wrote:

Grow up, Americans. It is immature to judge politicians by other than quantifiable public consequences, such as the growth of GDP. Your quaint, ridiculous political sensibility, reflecting residual puritanism, prevents mature acceptance of this fallen world's naughtiness.

To which, this riposte is apposite: Europe's political sensibility, sometimes called "realism" and accurately called the de-moralization of politics (politics in which the only important questions are, Do the trains run on time? Do the autobahns get built?), has been no impediment to the emergence of Lenin, Stalin, Mussolini, Franco and Hitler. So spare us your tutorials on political sophistication.[3]

Will's implication is that allowing Clinton to go unpunished could lead us, just as "realism" had led Europeans, down a slippery slope toward all manner of political evil. However he doesn't offer any proof that alleged Clinton-style vulgarianism had anything to do with the past political evil he identifies in Europe. Nor does he recall the fact during the late 1930s and early 1940s, a time he would likely regard as one of a higher moral quality than our own, it took a direct attack at Pearl Harbor to galvanize our nation behind the anti-fascist cause. For his part, *Los Angeles Times* writer Robert Scheer defended Clinton, not by addressing the substantive deficiencies in Will's logic, but by responding in kind by attacking Will as a hypocrite for having himself divorced the mother of his three children.[4]

The competition among talk shows prompted many of them to devote virtually every show for a year to charges and countercharges, leading up to and through Clinton's impeachment, ratcheting up the rhetoric. Judgments about Clinton colored partisanship in other important events, most notably Desert Fox, the December 1998 bombing campaign against Iraq, and even the spring 1999 war in Serbia.

Meanwhile, the planning for 9/11 was underway.

Laced throughout these controversies was a set of interrelated themes and assumptions concerning the nature of the relationship between personal and political life, between private character and public service. The most profound and we think most dangerous commentary to emerge was the implication that there is a determinate relationship between personal character as registered through private activities and beliefs, and the moral quality of one's political agenda.[5]

As we will see, there is an important conceptual distinction between demonization and appropriate and very strong criticism, although that line cannot simply be determined by abstract definitions. Deciding where that line is and when one has crossed it is itself a deeply moral and political decision.

When demonization does occur it is especially harmful because it obscures policy and leadership differences *and* similarities between political opponents, and may reinforce existing racial, ethnic, gender, and other stereotypes. But rather than simply lament demonization in politics, it is important to understand why it is prominent and what can be done about it. Demonization is both a consequence and a contributor to political polarization in America today, and for that reason it merits a more focused and broadly based analysis than it has received.

Defining Demonization

To demonize, the dictionary tells us, is "to convert into a demon," or "to infuse the principles or fury of a demon into" someone, or to turn "persons into or as if into a demon." Demons are "evil or malignant spirits," for example, a devil, or a "very cruel, depraved, or wicked person."[6] In this book, we do not use the verb "to demonize" in this more classical descriptive sense of denoting how someone becomes demonic, but to describe and hold responsible those who cast the aspersion of being demonic on others too easily and without proper cause. In this we are close to how the term is used in ordinary language.

To demonize is to use language or other symbols in ways that meet two requirements. First, to strongly imply or directly suggest that others have very bad, immoral, or evil qualities, and often that they are capable of quite immoral deeds; or to directly suggest that they have done reprehensible deeds. Second, to do so without sufficient evidence, inquiry, justification, or consideration of the consequences. It is our contention that demonization, as here defined, weakens our ability to deliberate in the most interesting and creative ways for the purpose of improving the quality of our lives.[7]

The idea of being demonic has origins in older beliefs about the world of spirits, particularly of evil spirits. In the modern world, we think it makes sense also to use demonization to denote the illicit attribution of extreme forms of abnormality and deviance to others. In this sense, to demonize may be to "abnormalize" some individual or group. Sometimes demonic as evil and demonic as depraved come together, as, for example, in extreme homophobic beliefs in which gays are thought at once to be both abnormal and possessed by the devil, in need of therapy and conversion. In fact, attributing deviance to others has some of the power it does because it trades on older fears of evil spirits. This is unsurprising because before the advent of modern psychology, this was one way in which what we today call deviance was understood. In some quarters, particularly on the religious right, it still is.

Accusing others of demonizing is a strong charge. We recognize that when *we* ourselves claim that certain writers or political leaders are engaging in demonization, we open ourselves to the charge of demonizing them. Claims against us, just as the claims we make about others, are each subject to evaluation. Proving one is engaging in demonization is not simple, however—in the first place because determining whether someone is actually moving down the road of attributing evil or depravity to others is not always self-evident. Second, determining whether the charge of evil or depravity is reasonable is perhaps even more contestable. The fact that demonization often involves a blending of tactical, strategic, personal, and moral motives makes evaluation of one's own role or the roles of others in it quite difficult to assess, and most difficult during periods of escalating rhetoric.

Demonization as we use the term is a *sustained* and *illicit* effort whose purpose is to thoroughly stigmatize individuals, types of persons, or groups whether for political or other advantage, righteous belief, or both. We sharply contrast it with knee-jerk attacks against, reflective criticism of, or even extremely harsh censure of positions or persons one has come to abhor. Appropriate moral censure is distinguished from demonization by the care given to the charge as well as by the truth of the claim. We can always press ourselves and others to ask, if not always succeed in fairly answering, whether we or they put in the effort to avoid the temptation of demonization.

To illustrate how some of these complexities involving demonization play themselves out in political life, let's go back briefly to the first Gulf War. There is no doubt that when President George H. W. Bush called Saddam Hussein "another Hitler" in 1990, his point was to paint him as "evil" in order to strengthen the president's political hand in using military force against the Iraqi dictator. Recalling the actual history of this period, however, how are we to think about Bush's claim? During most of the 1980s Hussein was a quiet ally of the Reagan-Bush administration, instigating and then fighting a brutal war against Ayatollah Khomeini's Iran, then believed to be our most serious (noncommunist) foe. It was during this period that Saddam Hussein used chemical weapons both against Iranians and "his own people" (a charge made quite often by George W. Bush to build support for the second Gulf War), the Kurds in northern Iraq. It took Hussein's invasion of the oil-rich sheikhdom of Kuwait, however, for him to become the moral equivalent of perhaps the most reviled person in history. If Bush was essentially right about Hussein's lack of regard for human life in 1990, and we think he was, would we be demonizing Bush if we were to claim that it was hypocritical and wrong, perhaps immoral or evil of him to have supported Hussein in the 1980s when he did in fact use "weapons of mass destruction," that is, chemical weapons? Could someone reasonably reply that, compared to Khomeini, Hussein was the lesser of two evils, therefore our characterization of Bush Sr.'s support for Hussein as evil amounts to demonizing Bush? How could we adjudicate whether this reply or our charge is reasonable? Could all reasonable people, even all honest brokers, agree?

This example suggests why simple definitions alone will not solve the problem. Deciding whether someone is engaging in demonization is itself an irreducibly political question. The best we can do is know as clearly as possible what we mean by demonization, and understand those demonizing tendencies most characteristic of ourselves as individuals, as groups, and as a political culture. And then we must do our level best to resist the temptation to demonize even as we engage in vigorous, even vituperative, political contestation, even over the question of who is demonizing whom.

Types of Demonization

There are three fundamental types of demonizing "strategies." In one, the target is an easily identifiable "group" of people, whether a nation, race, ethnicity, political affinity, gender, or associational activity. In the second the target is an individual, although the real objective is often much broader. In the third, the target is a policy, agenda, or political philosophy. The borderline between the three is permeable and the links between them are profound. For example, attacking an individual's character most resonates when the group that individual represents (or is seen to represent) is stereotyped as having similar group character flaws and the policy that person proposes is purported to reproduce such flaws. In this way, attacks on individuals or policies often become surrogates for attacks on groups, which, if made explicitly, for example direct racist attacks, would have political costs.

Political demonization, therefore, is best understood as a complex mosaic of interrelated mindsets, each of which is related to and often reinforces the other, but none of which is simply reducible to any one seminal component. There is, however, one constant. Demonization relies upon imputation of moral or spiritual failure, or deviance, or extreme incompetence (that is, moral failure for having illicitly assumed leadership). Thus, whether leveled against another culture, group, or individual, it always has a characterological component.

Today this is even true when the allegations are launched against foreign cultures that at one time could have simply been branded with racist stereotypes based upon purported natural characteristics. Even with today's fear of radical Muslim terrorism, public denunciation of Muslims will focus on the kind of people Muslim teachings produce rather than on the intrinsic "nature" of Muslims and Arabs. The issue, at least in respectable public discourse, becomes one of sociology and character, not one of intrinsic or genetic ethnic or racial characteristics. There is always the danger, of course, that these older stereotypes lurk in the background.

Group demonization includes defining the enemies of one's own nation in such a way as to ratchet up national chauvinism. In its most obvious form this occurs in run-ups to wars, whether secular or religious, and is nurtured, perhaps even necessary, in the execution of an actual war. President Bush's articulation of an "axis of evil" is one example, but the history of threat and warfare is replete with others. Recall, for example, Ayatollah Khomeini's characterization back in 1979 of America as "the Great Satan." Always important, this type of labeling deserves especially close attention today because of the real threat of terrorists, and their possible acquisition and use of weapons of mass destruction. This confluence creates simultaneous pressures toward exaggeration of foreign threats and marginalization of domestic leaders who resist such rhetoric, and toward temptation to demonize both foreign and domestic foes.

Demonizing foreigners has a domestic analog informed by traditional ethnocentricity and racism. It treats minority groups of different ethnic, racial, religious, and/or cultural origins as not merely a burden on the nation's resources, but as a deviation from the nation's character and an intrinsic source of the nation's problems. It scapegoats them. America's immigrant and racial history makes this kind of demonization an important one to keep in mind.

In today's more ethnically and racially tolerant political climate, overt domestic racial or ethnic demonization is at the fringe. Yet similar objectives can be achieved in other ways. Perhaps the most recognizable example is the way in which "welfare" was increasingly used as a "racially coded" term going back over three decades, most notably through Ronald Reagan's fable about a "welfare queen" who drove a "welfare Cadillac," which became political folklore. Demonizing welfare recipients was effective because of America's racial history, its denouement of disproportionate numbers of African Americans on welfare, and the racist and stereotypical traits imputed to African Americans such as laziness and low intelligence that, in turn, allegedly forced "hard-working" people to pay unfairly high taxes to support "them."

Individual political leaders may be demonized for their alleged bad character; the result of such demonization may simply be to discredit them or to serve the broader political objective of defeating their party in an election. Sometimes the effects, even the goals, are broader yet. The attacks on a leader's private behavior, for example, can be a proxy for a larger social cause in which the political agenda of one's opponents is reduced to and equated with, and thereby condemned by, charges about the personal character and private behavior of the leader. For many on the right, Bill Clinton's affair with Monica Lewinsky was most important because it was emblematic of the moral depravity and relativism that they believe has infected liberalism since the 1960s. This depravity could be as easily discerned in liberal policies as in the man, they believed—from affirmative action to welfare to gays in the military.

Demonization of this type flows in both directions. Thus, liberals accuse conservatives of the racist policy of victimizing blacks by cutting off welfare in spite of our racist history, and conservatives return the accusation of racism, blaming liberals for supporting a welfare state that creates a sick mentality of victimization. This conservative charge is worth considering. Policies such as welfare can easily be demonized because they inadequately address problems of historical magnitude, and therefore may seem to reproduce them or create insidious new ones. Thus African Americans may allegedly become dependent on welfare and, in the post–civil rights era, disempowered from making use of the full equal opportunity now claimed to be afforded them. Welfare, not racism, becomes the problem. Yet it remains the case that different social policies can create undesirable characterological traits in people. Therefore, raising questions about the consequences of public policy for character is a necessary part of serious political discourse.

Taken together, these three types of demonization are distinct yet often interwoven, and each can build upon the other. Policy agendas are treated as contemptible and simultaneously caricatured as "foreign" manifestations of a particular ethnic, socioeconomic, or racial group and/or flowing from the character of a particular leader. The whole process often culminates in and is reinforced by a process of condemning policy agendas through examination of the life—including the private life—of the political leader. That leader is seen as a symbol of a certain socioeconomic, racial, or "foreign" demographic type and a certain political perspective, and all are condemned through reference to the individual's private life or purported character.

When all types of demonization come together, particular policy agendas are thoroughly stigmatized and effective contestation and productive debate become almost impossible. At worst, an agenda is seen as unspeakably evil, fostered by a socioeconomic class or racial/ethnic group seen as the origins of the polity's most important problems and promoted by a leader whose despicable private behavior is typical of those to whom he appeals. The leader's purported depravity becomes emblematic of the values inherent in the policy agenda in question, as well as the type of person produced by its socialization process.

It is still the case, however, that whether demonization is occurring cannot usually be discerned simply by the content of the charge. Nor is all demonization intentional. To evaluate whether demonization is occurring therefore requires analysis of the care with which particular charges are constructed, the subcurrents on which they are based and designed to appeal to, and sometimes the motivation of the actors. And of course, in the end, what counts is the relationship between the accuracy of the charge—often enough, criticism is true—and the quality of the case the critic has made to herself or himself before actually making the charge.

Demonization is a process from which neither the left nor right is immune. Blaming economic extremes on wealthy individuals who are deemed inherently greedy or "malefactors of great wealth" is hardly more useful for understanding inequality than attributing the high school dropout rate to modern teenagers who are deemed willfully or inherently lustful and indolent. In each case, little effort is expended to define key concepts or specify just how the behavior of the "accused" is radically different from that of others. Neither do accusers, even when correct in their judgments about bad behavior, generally demonstrate that those found "guilty" have consistent patterns or histories of acting in these defined ways. Nor do they often explore conditions that might provide partial exculpation, or make a serious effort to see if there are extrinsic factors that may have induced the bad behavior in the first place. Why hordes of businessmen suddenly become inordinately greedy or packs of teenagers scandalously lustful is hardly self-evident and rarely explained in such jeremiads. Instead of regarding such problems as teenage pregnancy, poverty, or even greed as dilemmas rooted in the complex interplay of institutional practices, reigning moral codes, and wide-ranging human attributes, we treat these as proof of the inherent depravity of selected citizens. Those thus stigmatized readily return the favor.

We conclude that analyses that blame widespread social problems on the individual character of leaders or large numbers of people or the character of groups, while not to be ruled out by fiat, are often quite suspect. Seldom are they useful guides to comprehensive political action. Character is without question important, and people surely do make choices in their lives, but they do so as members of groups that may have different cultural expectations, experience inequitable political opportunities, and may be in dissimilar economic circumstances.

Attention to such details will certainly elicit charges of moral relativism by those who seek simple solutions and who have an interest, whether personal or political, in having an enemy to blame. Such moral postures, however, make both understanding *and* proper moral judgment impossible. Examining the political and cultural reasons of why we focus inordinate time and thought on the politics of collective or individual character is therefore itself an important endeavor.

Fundamental Ethical and Political Assumptions

Every society needs common standards that citizens can both fashion and embrace in a relatively consensual way. In a world where tradition and organic hierarchy have broken down, citizens still need the coordination and sense of security that standards set. Participation in their development and implementation is essential if these standards are to have legitimate claim to our allegiance. But much in human experience leads us to suspect any group, even a majority, that proclaims to have final and all-encompassing standards. The task is to build a community that respects both its own standards and the rights of its members to pursue their own individual course. For it is through such pursuit that we learn not just about individuals, but also about the moral purchase of the standards themselves.

A commitment to community based upon shared precepts and to individuality in which precepts may be imperfectly shared requires that we remain open to how we negotiate the terms of our compact. Accepted codes of appropriate behavior, however, are hard under the best of circumstances to criticize, because they can easily be used to impute that the critic is not just mistaken, but deviant or worse. Contrary to some political writers and thinkers, therefore, we also suggest that political rhetoric that alienates some people and which can do harm may emanate from the political center—where it is hardest to observe. There can exist a kind of centrist fundamentalism, reminiscent of what Cornell University political theorist Theodore Lowi once called the "politics of dead center," an ossified consensus defined and elaborated by contemporary coalitions of power and interest. If you fall outside the bounds of such reasonableness, be careful. Moreover, those who appear to the center as "extreme" are the ones most often accused of demonization. The answer then advanced by the center to solve the problem of demonization is a return to the center, which it accomplishes in part by employing a style of rhetoric that itself demonizes the "extremes."

Let's take two brief examples of steps in this direction from the work of journalists we respect and with whom we quite often agree. E. J. Dionne claims that "Americans hate politics" because activists in each party, more "extreme" than average party members, distort politics by moving it away from where the average American really is on key issues. Be that as it may, is it far-fetched to think that the center may from time to time be sitting out fundamentally important moral debates engaged by the partisans? *New York Times* correspondent Tom Friedman's work can yield to a similar temptation with a rhetorical style sometimes suggesting that, on the one hand, you could irrationally do this, and on the other you could irrationally do that, so why not do it in the only rational (and moral) way, that is to say, my way. Consider, for example, his support for the Geneva Accords, an agreement hammered out by nongovernmental

Israelis and Palestinians and presented to the public in October 2003. It is an agreement that we also strongly support as a way to resolve the conflict through compromise. Friedman strongly praises the Israeli negotiator Yossi Beilin as a "fanatical moderate—as committed to his moderation as the extremists are to their extremism."[8] Undoubtedly, Friedman is partly responding to the often mindless violence rather than simply the intransigence of each side. Yet does he advance his case (our case) or deepen the rift by attacking not only terrorists but also by demonizing what could turn out to be principled, nonviolent positions held by "extremists" on each side of the center that he and we stake out on this issue?

Dionne and Friedman's style of argumentation in these instances is very alluring, and most of us succumb to it. The temptation to cast one's own position as the only reasonable one is also hardly reserved for the political center. It traverses the entire political spectrum, built as it is into modern political discourse.

The premise of our overall approach to demonization is that the paradoxical need for both community and individuality commits us to democratic politics as an ever-present necessity. We contrast our views with those who suggest that ideological distortion, which we suggest includes demonization, is best combated by framing one set of "neutral," rational, or commonsense assumptions to which all reasonable citizens can agree and from which discussion and debate needs to proceed.[9] Our fundamental commitment in this work is to political practice and discourse that actively seek to minimize demonization as part of their project. Demonization-free discourse is an ideal that will never and perhaps can never be achieved. Yet political discourse freer of demonization is a worthy and obtainable objective.

Most of life must be lived in common. Living in a modern productive community, while fostering space for individual differences, requires a notion both of responsible agency and rationality, and one of openness to people, ideas, and codes more or less foreign to us. It requires, in other words, a capacity both for control and for surprise. Reasoned discourse itself is facilitated when we acknowledge we all work from worldviews that we can neither put aside nor fully prove; each limit we are brave enough to admit should inspire humility in our attitude toward others and in our own certainty about ourselves.

Assuming a complex, protean, and yet social world never fully expressive of our purposes, we suspect that the need for both individuality and common purposes will never end. Difficulties between these needs will remain and have to be negotiated within a regime that respects and protects individual rights by people who also have a sense of social responsibility.

Our fundamental commitment here is this. Anything does not go. Some beliefs and actions are simply wrong. Precisely for these reasons it is incumbent upon us to shoulder responsibility to better understand why we think and feel the way we do, and why we are drawn to certain styles of political commentary or particular political agendas. A desire for such understanding commits us to know ourselves more fully, yet with less certainty, to be more rather than less open. Easy demonization of others precludes precisely these qualities.

We know it is desirable and think it is possible in democratic politics to step outside of narrow bounds in the ways we frame identity and social purposes, and thereby make the effort to tame demonization. One step in this direction is to understand the distinctive and contemporary ways our western heritage, often believing itself free of superstition, nevertheless disciplines its inhabitants to singular purposes. At the same time, this tradition also prepares us for self-conscious reflection and analysis, and tolerance. This two-sided theme is a major subtext of the thesis we argue throughout the book and the proposals we present in conclusion.

We draw critically upon several seemingly disparate strains of thought. Some cultures, such as a number of Native American nations, adopted attitudes toward difference that have important points of contact for what we are suggesting. Nineteenth-century American thinkers such as Henry David Thoreau and Walt Whitman celebrated the natural and social worlds not primarily as sources of final harmony and truth but as purveyors of surprise. Reinhold Niebuhr and other theologians have tended to regard sin not as a licentious individual act but as reflective of the pretense that our values and purposes can represent or contain all of life. Liberal political thinkers such as George Kateb stress tolerance, political equality, and individualism. Conservatives such as Robert Nozick stress accountability, responsibility, and liberty. Critical theorists such as Theodor Adorno and poststructuralist thinkers such as Michel Foucault emphasize different ways in which Enlightenment notions of rationality or even science can create regimes of power, which marginalize. Yet the very idea of being self-conscious of belief systems and their enabling and constraining features is itself indebted to modernity's break with traditional culture and its effort to know the world more fully. Each of these schemes has in different ways influenced us, although some more than others.

Regardless of origins or precursors, any argument suggesting as best those worldviews that advocate a critical stance even toward the fundamentalist verity of their own standards is often denounced. Openness to the possibility of limits and injustices of received truth is often portrayed as undermining moral foundations. We challenge this perspective.

Resisting the lure of fixed and fully encompassing moral and political truths puts us in a better, not worse, position to ground our thought and action. It allows us to know more fully why we think certain courses of action are wrong, and thereby test our judgments and act more confidently as to our motives when we believe a course of action to be right. In our view, truth is not relative. Neither, however, is it a gift easily given, graciously received.

Our meta-ethical perspective, like any fundamental perspective, is not fully proven, nor is it simply chosen like a new car. It is elicited in us through awareness of the elements of anxiety we detect in fundamentalist postures, especially when they are our own, and the harms they do. It is also derived from the faith we confess to having in the human ability to find delight, fulfillment, and moral generation in discovering things that are new.

Rather than enter into a fuller defense of our position in philosophical terms, in this work we point to its advantages for democratic theory and political practices.[10] We hope that our discussion of contemporary issues and rhetoric exposes some characteristic yet underlying anxieties that we have as contemporary Americans, which make us more receptive than we need be to demonizing political strategies.

The narrative we elaborate encourages and is encouraged by political participation that is at once broad, plural, and deeply self-reflective. In our belief that deeper understanding, and therefore deeper participation, can point us away from a politics of demonization, we show our hopefulness. One effect of demonizing rhetoric is to create a constricted political agenda in which debates and arguments about how best to improve quality of life, both material and moral, are marched outside. The chapters in this book examine some reasons the scope of debate too often becomes constricted in this way, the consequences for American democracy, and what needs to be done to reshape political discourse. The 2004 election notwithstanding, our bet is that many Americans are ready—perhaps even hunger—for higher-quality debate and can be sufficiently tolerant to participate respectfully.

Overview

In Part I we outline the key elements of the problem of demonization in politics. In chapter 1, we review the background of demonization in America and some recent distinctive trends. In chapter 2 we elaborate a particularly modern and American form of demonization we call the "politics of moral personae," in which the character of leaders becomes enmeshed with policies, constituencies, and philosophies. In chapter 3 we examine the origins of one particularly salient form of that politics. We call it "America's moral paradox," our simultaneous economic and cultural need to be pulled simultaneously in puritanical and hedonistic directions, and suggest its consequences for political demonization, American-style. In chapter 4 we examine the depth and nature of the political and cultural divisions in America, and who is most harmed by them.

In Part II we examine aspects of important cultural and military wars in which we are now engaged. In chapter 5 we analyze the idea of the enemy, and how enemies come to be constructed. In chapter 6 we discuss terrorism and the meaning of evil, and what our response has been and should be to each. In chapter 7 we directly relate the terror and culture wars to each other, and address issues of fundamentalist responses among politically active citizens and some intellectuals. In chapter 8 we analyze how the culture war plays itself out over the environment, and how environmentalists can better position themselves to achieve reforms.

Finally, in our conclusion, we develop a perspective and set of proposals to foster a more generous democratic polity—one thereby better positioned to mitigate tendencies toward demonization. We suggest a specific program to advance the goal of "democracy without demons" based upon a renewed democratic covenant that includes five essential commitments.

Democracy will never thoroughly free itself of demons. Perhaps that is an impossible goal or one that would produce other harms. Our democracy, however, can be freer from demonization than it now is. If it were, we would be freer, too.

PART I

Demonization in America

1

Demonization American-Style

Demonization of political leaders in order to discredit their programs and allies is as old as our republic. Two centuries ago, newspapers blasted the morals of President Thomas Jefferson. Abraham Lincoln and even George Washington were targets. Debates over political agendas themselves have often included conflicts in which each side has accused the other of being of bad character. Prohibition is a good example, McCarthyism is another. Even issues of distribution or redistribution of income and wealth are often argued in ways that demonize character.

While there is of course significant overlap in the content of demonization by various ideological viewpoints—epithets such as "liar" or "cheater" are bipartisan—sometimes anecdotal patterns can be discerned. Using issues of sexual impropriety to attack opponents has often been a favorite of the more conservative party, from attacking Jefferson for his affairs with several married women and for having a child with Sally Hemmings, his slave, to President Grover Cleveland's out-of-wedlock child that inspired the ditty: "Ma, ma, where's my pa? Gone to the White House—ha, ha, ha!" Bill Clinton's Oval Office escapades will always be remembered. All but forgotten are Republican Warren G. Harding's two mistresses, one sent on a long cruise during the 1920 campaign, the other, overlooked by Republican leaders, later trifled by Harding in a White House closet.[1]

An obvious favorite tactic of the more populist Democrats is to attack opponents as being part of the greedy elite. From Jefferson's attacks on the Federalists, to Andrew Jackson's veto of the National Bank, presidential candidate William Jennings Bryan's 1896 "cross of gold" speech rejecting the gold standard, and Theodore and Franklin Roosevelt's denigration of "malefactors of great wealth," this theme has often been pronounced. More recent is the Ann Richards stiletto quip about George W. Bush: "He was born on third base and he thinks he hit a triple." Yet many leaders of the Democrats, from Roosevelt to John F. Kennedy to John Kerry, have been fabulously wealthy, while many Republican leaders from Dwight D. Eisenhower to Richard Nixon and Gerald Ford have not.

These styles of rhetorical flourish, excess, and sometimes demonization are related to the targeted constituency, the constituency being appealed to, and American political culture more broadly. To attack Democrats as sexual sinners has worked in part because they have often included recent immigrants and racial minorities, themselves at times thought by conservative leaders and nativist publics as lazy, indolent, and lustful. On the other hand, the Republican Party since its founding has been the party more solicitous of big business, making it the target of class resentments. In each case the cultural precept, deep in the Protestant ethic, that moral and spiritual salvation come through repressing desire and finding life's meaning through hard and disciplined work creates a code violated either by lust or greed. Savaging an opponent for being greedy or lustful may not advance debate on important issues, let alone structural crises, but it often works because we are moved by such attacks because of who we are.

Today personal attacks on leaders play out in a very different world than earlier in our history, and their consequences can even be international. Jefferson's world was one in which a relative degree of economic self-reliance prevailed and military action took a long time to carry out. Today, a global network of interconnected markets may react to declining faith in a president, for example weakening the dollar and thereby affecting trade. Or questions can be instantly raised and popularized about the reasons presidents initiate sudden military strikes (Clinton) or terror alerts (Bush). Our tools for scrutinizing private life have now also become immensely more intrusive and sophisticated, from e-mail as a permanently searchable record to DNA testing. DNA has reached back to touch even Jefferson and his out-of-wedlock child with Hemmings. If early 1800s rumors could be vicious, their very status as rumors was protected by primitive communication channels.

Rumors and accusations now explode upon the public with the emergence of instantaneous modes of communication. "All Monica, All the time" is hardly an exaggeration in a world of cable TV and the Internet. The emergence of cable and talk radio, and their scurry for ratings and profits, adds impetus to strive for the lowest common denominator in a way matched, perhaps, only by the earlier heyday of intense city tabloid competition. The pressure to unearth new and titillating detail and to find more avenues into the private lives of public figures is thus immense.

Still, most Americans fear and resent intrusive government, corporations, and neighbors. Such concern is likely to be deepened as new technology provides the means for ever-greater intrusion, and as some elites remain indifferent to this danger.[2] "You have no privacy, get over it," one captain of the information technology industry recently put it.[3] Reaction to the Clinton scandals itself reflected public ambivalence about moralizing in politics today, as a clear majority opposed impeachment even as the scandal gripped the nation's attention. We sometimes moralize because we yearn for greater certainty regarding who we are, yet we also seem to fear and dislike the kinds of total scrutiny—including self-scrutiny—such quests for absolute values seem to bring.

Polling data reveal that Americans have become significantly more "tolerant" in our lifetime,[4] even as some extremist hate groups take new and virulent forms. The data suggest that there was a major increase in tolerance in the World War II generation compared to their parents, and a significant increase again by the baby boomers over theirs, although not again by "generation X" over them.[5] Increases in tolerance did not come out of thin air. They are a mixture of the American ideal of equality as a putatively universal principle with hard, bitter, and often violent struggle for rights, through which American norms were extended and amended. Nonetheless, too easily concluding that increased tolerance settles the issue of respect can make us insufficiently attentive to the possible injustices even inside current practices and beliefs, including the expectations for conformity that sometimes attend toleration.

The temptation to demonize can prove especially enticing under contemporary conditions of close electoral competition, a dwindling "middle," and extreme partisanship. Studies over the last ten years have shown a deepening partisanship—not just among the political elites Dionne chastised, but within the American electorate itself—that didn't exist before, as political scientists find deep ideological and issue polarization among ordinary citizens.[6] Contemporary partisanship is abetted by deep cultural and political roots, which are also central to understanding how demonization works today.

Current divisions can actually be traced as far back as the Johnson-Goldwater election of 1964, part of what Robert Shogan calls "The Forty Years' War."[7] Just think what these names or ideas conjure up: Barry

Goldwater, George McGovern, "liberalism," "card-carrying member of the ACLU," Jim Wright, Robert Bork, Clarence Thomas and Anita Hill, Newt Gingrich, Kenneth Starr, "vast right-wing conspiracy," Hillary and Bill Clinton, and now George W. Bush and John F. Kerry. Deep vitriol accompanies debates over terrorism, the war in Iraq, gay marriage, affirmative action, immigration, teenage pregnancy, "partial birth abortion," stem-cell research, welfare, English as a second language, Social Security, health-care policy, "life support" for Terri Schiavo, and so on.

One great virtue of democracies with strong civil liberties traditions is that they can provide legal and institutional protections for individuals against the consequences of the tendency in politics to demonize opponents. However, the needs in democracies to manipulate public opinion and to mobilize an identifiable *majority* can themselves be siren calls to demonization that are abusive of identifiable ideological, ethnic, or other minorities. While demonization in democracies does not take the extreme forms it can in authoritarian and totalitarian regimes, less terrible forms can and do occur, and these have personal and political consequences for the targeted person or group. To suggest that demonization of opponents can be an effective political strategy is hardly novel. Negative campaign ads that cross the line from responsible, even harsh, criticism to demonization can work.

Difference and History

If we look back, we find that not all cultures regard those things that differ from their individual and collective norms as necessarily threatening to the overall order of their systems or as in need of reform.

Medieval Catholic thought was based on the notion that not only was society an orderly hierarchy, but that human society itself sat within a larger hierarchy, "the great chain of being" in Arthur Lovejoy's famous phrase. Within this worldview, everything and everyone had its place, albeit not equal power. In a way that we seldom acknowledge today, medieval society did often accord some place to nonconformity. The medieval notion of a "ship of fools," whereby the mentally ill were segregated but accorded a public role within the social order, was a kind of metaphorical statement of the notion that everything that exists is either part or expressive of a larger order of being. The idea that different facets of society have a role to play in the larger whole is represented by the idea of the jester at court, or in the role of "the fool" in English Morris dancing.[8] Christianity as a religion tended to regard conquest or conversion of the non-Christian as a divine responsibility, but in the New World Catholic and Protestant theologies differed in terms of the degree of assimilation sought. Papal doctrine, though often evaded in practice, also placed far more limits on the right of colonists to expropriate native lands.

Medieval thought, rooted as it was in a sense of total order, could provide some support for the unexpected or the unusual by affirming its place—albeit subordinate—within the comprehensive order of being. This medieval order broke down both at the level of philosophy and political practice. Its cardinal tenets that a unitary and omnipotent God stood at the top of the hierarchy and that there is an invariant hierarchy were in subtle tension. For does not the invariance of the great chain stand as a limit on God's power?

With the breakdown of this premodern order, the view of God and personhood changes. God no longer stands at the top of a fixed hierarchy of being. Psychic insecurity emerges from the tension between a world where change and the unexpected often occur, but where its inhabitants still on some level are indebted to the notion that order must be unitary and comprehensive. The breakdown of the medieval worldview was a pivotal political and philosophical point. Both thought and practice might have evolved from it in ways that emphasized the side of medieval thought that tolerated difference toward a form of monotheism that celebrated order through its accommodation to diversity. Instead, political and intellectual history took a different course, toward a new and potent form of monotheism.

During the Reformation, a new conception of the relation between God and the world emerged: that God can remake both human and nonhuman nature to suit "his" purposes. Later, of course, when traditional faith in God is challenged by science, this view is secularized, but it nonetheless retains a theistic residue. "Man" is now the maker and creator. Nature—including human nature—can be "his" handmaiden. The view of human beings as defined by their technological prowess and the material possessions carved out of nature underlies the very measures of progress and the politics that flow from them.[9]

Modern capitalism, of course, was built upon a celebration of work, material progress, and domination of nature. The famous Protestant ethic grounded this worldview through religion as economic success became an indication of God's grace. Thus, the meaning of life and one's place in the afterlife both justified absorbing strict discipline and marshalling self-discipline, and had little to do with personal pleasure. Yet this system, in a world not designed to neatly fit its still contingent purposes, had to overcome the resistance of other needs and desires people have, including those unleashed by the system of discipline and reward itself. If work is all there is to life, who will consume the goods society makes and why should they? Resistance occurred, therefore, not only in people uninitiated to the promise of the ethic, such as Native Americans, and immigrants from non–northern European cultures, but also closer to home in its own people. Human beings, it turns out, may not be designed for a singular commitment to the world of work.

The view of work and material progress as the purpose and essence of life may also underlay early puritan positions regarding sexuality. But the intrusiveness into privacy often blamed on such puritanical jurists as Kenneth Starr cannot be attributed solely to this heritage. At a deeper level, it lies in the urge to see all of reality either actually or potentially be embodied through one guiding ideal, through a unitary worldview.

This urge combined with a debt to the Protestant ethic, for example, can also be found in strands of environmental or "green" thought that repudiate material growth. The left in general has its own fundamentalist imperatives. An understanding of the human subject as realizing its purpose by finding its own inner vision and establishing perfect harmony between that self and the larger community underlies various communitarian, Marxist, and eco-fundamentalist views of the world. They share more than they would wish to acknowledge with their technocentric and capitalist relatives, housed also in narrow views of science and progress. For these views, there is ultimate harmony, either now or in the foreseeable future, between the individual, society, and nature. At the deepest ontological level, nature, including human nature, is without surprise or what appears to be surprise, and can be interpreted to fit within a unitary pattern.

How do these historical developments and philosophical strands play themselves out in contemporary politics? Welfare recipients, the poor, and some racial minorities have appeared to many middle- and working-class Americans to violate the disciplines they endure and have come to valorize. When laced with racial attitudes, the resentments become profoundly toxic, particularly in eras of instability in which real income stagnates and the relative value of one's previously acquired skills diminishes. "Reagan Democrats" were to some degree built upon a foundation of such resentments, but Clinton Democrats responded by also engaging them to buttress their own political position.

Clinton and the Treadmill of Demonization

There is one palpable irony in Clinton's receiving such animus for his lack of integrity in his personal life and his public lies about it. He did as much as any Democrat, and most presidents, to claim at the rhetorical level a central place for individualized personal responsibility as the best way to understand the causes of social problems. In this, important aspects of his own political rhetoric resonated with that of his fiercest critics.

Since at least 1968, the Democratic Party at the presidential level has been hurt by the perception that it is too liberal, not so much on so-called class warfare issues, but on issues such as race, crime, taxes, and rights, themselves often "race-coded" in their appeal.[10] Clinton is historically important for the party in that he fulfilled an ambition, fostered during his Democratic Leadership Council days as governor of Arkansas, of moving the party to the "center" as a way to reclaim a competitive position in presidential elections.

One of the essential tactical moves he consistently made in his truly remarkable political journey was to eliminate systematically some critical wedge "social issues" that have indeed hurt the Democrats, issues such as welfare, crime, and the death penalty. (He went so far as to return to Arkansas during the heat of the 1992 election to oversee an execution.) His primary rhetorical move was to make two related claims. There now exists a relatively fair set of rules for success and achievement in society (and we are working hard to correct the inadequacies that exist); government will assist those who play by the rules and act responsibly, but will go after those who do not.

The political conditions in which Clinton found himself (and then helped re-create) made these tactical decisions appealing. Clinton was a Democrat in an era in which organized labor had significantly weakened. The percentages of workers in unions had seriously declined from its high point in the 1950s. To compound the problem, a smaller percentage of workers voted than in the fifties, and of those who did more had been moved into the Republican column, in part through the use of wedge issues. They were called "Reagan Democrats," symbolizing at once their rejection of what they perceived to be liberal social values and their susceptibility to a populist appeal directed at their value needs. As the Democrats shied away from their own economic populist appeal[11] and were perceived to be giving "special preference" to racial and ethnic minorities, the conservative populist "values" appeal was given room to grow.

To win, Democrats needed a greater percentage of votes from higher up the economic ladder than before, and needed the campaign contributions in increasingly expensive elections that only the wealthy could provide. This need for money had become especially pronounced since the media, increasingly expensive, had become the main way to reach an atomized electorate that had fewer ongoing politically relevant associations,[12] including political parties that mobilize neighborhoods. Economic policies such as "free trade" rewarded some of the economically advantaged people whose support Clinton needed. But no Democrat wins without attracting a large share of the middle and working classes that vote. Democrats needed to retain and regain as much of their traditional base as possible.

A politics of economic growth, protection of middle- and working-class entitlement programs, welfare reform, and a rhetoric of personal responsibility worked well for Clinton. With the poor voting at half the rate of the wealthy and thus becoming even less relevant than they already were in an era of money-driven politics, welfare politics played especially nicely to the middle- and working-classes that were anxious about their own economic situation and about threats to their own values.

Clinton himself didn't engage in the kind of demonization of welfare recipients like many other political leaders, including even some Democrats such as Ed Koch when he was New York's mayor. Moreover, he did continue to support other policies despite their racial coding that some conservative Democrats connected to their party's vulnerability, such as affirmative action. However, the welfare bill that he signed into law in 1996 permanently cut off recipients after five years of eligibility, premised on the idea that the need for more than temporary relief in our society is caused by personal irresponsibility. Why have a mandatory cutoff after other disciplines had already been included, most notably workfare, unless failure to find work turns out to be a failure of character?[13]

As conservatives rightly suspected, of course, many of Clinton's moves were tactical in order to gain some of the benefits that had previously accrued to Nixon, Reagan, and Bush, Sr., or at least to blunt the assault other Democrats had absorbed from these antagonists. No doubt he also wished to use such moves to build political capital to first be elected and then create cover for the progressive policies he favored.

Ironically, however, having walked a bit down the character-is-destiny road, he too found himself lost on it. From the White House to the ghetto, it turned out that individual character was alleged to be at the root of our most important failures—from welfare policy to presidential leadership.

Why was it so politically tempting for Clinton to go down that road himself in the first place? Clinton understood that the implicit message that traditional welfare liberals were sending to employed workers, wittingly or not, was that they were "suckers" for accepting the discipline welfare recipients could ignore. For those whites who were struggling, the liberal subtext continued. Unlike persecuted minorities (whom they, Archie Bunker-like, were harming), they had no one to blame but themselves. In choosing to cut off welfare recipients, Clinton was appealing to the self-respect of these workers to get their votes.

When values and lifestyles feel threatened, the strong temptation to assert the truth of one's lifestyle is reinforced. People who had seen their income remain stagnant or fall, taxes increase, working hours grow, skills diminish in value, and hold on the American dream weaken were especially prone to resent those who seemed able to get by at their expense without working. Welfare recipients may actually have been less a threat to their wallet than to their sense of themselves, but being "on the dole" seemed to violate the kind of discipline that working and middle-class people endure and valorize. When laced with racial attitudes, their resentment becomes profoundly toxic.

Issues like welfare are powerful, however, for reasons that go beyond the racial poison in which they've been dipped. They reach deeply into the paradoxical relationship between discipline and working hard, on the one hand, and hedonism and consumerism, on the other—we will later elaborate this as America's moral paradox. Why, in an affluent society that celebrates consumption and leisure, do we need to work so hard? Although welfare as an issue calls subterranean attention to this question, the plausibility of not working hard is itself kept alive not just by the promise of modernity and technology, but by the self-centered impulses for convenience and pleasure that *must be shaped, nurtured, and honed* by any economic system heavily driven by consumerism.

Modern advertising, technology, and communications, of course, heighten these problems. Network and mainstream cable TV, radio, and the Internet rarely assess the effects on our politics of the simultaneous cultural pulls of discipline and pleasure, even as they pepper us with commercials or pop-up ads that encourage us to buy things for ourselves that will require us to work more in the "opportunity society" they extol. However complicit they may be, they do not create the paradox.

There is a huge literature that goes back many years on the subjects of "status seeking," "status anxiety," "working to spend," and consumer culture, and on the values and enervated sense of self that consumer culture produces.[14] What needs greater consideration today is how the very act of *not* bringing America's moral paradox and its consequences into political discourse and deliberation colors our politics. The 2004 election was but the latest example of neglect regarding these crucial questions of politics and culture.

Neglecting them will continue to promote the condemnation of—and the generation of anxieties within ourselves from—the behavior of those who seem to lack the virtue to hold the values we do. Neglect keeps us on a treadmill of demonization, modern-style.

Political positions designed primarily to appeal to or assuage resentments are not simply disputes about which reasonable people may differ. They become personalized wars in which each side feels its identity assaulted by an enemy whose own character is intrinsic to the wrong that was perpetrated. Consequently, one must expose the ways these wrongs flow from the private life of the individual. People too often are charged with being politically suspect for personal reasons because we have confused the *rhetoric* of personal responsibility with a sober assessment of it. Politically relevant assessment involves responsible discussion of the nexus between individual character, social structure, and public policy.

Personal responsibility is a necessary constituent, at a very deep level, of discourse that is freer of demonization. Humane political encounters require a specific kind of responsibility: the willingness of participants to resist the temptation to shield the self from doubts about oneself through the construction and illicit blaming of "others." Such willingness is a hallmark of responsible democratic participation.

Morality and Responsibility

The ability to reflect on critical moral concerns requires sober individuals relatively free of obsessive identity needs or the political pressure to denigrate others. The line separating legitimate moral concern and a politics of demonization is, within reason, contestable.

There is a vast difference between appropriate moral judgment and the self-serving efforts to affirm the worth of one's own or one's group's values, ideology, or identity. Our focus on the harm of rigid moralistic codes is inspired by a desire to foster a humane and sustainable *moral* as well as political discourse, as free as possible from manipulation that can cause harm. If every private act or public belief is seen as emblematic of a particular code, then ridicule, disgrace, and humiliation will proliferate. At the center of the derogation is the core belief in the depravity of one's opponent. Every act, private and public, becomes further political evidence for this belief. Hermetically sealed, mutually exclusive universes of discourse confront each other as politics becomes more perilous and less desirable, affecting the socialization process of who will or will not become a politician. Just where we can draw the line between private behavior and public office, however, is not immediately self-evident. Where such lines are drawn is an unavoidable part of politics itself and bears on proper application of moral concern regarding the publicly relevant character of candidates and leaders.

When these lines are drawn carelessly, hypocritically, or guided by partisanship, demonization of character becomes more likely. When all behavior is believed to be a legitimate target of scrutiny so as to determine the direction our polity should take, the temptation to place political actors and their programs in bins of good and evil will proliferate. The more evil (or deviance) we find, the more fearful we are and repressive we are willing to become. This cycle weakens compromise and reasoned discussion of the best course to follow. By protecting privacy, we can focus on public positions that keep us engaged in reasoned discourse over issues that really affect our lives. Contests in demonization are also dangerous, however, because of the chilling effect they have on participation. They can destroy a man or woman, destroy the movement she or he leads and, worse, demoralize the moral claims of its adherents.

The more we see the manifestation of good and evil in everything, the less we are able to distinguish when truly good or evil actions occur. To see ourselves consistently as saints and our opponents as evildoers is to lose the ability to tell the difference. The more we demonize, the more we weaken the imperfectly shared yet critical moral universe that grounds and enables members of our society to deliberate on and learn right from wrong. In the guise of morality, demonization of individual, group, policy, or ideology can destroy the capacity for sound *moral* judgment while also harming society's very moral foundations.

2

The Politics of Moral Personae

There is a characteristic mode of demonization in America that we call the politics of moral personae, in which persons become construed as embodied representations of either good or evil, normal or deviant. Demonization via the politics of moral personae implicates the entire relationship between the moral qualities purported to be inherent in and exhibited by leaders, followers, noteworthy individuals, policies, and political philosophies. This form of politics has particular resonance in modern electoral politics, and is of special importance in American politics today.

The most important signal that politics has shifted from simple demonization based on an opponent's ideology or ascriptive characteristics to a politics of moral personae is that the demonization of the private character and moral agenda of political leaders and followers becomes a dominant mode of discourse. As a consequence of such a regime, areas previously thought to be private and "personal" appear to become legitimate terrain of public scrutiny. Privacy erodes. Character becomes important not only for its own sake, or for completion of duties, but because it becomes evidence of the good or evil, normalcy or deviance, of policies promoted by a particular character.

The Personal Is (Sometimes) Political

Feminists have long told us that practices conventionally regarded as the foundation of social life—the domestic role of women, their deference to the leadership of men within the family, their subordinate roles in business, government, and the academy—were not inscribed by God. Some uttered a brilliantly turned phrase that was as complex in its ramifications as it was simple in its syntax: "The personal is political."

Spousal abuse, for example, although a hidden ("private") practice, was enabled by broader patriarchal roles and rules of behavior established and enforced by society and the state. Moreover, it was immoral behavior, feminists argued, that should be politicized in public and banned by law. Indeed, women's privacy depended upon stopping "private" practices of domestic tyranny, and this could only be achieved by subjecting those practices to public scrutiny. As this example indicates, the legal principle of sanctity of a "man's castle," which underlay the privacy protections outlined in *Rex v. Wilkes* (a 1763 decision that influenced our Fourth Amendment), could not be treated as absolutely inviolate.

Although it may be true that virtually all private relationships are founded upon public elements of language, tradition, culture, and law, it does not follow that all of these relationships should be politicized. Consider the ambiguity within the notion of personal privacy itself. Privacy can refer to what goes on outside the public eye, as in one's house. Privacy may also suggest matters viewed by the public that do not have substantial consequence for the larger society. The color of shoes one wears in public is a paradigmatic instance of the private, while murdering someone in one's own home is not.

These considerations suggest that understanding that the "personal is political" in important senses does not absolve us of having to do the controversial work of deciding where the lines should be drawn between private life and public acts, between power and legitimate authority, between privacy and politics and law. The very drawing of these lines is an exceptionally important political act, and the lines, as feminists have shown us, sometimes need to be challenged. Redrawn lines remain, however, to some degree, contestable and have crucial implications for the scope of politics. If all that is "personal" becomes "political," then wars of political demonization may know no bounds.

The Politics of Character

The emphasis on character and its relation to policy and associational activity is pronounced today because of the confluence of a number of factors. For the most part, it is no longer acceptable in American society to think of character in terms of ascriptive, socioeconomic terms, as tolerance has grown. Racial, gender, ethnic, regional, and other animosities may be suppressed or sublimated or they may be put to effective use through coded language, but they cannot be directly articulated if one has political aspirations, especially one with national reach. Yet the democratic nature of the American polity also insures that there exist public competitions for power, so that each side must gain whatever edge it can. Sometimes this quest leads candidates or their supporters to come very close to employing older forms of group stigma, such as racism, perhaps most famously in the Willie Horton ads used to undermine the candidacy of Michael Dukakis in 1988.[1]

Electoral contests may become vehicles for demonization especially in eras such as our own in which there is close electoral competition and deep partisanship. The advent of instantaneous mass media and intense competition for attention make sensationalized politics very attractive as a commercial as well as an ideological strategy.

Quite often it is the leader who is the lightning rod for the attack, in part because leaders who support certain policies may also be thought to have a character structure that must accompany such purportedly immoral policy ideas. This can also work the other way around, in which case the character of the leader becomes a guide to the lack of moral bona fides of policies and associational activity that have formed around those policies. Thus, the individual character of liberal leaders is suspect because they support welfare programs considered morally suspect, or the character of conservative leaders is suspect because they support the ending of welfare. Policies, leaders, and supporting groups become additionally suspect as the moral contamination is seen to migrate among them.

One important institutional reason for the saliency of leadership character in U.S. politics is our presidential system. Political scientists have long noted differences between our system, for example, and constitutional monarchies in which the king or queen is the symbolic leader of a nation and a prime minister is the one who governs. In the United States, the president must be a partisan party leader, governor, and symbol of the nation. Some add that the president also becomes the "father" of the nation, together with all the psychoanalytic implications of that term. All of these functions elevate the leader, who leads, rules, and ritualistically embodies the nation. Indeed, this is one reason that for many Americans the White House is hallowed ground, making President Clinton's dalliance with Monica Lewinsky all the more disturbing to them.

With presidential powers greatly expanding with the development and maintenance of the post–World War II "national security state," Arthur

M. Schlesinger, Jr., and others have labeled the office the "imperial presidency."[2] Although Schlesinger was criticizing the powers presidents and their administrations have been allowed to arrogate to themselves, Michael Rogin directly connects the charged symbolic role of the modern presidency to political demonology. For Rogin, the "imperial presidency" becomes one in which presidents "personified America by absorbing the members of the body politic into their own mystic bodies and leading the regenerated American nation against its alien, demonic foes."[3] He calls this the "climax of countersubversion," the tradition of demonization that he identifies as centrally important in American history. Particularly during a time of terrorist threat, this symbolic role gives presidents great power to cause harm to those they exclude from respectability.

Conservative *New York Times* columnist David Brooks nicely captures another way in which presidents and presidential contenders have become implicated in the politics of moral personae. "Have you noticed," he asks, "that we've moved from the age of the culture wars to the age of the presidency wars?" While we used to argue about cultural and social issues, we now focus on who lives in the White House. Whereas "culture warriors" were passionate about issues, "with the presidency warrior, political disagreement, cultural resentment and personal antipathy blend to create a vitriol that is at once a descendant of the old conflicts, but also different." Today, he argues,

> The warrior goes out looking for leaders strong enough to crush the devil. . . . It's about who can stand up to the other side. To the warrior, politics is no longer a clash of value systems, *each of which is in some way valid*. It's not a competition between basically well-intentioned people who see the world differently. It's not even a conflict of interests. Instead, it's the Florida post-election fight over and over, a brutal struggle for office in which each side believes the other is behaving despicably. . . . The warriors have one other feature: ignorance. They have as much firsthand knowledge of their enemies as members of the K.K.K. had of the N.A.A.C.P. . . . The core threat to democracy is not in the White House, it's the haters themselves.[4]

In describing today's politics in this way, Brooks points us toward important issues; however, the shift is not as radical as he suggests. What, after all, did Jimmy Carter symbolize to conservatives back in 1980 but an inept liberal do-gooder who was endangering America's security? For many liberals of the time, Ronald Reagan was bringing us directly to the midnight of a nuclear war. Was this simply a clash of values between opponents who recognized that the views of the other were "in some way valid," or was each man's character a perceived threat to a cherished way of life? Even more importantly, Brooks averts our eyes from the fact that character and policy have historically been intertwined in American political culture, even as they have been of continued relevance over the last forty years and have become the premier venue for demonization over the last ten. Do existing narratives within American political culture allow us to see into the minds and hearts of the "haters" about whom Brooks rightly alerts us?

Narrative and Genre

In order to win political support, all of politics simplifies, frames, provides points of easy reference, and draws our eyes from inconvenient facts. The politics of moral personae is best seen as a danger inherent in normal politics taken to extremes in particular ways. From Progressive-era reforms such as the primary election to the personality focus of modern mass media, the organizational focus of politics has shifted from party to individuals, making the saliency of individual character even greater than before. America's individualist and voluntarist culture is implicated in this tendency. But all of these and other political tendencies and structural changes are also built here on top of, as James A. Morone suggests, a culture of "hellfire nation" in which there is a "moral urge at the heart of American politics and society," with consequences for modern forms of demonization.[5]

Early settlers believed themselves to be creating a "city on a hill," an exceptional community fundamentally different from Old Europe. Drawn from different ethnic, national, and racial groups, in a process of continuous socioeconomic and ethnic change and often in anxiety, Morone argues, Americans have and continue to face the "primal question, Who are we?" The answer we have given is a "godly people," with a deep "moral urge" toward the puritan model.[6]

Contrary to popular misconceptions, however, the puritan religious impulse actually contains the seeds of two opposite answers to the "moral bottom line: Who do we blame for trouble, the sinner or the society?" Rather than just blaming the sinner, the puritans blamed both.

Salvation and perdition fell on individual souls; however, the Puritan covenants held the entire community responsible. In time, the two halves of that equation—the individual and the community—split. One moral tradition touts personal responsibility. Sinners impoverish themselves and diminish their community. . . . The alternative tradition, the social gospel, shifts the emphasis from the sinner to the system. . . . [Both traditions] run deep in the American psyche.[7]

Over the past century, Morone claims, "the two have alternated as the dominant moral paradigm," as America has not moved from religious to secular and back, but from "revival to revival," now Victorian, then Social Gospel. However, committed primarily to seeing America first and foremost as a liberal and perhaps republican denouement, based on belief in a strict separation between the public and the private, liberal political history tends to view moral movements as "anomalies," underestimating "the roaring moral fervor at the soul of American politics," including the soul of liberalism.[8]

Each of these distinctive moral visions was spawned by early puritanism's emphasis on personal godliness and an ideal of community that took responsibility for the godliness of its members.[9] The first tradition, the one most commentators associate with the puritans, portrays an unending struggle between good and bad people. Our national strength depends on the personal moral integrity of individuals. If all Americans work hard, lead disciplined, monogamous lives, avoid the perils of consciousness-distorting substances, all will enjoy at least a modicum of prosperity. The task of the community as a whole is simply to enforce these personal norms.

Against this moral vision, Morone recounts another moral tradition, the Social Gospel. It portrays the moral distinctiveness and greatness of this society in its willingness to provide both ample opportunities and a generous safety net for all. Within such a framework, individuals are far more capable of rising to the level of responsible citizenship and proper attentiveness to the needs of family. It is the ideal of inclusiveness that defines national greatness.

These twin traditions were related to a single experience. Early puritans came to a new world to escape the persecution in the old, to build a church and society that is in direct contact with God, to allow their identity to flourish. Yet paradoxically, in a land where all except the Native Americans were from abroad, and now freed from Old World persecution, it became hard for puritans to build and sustain a coherent identity. According to Morone, "The Puritans groped back to the tried and true— they found terrible new enemies to define them. The saints constructed their 'us' against a vivid series of immoral 'them': heretics, Indians, witches. Each enemy clarified the Puritan identity."[10]

We would add that persecution in England had left the puritans all the more determined to establish a direct relationship with and dependence on their God and to regard all that differed from that mindset as not merely different but evil. Moreover, the puritans in a sense were fortunate to benefit from two historical accidents. The Native Americans were different and they were formidable and successful enough to require the attention of the puritans, but not so strong that they could not be subdued. And the continent the puritans occupied was extensive and rich in resources, characteristics that could undergird both individualistic and mobile conceptions of freedom and an emphasis on economic growth.

Yet economic growth and the private market have never been without bumps along the way. So for example, when technology, markets and the rise of extraordinary economic inequality in the 1920s led to depression, these cataclysms encouraged the reemergence of the other moral tradition in America, the Social Gospel. The rise of public primary education, Social Security, and the GI Bill after the Second World War reflect this tradition.

Morone's work is a skilled and admirably accessible defense of the Social Gospel tradition. He provocatively probes the narratives of good versus evil presented in contemporary public discourse. The ways in which particular moral crusades against drugs, sex, or dissolute youth have often intersected with now properly discredited forms of racism and sexism, the almost ritualistic litanies of vices said to be morally connected to each other, the gaps between the enormity of the charges and the evidence provided, the willingness to suspend conventional civil liberties and standards of evidence all suggest more than a desire to cope with real risks. They bespeak an urge to impose a narrative of a good us versus the destructive bearers of other values and lifestyles in order to build up a core group's sense of self.

To his great credit, however, Morone is not an unqualified defender of the Social Gospel tradition. He recognizes that advocates of that tradition, such as Franklin D. Roosevelt, made compromises with older forms of moralistic and exclusionary politics in order to enact some of their visions. The original Social Security legislation excluded agricultural and domestic workers from its definition of the "workers" eligible for pensions.

Morone is right to recognize the compromises built into the original "universal" entitlement programs, but we would be inclined to go deeper. Morone cites the neo-orthodoxy of such mid-twentieth century Protestant theologians as Reinhold Niebuhr, but from our perspective he might have done more to elaborate on Niebuhr's challenge to the Social Gospel. The problem with unequivocal celebrations of this gospel, which Niebuhr resisted, lies not merely in the inevitable compromises one must make to enact it, but also in the claims to the universality of even the original unsullied proposals and agendas. The Social Gospel portrait of the good society bears a striking resemblance to conventional moral notions of the good and bad individual. In the Social Gospel tradition, individuals may not be solely responsible for their behavior, but the world can often still be starkly divided between good and evil societies and ways of life. The onus in achieving the good society now shifts to a proactive government.

Morone points out that at the heart of Niebuhr's theology lay a "demanding existentialism reverberating with irony, paradox, and historical contingency."[11] Niebuhr would also have been the first to remind us of the depth of the eschatological similarity between the Social Gospel and more conventional Protestant religious discourse. Social Gospel advocates envision reforms that bring citizens into full conformity with and willing acceptance of a range of important familial and social norms. Conventional discourse imagines the eventual triumph of saints over sinners. History may end with a bang or a whimper, but in either case it ends. We doubt that history will end, and fear for our boredom if it did.

The Social Gospel tradition in America today, represented by the legacies of Progressivism, the New Deal, and the Great Society, is a proud legacy that has encountered at least three limits. Its commitment to economic justice grew out of, and was a means toward, further economic growth, the production of more goods and services. Such good was itself based on a faith in a nonhuman nature that is both inexhaustible and subject to ever-greater comprehension and control. In a world where growth is both the means toward and the substance of the good life, must not the question arise of the purpose of growth—at least as long as generous subsistence needs are being met for middle-class and even many working-class Americans? Finally, the Social Gospel tradition, just like the welfare-state tradition in Western Europe, was premised on a view of the sovereign state as the instrument of justice and freedom. But what will happen when the very processes of economic growth and technological development enable and even require increasing contact with foreign peoples and cultures?

Every universal right or entitlement—even that of the more capacious Social Gospel tradition—is articulated by finite human beings standing in particular historical and cultural space. What if the world—both human and nonhuman—is not designed to be fully understood or controlled by mortal creatures whose insights are limited by the senses, memory, perception, death, and what must remain *human* spirituality? What if the unfolding of any tradition runs into and generates surprises it could not anticipate? What if these gaps lead to new rights claims? Human beings may respond to the inevitable gaps and limits that seem to transcend their every claim with more and more desperate efforts to claim finality for rights long held to be comprehensive and universal. But in the face of a world that may always exceed our grasp, perhaps those universals that are the most true are the ones articulated with an openness or critical sensitivity to their possible, indeed probable, limits. In such a context, one must be attuned to the possibility that universal rights may be too narrowly extended and that the rights themselves are inherently incomplete.

The culture of economic growth—projected in various ways by both left and right—seems to have encountered a broad set of environmental, cultural, ethnic, and religious questioning and resistance. Understanding our history of demonization may help foster a more generous response to these currents, and better understanding of this resistance may in turn deepen our understanding of demonization. At least this is the faith that governs our work.

To say that the politics of moral personae in America can be tempered is not to suggest politics would or should ever become a group sing-a-long of "Kumbaya." Politics is and will remain a contest of power, interests, ideas, and identity, even as democratic politics tries to allow clashes to occur peacefully through the principles of political equality and individual liberty and rights. Although limiting demonization in contemporary America is important for a more humane and civil discourse, there is another reason to impose limits on it: to allow all people, whether harried middle-class professionals or society's most vulnerable and disenfranchised, to reach the best assessment of what they really want and need and how best to achieve their goals.

According to Morone, today's culture war is really not a clash between secularism and fundamentalism but one "between two American moral traditions." One focuses on "reforming 'them,'" the other on "redeeming 'us.'" Both are entangled in American political history.[12] In each of Morone's examples—although his stories are often quite textured—it is the "reforming them," or Victorian tradition, that produces the major harms. In his narrative, the Social Gospel, not its Victorian (evil?) twin, is the hero. He passionately defends the civil rights advances of the sixties as examples of a Social Gospel revival. Further, he charges that social conservatives today demonize the sixties, wrongly mischaracterizing the era as primarily a time of hedonism and nihilism, precisely because it represents "an undiluted version of the Social Gospel" that challenges the priorities and purposes of the Victorian moment. What, however, of the Social Gospel tradition? Where might it fit into the schema of demonization?

Beyond Innocent Victims

For insight into the relationship between demonization and progressive moralizing, we now turn to film, in particular, to Warren Beatty's innovative and brave 1998 film *Bulworth*. Film is an excellent medium by which to explore the politics of moral personae because it is so dependent on audience *expectations* about character and narrative, much as the politics of moral personae does.

Bulworth is about a middle-aged California senator, J. Billington Bulworth, deep in despair at the end of a personal and professional midlife crisis. Played by Beatty, Bulworth trades a promise to a lobbyist that he will subvert health insurance reform in return for a substantial life-insurance policy. He then takes out a contract on himself to end his life. Liberated by his impending death from the burdens of his old life, Bulworth finds a new identity and reason for living. Inspired by an intelligent, beautiful, engaging young African American woman, Nina, played by Halle Berry, Bulworth puts aside the vacuous clichés of contemporary politics for the style and rhetoric of political and cultural critique. He literally raps his new message about race, class, and corruption of politics. He is redeemed, but can he redeem us?

Bulworth is a film with texture. Senator Bulworth is certainly no victim, and Nina is no innocent. Nina's family is interesting and multifaceted, although there is also something very innocent about most of its members. *Bulworth*, however, is more often than not a movie of black and white in more than one sense. It is an old-fashioned morality play.

The rich are evil. They control the media and entertainment industry and thoroughly dominate economics and politics. The system is theirs. African Americans are victims and white Americans victimizers.[13]

In this film it is Nina who presents the critique of globalization. Although her argument is hardly novel, it is an important one to hear from *her* and to bring to the theater. She believes the notion that weakness in black leadership can be explained by past assassinations is wrong. Wealthy corporations have shipped the whole urban industrial base offshore, depriving blacks of the economic resources upon which community power must be built. Nonetheless, her overall jeremiad, the one Bulworth (and Beatty) endorses, is another in a long line of power-elite theories that have gripped the left at least since the Populist era. All of these theories operate on the assumptions that (1) there is a tightly unified group, the wealthy, (2) that dominates not only our economics and politics, (3) but even controls the content of our thoughts. Nina is correct in pointing out the implications of outsourcing not only for African American communities, but also for much of the white working class. And wealth, coupled with the corporate prerogative to relocate and redesign production processes, is surely a form of power. But are liberals, African Americans, and workers wholly blameless (wholly powerless) in the face of these scenarios? The AFL-CIO until recently had a long history of support for U.S. government efforts, in part motivated by the Cold war, to repress populist unions abroad, just the sort of foreign union whose equity demands would make business flight more difficult in the first place.[14]

Money is power, of course, but so too are large numbers of people. The major media are becoming increasingly concentrated and are far too monolithic, although not to the degree *Bulworth* implies. If money really were all-powerful, resistance would always achieve only the cul de sac that Bulworth's "assassination" seems to make inevitable. Yet in addition to defeat, American history is full of examples of resistance and change. Might there be other reasons beyond elite manipulation and control and white racism that prevent majorities from rising up to right the wrongs that Beatty sees?

Bulworth doesn't explore these possibilities. Beatty has both political and cinematic reasons for constructing the film's main thrusts in the way he does. They are not unrelated.

Film language builds the art of expectation directly into its theory.[15] Films rely on our expectations about the nature of certain types of characters and situations to tell us a story in a limited amount of time, during which we have no opportunity to go back to reread what we missed. The script plays a role, of course, but most films tell stories through pictures and sounds, through camera angles and position, through editing, style, and music, through audience expectations and genre codes.

The most important aspect of film language for this discussion is genre. The telling of stories through film often depends on the expectations of the roles and plots that we bring into the theater. Classic film genres have representative codes. The Western, sci-fi, murder-mystery, film noir, and even the political thriller (think of a younger Beatty film, Alan J. Pakula's *The Parallax View*) are some examples. Putting the more avant-garde film to one side, filmmakers rely on our knowledge of genre to tell a story.[16] While not all films are generic, and films are made that defy, play with, or pay homage to a variety of genres, generic expectations are important in most films.

Through genre, visual and audio power, and audience willingness to suspend disbelief, films create an impression of reality with the "consistency of a possible world . . . organized so that every element of the fiction seems to respond to some organic necessity by appearing essential to the imagined reality."[17] Through generic expectations, identification with camera and character, and the medium's iconic representations, the spectator-subject becomes inscribed into the film's representative system as if in the film's diegetic space.[18] Thus, a film rings most true when we were "in" it before.

Bulworth is most intelligible to us as a morality play of (failed) social redemption in which each character is not so much a person as a persona with a specific role to play and a moral code to embody. These expectations are both tied to the populist ideology of the film and the need in film as a medium for expectations to be established and fulfilled. Nina is, if not completely virtuous, the oppressed African American who refuses to be a victim. Bulworth is the redeemable (indeed redeemed by love), caring, if adorably quirky, white guy who rediscovers his true self. In finding their inner power, Bulworth and Nina empower others. Discovering who they are as they propagate the Social Gospel, Beatty-style, however, requires defining them against the wholly unsympathetic forces of evil arrayed against them, making them all the more sympathetic.

Assassinating Bulworth serves three objectives. Rather than having a nihilistic ending, it fulfills the populist generic expectation that a system headed by an evil all-powerful elite does exist. For who else but evildoers could *do* such a thing to *defend* such a system? It also keeps Beatty the director from having to show us what Beatty the reformer would do. For that would require more assessment of what is wrong and how the world might be different in new hands. The ending, of course, is stirring, but it is so in part because it confirms Bulworth as the latest victim in the slaughter of the reformers, from Christ to Gandhi, Kennedy and King (and Beatty's earlier murder in *The Parallax View*). We are all innocent victims of a corrupt and racist political system. Our innocence is proven when Bulworth—and we are all Bulworth by that point—is assassinated by those complicit in the system. In some ways, a better answer to the question of powerlessness was given by Robert Redford's character in Michael Ritchie's 1972 film *The Candidate,* after Redford's character's improbable election to the Senate. A reformer corrupted by the art of winning, he turns to his campaign manager and asks inaudibly against the crowd's roar, "What do I do now?"

Stirring narratives are needed in politics perhaps even more so than in film; but when they become too self-assured, the consequences can be grim. Innocent victims—and many people join hate groups precisely because they believe they have been victimized—can become "innocent" demonizers.

Many in our society have been exploited, and each of them properly draws on that experience to frame his or her view of the world. To portray a world divided inexorably between demonic oppressors and virtuous victims, we must deny or belie parts of our own experience, forms of evidence accepted in other contexts, and even the logical consequences of our own theories. We move away from an analysis positioned to understand real people and real movements toward one that has already decided on the roles we expect people and movements to play in order to fulfill the gospel we wittingly or unwittingly preach.

3

America's Moral Paradox

The cultural wars dating back to the 1960s, which often led to a willingness to treat moral and political positions opposed to one's own as utterly evil, have spilled over into the American tendency to focus unduly on the private lives of public figures. In the previous chapter we identified a characteristic mode of demonization and the context in which it occurs. Here we try to identify structural, ideological, and psychological sources that help explain why the politics of moral personae has taken the particular forms it has over the last forty years.[1]

Some have understood the political battles over President Bill Clinton's impeachment as a struggle between conservative/puritan and liberal/hedonist responses to the allegation of sexual improprieties—or the morally uptight crowd, as liberal detractors of conservatives would put it, and the anything-goes crowd, as conservative detractors of liberals would respond. Undoubtedly, there was hypocrisy on each side.[2] Our contention here is not that moral critics of Clinton were all "puritans" or that his defenders were all "hedonists," although some in each camp may have been. Moreover, critics and defenders of Clinton could reasonably come to opposite conclusions on his fitness for office without being involved in the politics of demonization.

We do contend that there is a moral paradox within America that may play a role in political contests that are as rife with demonization as was, for example, the struggle over Clinton's impeachment. The paradox is indicative of our doubts about the course of modern progress, and it produces anxieties and pressures that make our identities less secure and make us more likely to seek relief through demonizing thought and rhetoric. When one's values and lifestyles seem threatened, there is a temptation to assert the validity of one's own path in life. Such anxiety and threat can be exploited for political gain through political demonology of the kind leveled at Clinton and his critics. The fervor with which it was pursued is further indication that Morone's characterization of the two strains of puritanism is worthy of our close attention.

A Cultural Dilemma

Almost thirty years ago, Daniel Bell argued that there exists a "cultural contradiction" within capitalism that undermines the moral character and legitimacy of our society. In capitalism from the start, the impulses of "asceticism and acquisitiveness were yoked together," he says, but disappearance of asceticism has taken with it a central moral legitimation for capitalist behavior:[3]

> American capitalism . . . has lost its traditional legitimacy, which was based on a moral system of reward rooted in the Protestant sanctification of work. It has substituted a hedonism which promises material ease and luxury, yet shies away from all the historic implications of a "voluptuary system," with all its social permissiveness and libertinism. . . . [A] hedonism that has undercut the Protestant ethic which provided the moral foundation for the society. The interplay of modernism . . . [and] hedonism as a way of life promoted by the marketing system of business, constitutes the cultural contradiction of capitalism.[4]

For Bell, the most fateful division in society is between industrialism and modernist culture. Where one emphasizes functionalism, rationality, technocratic decision making, and the rewards of meritocracy, the other features "apocalyptic moods and anti-rational modes of behavior." One is based on rational economic principles, the other on "anti-cognitive and anti-intellectual modes" that look inward "toward a return to instinctual sources of expression."[5] He leaves little doubt about which is to be reformed and preserved and which exorcised.

Where interests rule, society needs to be held together by a reaffirmation of liberalism, a "social compact," maturity, recognition of limited resources, greater equity and fairness and common purposes—in short, a "priority of *needs,* individual and social, over unlimited appetite and wants." The polity needs to play a crucial role, but can do so only if it is redesigned as a "public household" that promotes social purposes, especially through the public budget, and a new social bill of rights. The relegitimation of capitalist society can occur only if the values of political liberalism save it from "bourgeois hedonism."[6]

While Bell's work is richly suggestive, he too easily turns his eyes from the disciplines modern society needs and is able to maintain for the sake of the productivity that drives the hedonism he chides. His argument turns from an interesting examination of history, social structure, and ethics to a cultural critique and call for a higher moral tone in the new liberalism of the public household. The deviant impulses that guide one's life, however elicited by modern capitalism and modernist culture, turn out in Bell's account still to be mostly the responsibility of the people they guide or the cultural cues that lead them astray.

It may be that some of the individualism that Bell eschews is a reaction to more than advertising or modernism. An assortment of modern disciplines, including the competitiveness of meritocracy and need for performance even in noneconomic realms of life, may spark rebelliousness, as it did with the antimaterialistic views of many in the 1960s counterculture. Corporate capitalism may be both promoting unlimited desire and sparking rebellion through its own kind of organization, which it tries to placate with the promise of meeting even more material demands, which it can then promote.

Bell may also be giving capitalism and modernity too little credit. Some aspects of economic abundance and modernist culture may have liberated parts of ourselves from disciplines, superstitions, and needs, of older-style, harsh moralizing regimes, making room for new possibilities. Instead, there is a kind of nostalgia for values-gone-by in Bell's scolding moral critique.

Bell offers a trenchant critique of important cultural implications of advanced capitalism as economics and of modernism as culture. In the end, however, he implies too strongly that we can keep what is essential to the economic engine if we can bring about changes in our hearts. If there really were cultural *contradictions*, neither such changes of sentiment nor their institutionalization through a "public household" nor the reforms we offer later in our conclusion would suffice. Political *and* cultural revolution would be required, hardly something he desires. In the end, Bell helps us identify America's moral paradox but remains insensitive to its texture.

America's Moral Paradox

Although Americans are a religious people driven by a strong moral sense of themselves, they still want, here and now, material and psychic rewards for submitting to the disciplines modern society still, sometimes increasingly, demands. In the economic arena, even in a technologically advanced society such as our own where most have basic comforts, demands for increased productivity have grown to try to keep pace with intensified competition. Fear of job loss, of course, plays a role in people's willingness to submit to economic disciplines and pressures. Escalating lures and promises of possessions that will increase comfort, leisure, pleasure, passion, free time, or escape, however, remain essential both as reward and as the motivating engine of the economy itself.

Desires for such goods, however, call into question the very disciplinary codes essential both to increase productivity and to attain the income needed to purchase the rewards. As time and psychological space needed to enjoy the possessions worked so hard for are themselves put under pressure, the meaningfulness of the discipline/reward bargain is further questioned. Although the broad strokes of this dilemma are familiar elsewhere, our puritan heritage, individualism, Protestant ethic, faith in unbounded opportunity, and relentless commercialism give it distinctive power here.

Indeed, that's why we call it *America's* moral paradox. The nature of the rewards we expect and the kinds of discipline we require call each other into question. Yet we simply cannot dispense with either. It is a paradox worth negotiating with care. It is too easy to resent either those who *seem* to embrace the disciplines too tightly or who *seem* to view the rewards as the ends in themselves.

The disposition we identify has partial roots in the Protestant ethic, its celebration of work and material progress, and the abstemious attitude toward personal pleasure such an ethic entails. This ethic has been a consistent theme throughout much of our history, but it has never lacked domestic critics. Nor has it been without its own internal problems. The long-term survival of the very capitalist system that emerged through that ethic also came to require a blatant consumer culture and even the celebration of a culture of excess. Yet the paradox has never been fully acknowledged, as the political economy and its culture of work and growth are continually celebrated as a simple and unproblematic good. In the process, puritan and hedonist fundamentalism develop together, and each provides ideological and psychological fodder for the other.

Consider the unadvertised meaning of the coda of an ad for Saab. "All they did was eat, sleep, and work. Be glad you're not a Puritan." Because we are not puritans, the ad suggests we have the sense to buy a Saab, close its doors, and drive out into the countryside. We can know how to really live, if we *choose* to know how. What the ad does not tell us is that a healthy dose of Protestant work-ethic self-discipline is still necessary for most of us before we can make the purchase. Or that the time needed to take that drive may be hard to find because our work days have lengthened. Or that the coordination needed to make that drive a family drive is more difficult than it once was, with both spouses working and even children fully scheduled. Or that with increased debt, the credit rating we won through work and discipline will require new discipline for its maintenance.[7]

The motivation for hard work has changed in important ways since Puritan days, and even since the late nineteenth century, as many commentators have already pointed out. Once seen as no less than the meaning of life as endowed by religion, work is now often seen as the means to the good life. Strict Calvinists believed that one's position in life was predestined, that how hard and well one worked reflected God's plan for you.

Today, beer ads preach a different story about fate: "You only go around once in life; grab all the gusto you can." The faiths of Calvin and Budweiser appeal to radically different motivations for laboring. Work to reveal God's plan for your salvation. Work to buy the only salvation available in an amoral, godless world. Nevertheless, beer theology has some things in common with Calvinism. Work and its rewards are the best medicine for confronting finitude, and to show that one is saved.

Hard work at the job, at home, in leisure requires discipline, which, even when needed for the best of reasons, can breed rebelliousness and an external or internal reassertion of control. The purposes of hard work give meaning to these disciplines, which are usually codified in accepted standards of behavior. Those who seem to deviate from such codes and those who seem always to submit become problems for each other. The more one has a traditional, Calvinist orientation, the more likely deviation is experienced as evil, and the more one feels guilt, shame, and remorse as internal self-regulatory mechanisms kick in. The more "modern" the orientation, the more the deviation is experienced as dysfunction or abnormality, the more the disciplinary feelings are anxiety and self-deprecation. Whether "modernist" or "Calvinist," easing these self-denigrating feelings may be achieved by projecting forbidden desires, or fear of failure to meet standards, or fear of desire to be held to standards—to be disciplined—onto a pool of soon-to-be-despised others. "Puritan," cries the modernist or postmodernist. "Hedonist," replies the Calvinist. When these categories seem to overlap with groups whose beliefs or ascriptive characteristics are already viewed as suspect, the power of these techniques of self-validation grow. One's identity and group identity are buttressed, one's values and moral worth are demonstrated, by placing them all in stark relief against that of one's antagonists. Resentments, anger, and outrage are cultivated.

Social "puritanism" and material "hedonism" have an ironic and unstable relationship: the latter creates a rationale for the former—it offers an answer to the question: Why work so hard? Why, in an "age of affluence," are we still subjected to so much discipline? Nonetheless, it is a rationale the former must deny so it can be true to its own moral code. How much can escape the net of puritanism as it seeks to validate itself as a complete truth? How does puritanism react when signs of escape emerge? In periods of moral ambiguity and social and economic uncertainty, condemning the most blatant signs of "hedonism" may become necessary to suppress just how much cultural pressures toward (morally certain) puritanism now depend on (amoral) "hedonism" to justify the sacrifices puritan codes entail. In the short term, hedonism may ease feelings of deprivation, but it cannot really escape them. For it promotes its puritan twin by demanding growing self-centered rewards, and thereby the discipline necessary to achieve them.

Perceived threats to puritan codes of rectitude are inflamed by the very desire for pleasure and reward that is important in making economic disciplines today palatable and in creating new markets in a society where most middle-class citizens enjoy the basic comforts. Replying to "hedonistic" tendencies with calls for greater rectitude and discipline therefore runs the risk of undermining a critical modern motivation to accept the discipline. Dismissing discipline undermines the possibility of the rewards. Yet the resentments this system of discipline and reward breeds impel those who would require the adoption of one posture or the other, while making their arguments more compelling. Trying to do the right thing by condemning either the discipline or the rewards cannot succeed. That is the *moral* paradox.

There are two poles of reaction to this paradox: one is conservative, edging toward the puritanical; the other is libertarian and liberal, edging toward the hedonistic. The first we can call puritan-conservatism. It was exemplified by the now-defunct "Moral Majority," and the kind of prudishness that Clinton special prosecutor Kenneth Starr was accused of exhibiting. One of the most interesting and disheartening developments in conservative thought has been its inability, as a movement, to locate the structural sources for the seeming decline in cherished values. Perhaps this is one reason William J. Bennett, the former Reagan education secretary and Bush Sr. drug czar, seemed bewildered when he asked "where's the outrage?" when too many citizens, for his taste, seemed indifferent to Clinton's behavior. He questioned the public character because he knew what he perceived as misplaced tolerance extended well beyond the familiar conservative targets comprised of liberal elites in government, media, Madison Avenue, and Hollywood. What else then could be the cause of such perverse indifference than millions of individual characters suddenly gone wrong? That at least some of the sources of the problem might actually be in the economic and social system he lionizes didn't seem to occur to him.

For many conservatives, blaming liberal elites for perceived public immorality remains sufficient. Advertisers, for example, are accused of stimulating the prurient interest. Less attended is the source of those "needs" in people that give even the most salacious ad designer a foothold, and the intense competitive pressures that can also drive consumption within the social-status matrix of the workplace and community. Indeed, much of modern advertising combines an appeal to status and class insecurity with a promise of sexual fantasy, release, and success. The advertisers who succeed in this world work in a competitive environment that is celebrated by most conservatives, and they are rewarded for finding ads that sell, whatever their content. Unwilling to locate such structural sources of perceived problems, social conservatives such as Bennett tend to focus on individual culpability. If only people had the strength to retain the old verities in the new order, the new would be as good as was the old. Misunderstood change causes anxiety and guilt at not being able to be responsible in the same way as one's forebears were. It leads to further blaming of individuals, whether oneself or others. In our view, the consequences of political puritanism can have especially severe consequences in the present era, in which there exist intrusive and omnipresent modes of communication and information gathering, intense multimedia competition for the public's attention, and unsettling political challenges such as terrorism, economic globalization, and a growing inequality.

We can call the second pole hedonist-liberalism. It may put a brake upon the intrusiveness of political puritanism. However, it too is ill-equipped to navigate the moral paradox. Regarding the Clinton scandals, knee-jerk reaction against "prying" into his private life and especially calls to let him "do his job"—as if he were a technician—let him off the moral hook too easily, deflecting attention from his specific moral choices. Such a posture misses the important point made by social conservatives that *anything* simply does *not* go. "Do your own thing" overlooks both the sense in which our own "thing" sometimes displays the dominant culture more than unique individuality, and also the possibility —even probability—that individuals' desire for personal freedom is in subtle ways itself indebted to that culture. Moreover, hedonist liberals eschew a need for coordination and consensus in some cases while valorizing it in policies they favor.

The question most pertinent to the protection of real individuality is what should be coordinated, how and by whom, and what should not be. Hedonist liberal lapses in this regard reveal that this style of thinking also lacks appreciation of social structure. Like its puritan conservative "opposite" it also projects its anxieties outward, in this case perhaps a fear that being "free" may still leave one morally running on empty. Favorite targets, of course, are the puritan conservative moralizers who seem to threaten the hedonist liberal lifestyle.

Hedonist liberals and puritan conservatives need each other. For example, when critics of the intensive work life within the abundance of corporate capitalism propose limiting the demands of the system, defenders of corporate discipline can point to the mindless and destructive abuse associated with contemporary forms of hedonic escapism. On the other hand, an ethic of work for work's sake creates appeal for hedonism's promises of more pleasure. This appeal can then be channeled to workers through the form of promises of newer and better goods as reasons to follow the needed disciplines, also creating more questions about the need for further disciplines, and perhaps reluctance to adhere to those disciplines. This brief sketch shows how each pole of the moral paradox is tied to the other.

While individuals may sort themselves (or be sorted by their opponents) into one camp or the other, each pole of the paradox exists in most of us because it is implicated in important legitimating ideas and into our social structure and political economy. So, for example, someone who appears "hedonistic" may actually be doing prodigious psychic work, ironically, to defeat "puritan" impulses. Our point here, therefore, is not to condemn particular individuals or movements by labeling them as "puritans" or "hedonists," which is not to deny that there may be times that such appellations fit. Rather, it is to uncover and bring to awareness politically relevant impulses we share as a culture in order to enable a more generous democratic politics.

When either pole of the paradox dominates a person, or the paradox's influence is discounted or repressed, the temptation to displace resentments and anxieties onto others intensifies. This may even occur among those who, in resisting the pull of each poll, adopt a hyperpractical stance with regard to the meaning of daily life, resigning themselves to the way things are. They seem to avoid the paradox. Yet their stance too is molded by it.

How people negotiate America's moral paradox is important in studying contemporary patterns of demonization, and may provide clues about what differentiates demonization today from earlier periods. A more civil, respectful, yet more intensely participatory democratic politics could help us better situate our attitudes toward others within the context of paradoxes such as this one. Yet this is precisely what puritans, hedonists, and avoiders resist with their particular stance, making fruitful discourse and debate less likely.

Easing the Paradox, Understanding the Price

America's moral paradox will not be eliminated, but its pressures can be eased if we learn how better to negotiate its terrain. While discipline and sacrifice are essential to important goals, the question remains to what degree "progress" as presently construed is leading us to a higher quality of life. This quandary is difficult to disentangle because we sometimes confuse our cultural and economic pulls toward puritanism and hedonism with the necessary and desirable needs of discipline and pleasure.

Negotiating the paradox, put simply, will entail a broad discussion of national well-being centered on a sober probing of the quality of contemporary American life. Having a fruitful discussion is made more difficult, and interesting, however, by the ways in which the contradictory urges of Morone's two strands of puritanism may be laid over (or inter-mingle with) the puritan-hedonist pulls we describe in this chapter. As this overall matrix of orientations and sensitivities plays itself out between individuals and groups, and within them, how will it affect our ability to lessen demonization in day-to-day practices and to hold the kind of national discussion that will ease the demands more generally of demonization in politics? It is hard to say. We do think, however, that this conversation is best begun with a discussion of how we as a nation can best assay the price we pay for "progress."

Progress has a price that is obscured by an uncritical stance toward the most common ways in which we "measure" its achievement. National prosperity grew enormously in the twentieth century. By the turn of the century we had twice the GNP per capita that we enjoyed in 1950. Many Americans worked hard to achieve this result and should take pride in its accomplishment.

Studies show, however, that many citizens since then have become less satisfied with their lives.[8] This dissatisfaction may of course be related to overly inflated expectations, but these expectations would also need explanation, which is relevant to gauging quality of life.

Socioeconomic pressures and disruptions play a role in this unease and create an environment in which rhetorical excess may flourish. They have historically been designated as proximate causes for historical tragedies in which scapegoating and demonization figured prominently, most tragically in the collapse of the Weimar Republic and the rise to power of the Nazis in Germany. Pressures often are felt as problems within daily life, the practical tasks of getting and keeping a job, paying the bills, and keeping the family whole and on the right track. The sources of pressure can sometimes be misunderstood when we neglect tracing the private troubles we feel to the social, economic, and political milieu in which we live. Such neglect is abetted by inadequate political and social deliberation, making it more likely that we will cling to or even seek ways of thinking that do not serve us well.

Quality of life and quality of political deliberation, therefore, are interdependent instruments of national well-being. Yet, much political discourse fails to analyze either the meaning of the trends in which we find ourselves embedded, or the concepts that are used as gauges to mark the adequacy of those trends. Too often the current scope of discourse on economic well-being is at once fueled by partisanship yet limited by ideology in ways that heighten rhetoric while limiting understanding.

To illustrate, consider recent debates in the 2004 presidential election over job growth. Much was made by the Democrats and candidate John Kerry over how many jobs were lost during the Bush administration's first term, compared to the Clinton "boom" years,[9] yet far less attention was paid to the structure of the job market in either period.

In 2002, while there were 8.4 million officially unemployed workers, there were also 4.2 million involuntary part-time workers and 4.7 million people who stopped looking but still wanted a job. If there were a widely accepted statistical gauge in our political discourse that reported the rate of these 17.3 million people willing to work but without real work, it would tell a grimmer story about employment prospects than does the unemployment rate alone.[10]

The question of job growth even during Clinton's years, however, invites close scrutiny because it helps us understand pressures that persist even when key economic indicators tell us we are doing well. In 1995, the official unemployment rate stood at 5.7 percent. That figure did not, however, include 4.5 million Americans working part time but seeking full-time jobs. Another 8.1 million Americans worked in temporary jobs, and 8.3 million Americans were downsized professionals who now call themselves "independent contractors" but whose work is often sporadic at best. Finally, 5 or 6 million workers gave up looking for work. Lester Thurow estimates that when all these factors are considered, nearly 28 percent of the labor force was unemployed or underemployed in 1995.[11]

Thurow's data also help explain one of the most important anomalies of the 1990s "boom." The wage of the median worker fell throughout most of the Clinton recovery. Although many economists and business press writers anticipated a surge in wages occasioned by the relatively low rate of unemployment, these gains appeared only briefly and very modestly at the end of this period. It wasn't until the first quarter of 1999 when, adjusted for inflation, the median wage reached its 1989 prerecession peak. Economic insecurity, a prevailing ideology emphasizing individual efforts as the route to wealth, as well as internal problems within the union movement, made it very difficult for most workers to achieve the leverage necessary to gain significant pay raises, let alone ones that would keep pace with productivity growth.

An official unemployment rate of around 5.5 percent in 2004, therefore, is very different from a similar rate thirty years ago. More of today's workers hold only part-time positions, temporary jobs, or are downsized professionals. Others have given up looking for work because of lack of opportunity or because the costs of work, from childcare to transportation, greatly diminish the rewards of the job. When we consider these facts and recognize that European governments generally do factor part-time workers seeking full-time jobs in their definitions of unemployment, the U.S. labor market is hardly superior to Europe's,[12] contrary to widespread perceptions in the U.S. business press. For many of those who hold full-time jobs, soft labor markets and the absence of strong unions and low-wage standards have taken a toll. In 2002, 16.4 million full-time year-round workers earned less than the poverty level of $18,104 for a family of four.[13]

Health insurance coverage, which is quite expensive but a necessary economic protection, is also a mark of the economic health of citizens. In Europe, of course, comprehensive national health insurance is the norm. When President Clinton first proposed his national health care plan, 37 million Americans had no health insurance coverage. Two years after the demise of the Clinton effort, the figure reached 41 million.[14] Today it is 43.6 million, or more than the population of twenty-four states plus the District of Columbia. Equally troubling and less well known is that over the last two years, some 75 million Americans were at some point uninsured.[15] Even Americans who have coverage are vulnerable. Of the 2 million Americans who were bankrupted by health costs last year, 85 percent of them had some kind of health insurance.[16]

Sometimes when questions arise about quality of contemporary life, we like to remind ourselves that we are the most free, affluent, and powerful nation in history. Yet disturbing social and economic questions linger. For example, how do we explain the fact that the United States incarcerates more people, at more than 2 million, than any other nation except China, and possibly equals China with five times its population and a very repressive state? Or that the United States also has the highest incarceration *rate* in the world, at 702 persons per 10,000, three times higher than theocratic Iran, and 4.3 times higher when compared to its own rate in 1971? If our incarceration rate were equal to that of Iran's, approximately another 1.5 million jobs would be needed to take up the "prisoner" slack, and hundreds of thousands more to absorb layoffs from a "corrections industry" that now employs another 2.2 million Americans in the jobs of catching, putting, and keeping criminals behind bars.[17] Indeed, it is becoming more common, as the *Wall Street Journal* has done, to talk about the "corrections industry" as the "prison-industrial complex." When we add to those now behind bars 100,000 minors in juvenile facilities, 4 million persons on probation, and 750,000 more on parole, we find approximately 6.63 million Americans under legal supervision. Add the system's employees to this figure and we find that almost 9 million Americans are directly involved in the criminal justice system in one way or another. Yet neither the high incarceration rates nor the huge amounts of dollar and human resources expended in these ways were mentioned in the 2004 presidential election. In national politics, at least, talking about them is taboo.

Just as conventional political and economic talk often omits questions of how success in the production of jobs is measured and should be measured, it also often omits discussion of the kinds of jobs our citizens have. To what degree are we producing quality, full-time jobs for people who want and need them? Quality here would at a very minimum mean reasonable compensation and job security, vacation (where we again compare very unfavorably with Europe) and leisure time, and real choice regarding overtime.

Unfortunately, many of those who have full-time work are working the longest hours of their lives. Juliet Schor has argued that U.S. workers put in 163 more hours per year than they did twenty-five years before. Schor found that on average we work 1,900 hours per year, while Germans work about 1,600.[18] (Is it quaint to ask what happened to the freer-time promises of automation?) If government statistics show that I'm doing better, a fully employed worker might ask, Why do I feel that I can never catch up with all the things I need to do?

And where does all the money go? Following up on her work on increasing work hours, Schor also describes strong advertising pressures that no longer urge us to "keep up with the Joneses" but, worse, actually to spend as if we were in an economic class higher than our own. Consumerism in America has resulted in massive personal debt. Therefore people feel they are in a bind: to live the good life, one must find more time to make more money.

Our debates over jobs, therefore, echo rather more than reveal the prejudices hidden in the statistics. Should those who have given up looking for work not count as "unemployed"? If you believe that any person who tries hard enough has a good job awaiting him or her, why would you count quitters?

Yet a political debate over jobs that cannot probe deeply into issues such as structural job insecurity, underemployment, and desperation in finding work creates an interpretive deficit. If things are good, a newly part-time worker might ask, why am I not doing well? Is it my fault? Are foreigners stealing my job? How do I locate the source of the troubles I feel or the anxieties I experience when all the indicators I hear discussed tell me I should be doing well? Exactly whom should I blame?

Progress and Quality of Life

Even more than employment statistics, pride of place in the economist's statistical pantheon is given to the Gross National Product (GNP), referring to the total dollar value of goods and services produced by an economy. This figure also becomes a mainstay of political dialogue with economic debate between the parties focusing largely on how we can "grow the economy," to use Bill Clinton's infelicitous phrase. The Bush administration celebrated a magnificent 2003 fourth quarter in which the annualized growth rates of the GNP was over 7 percent, and then experienced a sharp 4.2 percent rise in the first quarter of 2004,[19] figures reminiscent of the 1960s, the golden age of the U.S. economy. Republicans used this as well as better monthly unemployment data to argue that the "Bush tax cuts" were working and Americans' lives were getting better.

GNP is a concept used in economic analysis as a neutral statistical gauge of an economy's success or failure. But the concept imbeds certain assumptions and reflects and embodies a broader worldview it never explicitly acknowledges. We might call GNP the secular statistical artifact of the seventeenth-century Protestant work ethic. More goods and services are not only a value in themselves but are proof that a society is directed in the right way.

It is our contention that measures such as GNP, even if we were to add measures that would track the fairness of distribution, are partial guides to social progress or lack thereof. What, after all, does GNP measure? That a given dollar amount dedicated to prison construction counts as much as the same dollar amount devoted to school construction should raise some doubts about just what the GNP is measuring.

Equal expenditures in building prisons, or controlling pollution, or cleaning up the damage wrought from previous product and technology choices adds as much to the GNP as does the production of more food or housing for those in need. When individuals leave the labor market and provide their own childcare, GNP decreases. Conventional GNP also fails to take account of the depletion of natural and finite capital resources, although accountants are well trained in depreciating capital equipment. These are just some examples of oddities produced by current economic measures. Gross National Product reflects and perpetuates prevailing cultural concepts of individual and collective identity. And the inequalities and stresses that have emerged from resulting patterns of growth in the GNP help to strengthen resentments that sometimes emanate from these conventional notions of the good life.

Maintaining steady economic growth, especially in the new competitive world market environment, and in spite of massive technological change, may require new disciplines. These include working harder and longer, having less security on the job, getting fewer services from government (as government frees capital for private markets), enduring constant "retraining," having one's children require ever higher levels of formal educational achievement, more homework, and less play. That work hours are increasing in our technological era rather than declining seems self-explained by new competitive pressures, but is competition by itself a satisfactory explanation of the prevalence of—even commitment to— lengthening hours of work?

An economic order premised on the need for relentless economic expansion, extremely demanding world markets, and the sanctity of acclimating oneself to the demands of the changing labor market presents an especially intense challenge today—not only in conventional economic terms but in cultural and ethical ones as well. The blue- or white-collar worker now expected to work longer hours does so in a world where not only products but workers from abroad can threaten one's immediate economic future. The pace of cultural and economic competition and confrontation grows just as those economic anchors that once provided security in daily life are being eroded. For employees deeply invested in traditional notions of personal and social identity, the urge to fall back on what they believe to be fundamentals in the midst of wrenching changes over which they had no control could become compelling. Recent discussion over the outsourcing of tech jobs to India could be the tip of a dangerous iceberg if we are not careful. These tensions and resentments are worth our attention, particularly because the structure of partisanship in contemporary politics often makes exploitation of resentments such an attractive strategy.

The Future of Progress

For a long time now, far-thinking analysts have attempted to come up with alternative measures of a nation's economic progress. Some years ago, Herman Daly and John Cobb created an Index of Sustainable Economic Welfare (ISEW). Daly and Cobb's measure was designed to replace Gross National Product as our primary measure of economic welfare. In this measure they consider factors such as personal consumption, economic inequality, service household labor, net capital growth, change in net international position, a variety of measures of ecological deterioration, and others. For example, they include the cost of national advertising (as opposed to local) as a negative contribution to economic welfare because it provides no real information about price of goods or where to purchase them. They also include the cost of commuting time, and the cost of urbanization (measured in part by high land values in densely populated areas). Using their measure, they find, from 1968 to 1986, there has been a decline of about 12 percent in ISEW with much of it coming in the 1980s. During the same period, the GNP went up by about 40 percent.[20]

In devising their measure, Daly and Cobb seek to put into play a measure of economic welfare that addresses the shortcomings of GNP, which they argue all serious economists think exist. Daly and Cobb do not jettison "the individualistic bias of contemporary economic theory," or ask for a (presently impossible) fundamental shift in perspective away from per capita availability of economic goods, to social health itself. Nevertheless, they still believe that ISEW measures the overall health of communities. Because most policymakers see improvement of the economy as being of singular importance, they believed they would get a hearing. They saw their task in this way:

> Because evaluation of policy changes is so heavily dependent on their anticipated effects on economic growth, and because growth is so widely assumed to be the increase in throughput measured by GNP, we believe that a new measure is indispensable to gaining a hearing for proposals that would tend to reduce GNP, as ours would.[21]

A group of economists based in San Francisco and going under the name "Redefining Progress" has also devised an index of economic welfare that is attentive to growing economic inequality, the loss of leisure time, the depletion of scarce resources, and social pathologies such as crime. They have concluded that although total welfare increased between 1950 and 1970, it has decreased substantially since 1970. Their "Genuine Progress Indicator" places the decline since 1970 at an astounding 42 percent.[22] Since some of the decline is based on failure to account properly for depletion of natural stocks, we may not feel the loss now. Nonetheless, future generations will have to grapple with the consequences.

Discussions about the size of current resources, future damage to the ozone layer, and global warming are necessarily speculative. Even many of those sympathetic to the efforts of these economists question the magnitude of some of the revisions in current calculations. Undoubtedly, technological advances and broad arrays of consumer choices have increased quality of life in some respects. Nonetheless, their effort to provide measures of economic "growth" or well-being that are more attentive to the downsides and risks of our current patterns of living has received some support even from more traditional economists.[23]

Many individuals, according to Juliet Schor, are choosing what they perceive to be higher-quality lifestyles that reflect some of the values inherent in these alternative indices of progress. She reports a growing movement of "downshifters" who are finding ways to choose simpler and less expensive lives. Less consumerism, less work time, more free time, more time for friends, family, and pursuits more rewarding than working and buying. Downshifters are building for themselves, outside the system, as it were, a higher quality of life.[24] Their example is instructive but insufficient. We will not become a nation of "downshifters," at least not by choice.

A public debate on quality of contemporary life is therefore especially important to have today. Efforts like those of Daly and Cobb and the San Francisco group and Schor are excellent starting points. If successful at capturing some measure of public attention, they might provide a commonsense analytic framework through which to understand the gap between perceived decline in quality of life, and our dominant measures of economic welfare and growth. To the extent they gained a presence in discourse, they would provide a better marriage of economics and quality, help create a basis for a shared set of goals (or renewed "covenant"), and mitigate social and economic inequality, thereby also providing reciprocal support for mutual objectives.

Unfortunately the work of Daly and Cobb, Schor, and the San Francisco group has not penetrated our politics. In the 2004 campaign, important objectives of the followers each of Bush and Kerry would have been advanced by some of the concerns of these writers. Yet as the candidates argued over who would deliver the largest GNP to Americans, they failed to acknowledge that GNP growth itself often indicates slipping values. Conservatives should care that every extra hour at work is spent away from the families they value, and every corporation that makes the right economic move in leaving unmoored a previously cohesive community registers as an increase in GNP and a decline in values they cherish. And liberals should care that a piece of the economic growth of which they were so proud in the 1990s was built on unnecessarily punitive drug laws and consequent incarceration, prison construction, and prison personnel infrastructure. It would be quite interesting to observe liberals and conservatives together compare GNP to alternative indices of progress, to see to what degree GNP could be purged of trends that, upon agreement, would turn out to be indications of decline rather than progress.

A more open and probing discussion of the meaning of progress can support the building of a consensus around democratic values in profound ways. Some of the anxiety people feel reflects ambivalence about modern life, about quality of life, even about progress. Yet many also hear positive reports of economic growth, even as these do not always translate into an improvement in their own lives.

Equal Opportunity and Beyond

There is another question relevant in locating the tensions and resentments that probes even more deeply into some of our foundational beliefs. What is the downside to equality of opportunity? Connected to hard, bitter, and sometimes bloody struggles for basic civil rights and justice, equal opportunity is an ideal that is beyond reproach. It is a good ideal when applied to rectification of injustice. Yet at its core it, too, demands a price that should be assessed in public discourse.

What would an "aristocracy of merit" actually look and feel like?[25] As John Schaar brilliantly argued many years ago, what is missing in discussions that praise the ideal is its problematic and harshly competitive nature and consequences.[26] The idea of a fair race is problematic because some talents will be highlighted over others, fulfill one set of functions deemed socially useful rather than others, today often determined by the market and those successful in it. It is competitive because it endorses and ratifies harsh competition as the basic principle for virtually all aspects of public life. A fair race that is lost because one lacks the talent prized by the rules leaves you to blame no one but yourself for your failure.[27] *You* are the failure.[28]

Under the guise of a lofty goal, do we unwittingly encourage development of impoverished selves, forever discontent, forever striving to design an identity that proves itself better than its neighbors and co-workers, in fact, better than itself? Do we foster the development of individuals who are ill-prepared for democratic citizenship?

The "basic question," says Schaar, "is not whether competition should be praised or condemned, but where and under what conditions competition is a desirable principle of action and judgment and where and under what conditions it is not." Equal opportunity is valuable in those areas of life in which competition is the appropriate operating principle, but these areas should be far fewer and between than now compared to those that prize other values and equalities, especially equality of respect or equality of being. There could be, Schaar believes, a greater variety of "games" to fit more talents, needs, and interests. Compared to such possibilities "our present social order," he says, "is a mean thing."[29]

In the struggle for success, personal worth is accomplished by beating others in the struggle for wealth and status, thereby blocking an "ethic of personal validation through self-transcendence." Instead, those who fully embrace this struggle look upon themselves as commodities whose worth is determined not by their own standards, but "by the valuations others place on the position he occupies." Once equal opportunity as "dogma" is fully internalized, Schaar claims,

> the result is as humanly disastrous for the winners as for the losers. The winners easily come to think of themselves as beings superior to common humanity, while the losers are almost forced to think of themselves as something less than human.[30]

We would argue a bit differently. For winners and losers alike, the judge rarely rests. For even the biggest "winner" may have experienced harms that go beyond misplaced feelings of superiority, indeed that produce and reproduce anxieties and doubts. The harsh spotlight may produce a self that is prone to resentments, sometimes looking for someone else to blame.

It may seem that this is a particularly inopportune time to raise issues such as these. The emergence of more integrated trading, labor, production, and finance regimes puts pressure on the concerns we raise because of the increased premium placed on international competitiveness. The ideas almost seem naïve. However, it is a necessary time because internationalization reflected in trade policy, finance, communication, and immigration creates not only opportunities for commonality and tolerance, but also more venues and reasons for demonization, and thereby more need to understand how to ease resentments in order to lessen the temptation.

We don't present these alternatives as the *only* ways to think about progress while addressing quality-of-life issues. Indeed, the priorities in each of the model measures of progress presented by Daly and Cobb, and by the San Francisco group, are not the same. Nor do we find it inconceivable that these proposed practices wouldn't create resentments of their own. The very claim that we can frame only one way of looking at progress, not subject to debate or conceptual challenge, freezes political debate and blinds us to the problems simmering below the surface.

Discussion of other ways of thinking about progress does not settle any of the issues we have raised. It may, however, help people recognize assumptions and hidden individual and political choices inherent in what otherwise seem as "natural" watermarks of progress and ways of thinking about it. It may even lead some to consider personal or political alternatives.

Probing discussion can also help people bring to the surface the causes and reasons for some of the pressures and resentments they feel, and contribute to a better understanding of the resentments others harbor against them. At best it can even help in developing perspectives that are more aware of and resistant to scapegoating and demonizing temptations. Each of these is an important step toward a new politics of progress, open to more voices.

4

The Deep Divide
and the Most Vulnerable

U.S. politics has become more polarized and more partisan, and there exists—even after the 2004 election—close parity in the appeal of the two major political parties. Polarization, partisanship, and political parity are a formula to ensure continuity in harm for the most vulnerable. For under the terms of contemporary partisanship and division, what political leader will risk the attacks likely to ensue by appearing to identify with those who have failed all the modern tests of worthiness?

If Bill Clinton's former pollster Stanley Greenberg is right, this almost even division of the electorate puts a tactical premium on maintaining the current "bias of conflict" in politics—here he uses E. E. Schattschneider's famous phrase to denote the terms of what is included and excluded in discussion and debate—because each side can make a plausible argument that it has a chance to win under prevailing conditions.

With the Congress and the vote for president (and the Electoral College map) so evenly split, why risk a new strategy or propose an unanticipated program? Each side can easily design plausible short-term scenarios in which they can win over the elected branches. The temptation is strong in what Greenberg calls the "two Americas," not to rock the partisan boat. "With each party tantalizingly close to winning any election," he argues, "the goal now is to get your coalition inflamed, engaged, and united, perhaps to bring over some of the contested, to edge past parity."[1] Mobilize an increasingly polarized base and, somehow, win over enough in the middle by contesting around issues upon which the other side can be made to appear "weak." This formula for victory, we argue, keeps not only the marginal out of the game, but also the discussion that we think needs to take place about progress and quality of life.

How Deep the Divide

One measure of the deep divide between Republicans and Democrats is how each perceived the Bush presidency in the middle of an election year. Polls taken by the Gallup organization from May 21 to 23, 2004, revealed "extreme and unprecedented levels of polarization" with regard to President Bush's job approval ratings. Not only did members of each party evaluate the president differently, but their feelings were also very strong and the differences historically unprecedented. The "partisan gap" in approval ratings (between Republican approval and Democratic approval of the president) was 77 percent in this poll: "Never before has Gallup data shown such a high proportion of partisans with such strongly opposing views of a president." "No president, dating back to Harry Truman, has had a partisan gap above 70 points in any Gallup Poll in a reelection year."[2]

One is tempted by these data to conclude that George W. Bush is himself simply a deeply polarizing figure in American politics, and in fact he is. However, there are deeper forces of partisanship at work, and Bush is so polarizing in part because he appears to embody a side of the cultural and political divide that we have discussed.

Going back to the 1970s, a number of political scientists tried to make sense of the electoral era that was emerging out of the breakdown of the New Deal coalition. Some commented on the decline of the saliency of America's political parties. Some used a dealignment thesis to explain why, even though the time was right within the "realignment cycle" (every thirty-six years or so), a post–New Deal realignment of the electorate did not occur. Overreliance on such ideas, however, may have led some to miss what has actually proven to be a profound deepening of political partisanship and polarization over the last generation.

For example, David Lawrence finds that the strength and impact of party identification on voters has been growing for the last twenty-five years. While the 1950s is considered the "golden age" of the political party, he writes, "the impact of party identification on vote choice, for the population as a whole and particularly for strong partisans, has [now] exceeded [that era's] level."[3] Richard Fleisher and Jon R. Bond argue, moreover, that in the 1980s and 1990s citizens increasingly perceived important differences between the views of the two parties, and they report other research showing that policy preferences of party identifiers showed "an increasing divergence in citizen attitudes on social welfare, race, and sociocultural issues." Indeed, measures of "ideological self-placement" reveal increasing polarization from 1972 to 1996, with a break only in 1988. During that period, Democrats, who began slightly left of center, became "somewhat" more liberal, whereas the "Republican shift to the right started earlier and is more pronounced."[4]

Contrary to views suggesting that elite polarization caused citizens to turn away from or "hate" politics, Fleisher and Bond found deep polarization among nonelites as well, which in turn helps explain how elite strategies of polarization could be maintained at the polls. They conclude that, "in the aggregate, elites were not alone in displaying greater partisan polarization. The views of party identifiers toward a variety of political objects—candidates, parties, issues, ideological self-placement, and presidential performance—show a growing divergence." Nor was growing polarization limited to those who strongly identify with a political party; it extended even to weak identifiers and independents, and was not limited by region or age.[5]

Stanley Greenberg too admits to having missed many of these signs before 2000, as he and others focused on the revolt against congressional incumbents in 1990; the end of the Reagan coalition in 1992 with Clinton's election; the Gingrich revolution in 1994; and Ross Perot's historic 1992 and 1996 candidacies. He saw instead volatility and "a public pulling back from both of the parties." If there were rules in the emerging system, they were not apparent to him then. "But we now know . . . that there are new rules," he argues, "and they center on the parties and the parity itself."[6]

First, "the politics of parity has seemed to lock the country into a politics of culture," with the public dividing itself over issues of religion and secularism, government regulatory powers, and the uniqueness or diversity and openness of America. These tend to be "overlapping divisions," he writes, "which raise the barrier between two Americas whose politics are increasingly about their way of life, not just issues. Abortion, guns, taxes—all are incendiary devices under the rules of this new game." Second, the partisans themselves have shown increasing partisanship, as the percentage of strong identifiers with the Republican and Democratic parties have increased since the beginning of the 1980s. However, third, although the number of independents is only marginally higher than in the 1970s and 1980s,[7] "the political turmoil and intense partisan battle leave a lot of voters amenable to a different kind of politics, if one of the parties can break free of the current deadlock."[8] Yet, the incentives to maintain the status quo are very powerful. The present era, Greenberg concludes, is of such remarkable electoral stability that you have to go back 100 years to find another like it. If he is right, we may be in the "system of 2000."

What is partisanship and how deeply and in what ways does it reside in a person? This is an important question if the current impasse of polarization is to be breached or even understood. One question political scientists have long asked, in trying to understand the motivation for political behavior, is, How "rational" are American voters? "Rational" citizens, the presumption is, would be able to make choices undiluted by sentiment between parties and candidates, and instead base them on their preferences, interests, and values at a particular point in time. Strong partisan filters, as Angus Campbell put it (or passions as Thomas Hobbes might), get in the way of making rational choices. Recent evidence, after all, supports the view that perception does distort facts in favor of one's preferred political party.

Some contemporary writers, going back to an earlier tradition within behavioral political science, suggest that people form political attachments at an early age, even inheriting them from their parents, and don't change easily even in response to major world events. As Donald Green, Bradley Palmquist, and Eric Schickler argue in their book, *Partisan Hearts and Minds,* most people either inherit their party affiliations from their parents, or they form an attachment to one party or another early in adulthood. Few people switch parties once they hit middle age. Even major historic events like the world wars and the Watergate scandal do not cause large numbers of people to switch.

Moreover, they argue, people do not choose parties by comparing platforms and then figuring out where the nation's interests lie. Drawing on a vast range of data, they argue that party attachment is more like attachment to a religious denomination or a social club. People have stereotypes in their heads about what Democrats are like and what Republicans are like, and they gravitate toward the party made up of people like themselves. In this view, people choose parties not because they weigh issue platforms against their concept of the national interest, but because they want to be with people like themselves, much as one would in a religious or social affiliation. In fact, over time, people align their views to conform to their "political tribe."

After reading some of these studies, David Brooks concludes, "The overall impression one gets from these political scientists is that politics is a tribal business. Americans congregate into rival political communities, then embrace one-sided attitudes and perceptions. That suggests that political polarization is the result of deep and self-reinforcing psychological and social forces."[9] Yes, but how deep? And is this a problem to be solved, or a situation to be managed more or less effectively? If perception is like a filter, then rationality can be achieved by taking it off or by changing it. Alternatively, if rationality is an abstract quality of mind that can only serve to rationalize emotions it can never "master," then no solution is available to solve what is an insoluble problem. Is there another way to orient ourselves to the nature of perception?

There is a growing appreciation among political theorists of the relevance of recent insights of neuroscience and cognitive science into the study of the question of what constitutes perception. Taken together, some of these studies point to the inadequacy of models that reduce the biological to the genetic, or the mind to computer modeling. Instead, perception is seen as an enormously complex multilayered phenomenon, in which the mind is "embodied" in the sense of being situated and complicit in an enormously complex and rapidly fired set of connections and relays between culture, brain, and body, and heavily dependent on affect-imbued responses.

One relevant example is neuroscientist Antonio Damasio's approach to memory. Damasio believes that because memories cannot be separated from the affects that partly constitute them, remembrances in the course of acting are better thought of as dormant and implicit dispositions rather than as active and explicit recollections: "As a consequence when we recall an object, when we allow dispositions to make their implicit information explicitly, we retrieve not just sensory data, but also accompanying motor and emotional data." This intimacy between affect and thought, however, is neither an impediment toward rationality nor an unproblematic marriage. He gives the example of a brain-damaged patient who cannot access what Damasio calls "somatic markers," the visceral embodiments of culture relevant to dispositional memory. Somatic markers assist our deliberation by highlighting options, sifting through detail, and "reduc[ing] the need for sifting because they provide an automated detection of the scenario components that are likely to be relevant" in particular situations. In one instance, the patient's ability to negotiate an icy road was advantaged by the ease to which his defect allowed him to ward off the "natural" impulse to hit the brakes. In another it was greatly disadvantaged when he tried simply to pick a date for his next appointment—the patient engaged in an obsessive and endless cost-benefit analysis of the pros and cons of the options available. As Damasio puts it, in this case the patient's behavior "is a good example of the limits of pure reason" as damage to the *affectively imbued memory* inhibited rather than aided reasonable thinking.[10]

Rather than thinking of affect as an impediment to reason, or as a separate force that dominates it, studies such as Damasio's highlight the deep connections between rational thought and bodily states, including in the brain and other viscera. Several implications are pertinent to this study. The filter model of perception is misleading because "somatic markers" cannot be removed without altering the *capacity* of perception. Perception is deeply rooted and not easily changed by "rational" appeal. Indeed, such appeals may aggravate the differences between partisans, denying the validity not just of the logic of opponents, but their inner emotional life as well. This point is particularly lost on some liberals in the Democratic Party, as they try to understand why anyone would oppose the rights and social provisions they endorse.

Perception moves very quickly. Rather than relying on conscious reflection, it occurs at the meeting place of the sensory experience of an encounter and the instantaneous "virtual" memories it summons. The fact that culture helps constitute the visceral component of thinking suggests that, within modest limits, perception can be remapped once the process of drawing the current map is understood. Changes in perception are possible, even as rooting the emotion out of perception is not.

Precisely because we are beings whose capacity for perception is constrained by limits in our ability to *consciously* process information and emotion, as William Connolly puts it (or enabled by our ability to keep much implicit, as we prefer to say), when

> we are confronted with the cruel effects our perceptual habits have on those marginalized or demonized by them . . . [it] becomes ethically incumbent or prudentially important to examine the structure of perception and, sometimes, to devise strategies to work on the cultural dispositions now installed in it.[11]

Structures of perception, according to Connolly, are formed through the intermingling of individual sensibilities (what he calls "relational techniques of the self"), the deployed techniques of institutions that acculturate us to their practices (what he calls "micropolitics"), and the big-ticket items that more formally stipulate the terms of our political economy and political culture, for example, markets, laws, and elections. Taken together, sensibility, micropolitics, and macropolitics connect "memory, perception, thinking, judgment, institutional design, and political ethos."[12] In the remaining sections of this chapter we discuss some facts of our macropolitical world to see how they become translated into that aspect of micropolitics (we will have more to say about sensibility in the conclusion) that influences our politics and our political ethos in ways relevant to demonization of vulnerable groups.

Inequality as Context

Demonizing invective is not only directed at the marginal (the rich, for example, can be easy targets), but the consequences for those on the edge are the most severe. These effects are intimately tied to the varied and overlapping structures of political and economic inequality in our contemporary culture of progress. Context matters.

Edward N. Wolff's 1995 study for the Brookings Institute, *Top Heavy*, provides a superbly detailed, comparative and historical examination of inequality in America. The United States, which once was more egalitarian than such aristocratic entities as Great Britain, is the most inegalitarian advanced industrial nation in the world. The top one percent of the social pyramid holds an astounding 42 percent of all marketable wealth. Wolff points out that even when we consider such forms of wealth as consumer durables and other household assets, inequalities have grown dramatically in recent years.[13]

Updating his detailed study recently, Wolff does acknowledge that

despite slow growth in income over the 1990s, there have been marked improvements in the wealth position of average families. Both mean and median wealth grew briskly in the late 1990s. The inequality of net worth leveled off even though income inequality continued to rise over this period. Indebtedness also fell substantially during the late 1990s. However, the concentration of investment-type assets generally remained as high in 2001 as during the previous two decades. The racial disparity in wealth holdings, after stabilizing during most of the 1990s, widened in the years between 1998 and 2001, and the wealth of Hispanics actually declined in real terms between 1998 and 2001. Wealth also shifted in relative terms away from young households (under age 45) toward elderly ones (age 65 and over).[14]

Wolff's work clearly indicates that substantial inequality in wealth has been persistent, with any stabilization or reduction in wealth inequality limited only to the period of *relatively* full employment during the last two years of the Clinton administration.

Many conservatives suggest that whatever the extent of inequality, in the United States anyone can work his way out of poverty and that the wealthiest citizens have often done just that. Yet in a careful rebuttal, Chuck Collins, of United for a Fair Economy, points out that 50 percent of those in Forbes's top four hundred in 1996 started their business lives with $50 million in family wealth or by inheriting a large company.

Inequality, as well as social change, is supposed to be the price we pay for steady growth in the standard of living and quality of life for everyone. Inequality, the argument goes, is necessary to motivate productivity, and increased productivity creates a rising tide that lifts all boats. Unfortunately, American working-class incomes largely have been stagnant for most of the last quarter century. Society may pay a high social, moral, and perhaps even economic cost for failing to nurture the talents of all.

Political "Apathy" and Inequality

There is nothing new about being concerned about social and economic inequality in the United States. James Madison, among many others, worried about what growing inequality in the commercial society of his day would do to our republican prospects. The great hope of democrats, articulated by E. E. Schattschneider in his classic *The Semi-Sovereign People,* has been that equality of political rights could provide some measure of balance. Democratic government would offset the undemocratic market. There would be a balance of power. This hope, however, depends not just on formal legal political rights, but also on *real* political equality in the practices of American democracy.

These practices, however, have serious problems. American rates of electoral participation are very low. A survey by the International Institute for Democracy and Electoral Assistance shows that from 1991 to 2000 average U.S. turnout in national elections ranked thirty-first out of thirty-four nations in Western Europe, the Americas, Turkey, Thailand,

and Australia, just behind the Dominican Republic and trailed by Switzerland, Columbia, and Guatemala. (If we take out our lower-turnout non-presidential-year elections, we improve to twenty-ninth, tied with Venezuela.) In the highly partisan election of 2004, U.S. turnout did rise slightly above its 1992 level of 58.1 percent of eligible citizens (our post-1960s highpoint) to 59.6 percent. This is the highest rate since 1968, when turnout was 61.9 percent. Even the 2004 figure, however, leaves the United States lagging behind most of these nations and way behind when compared to Western Europe (except for Switzerland) where turnout is often 80 percent or higher.[15]

These enormous turnout differentials between the United States and its important trading partners and main military allies translate into an even greater *class voting gap*. Political scientist Mark N. Franklin concludes that, except in the United States, "whether people vote is hardly at all affected by their socioeconomic status (SES) and hence the resources they bring to the political world."[16] Frances Fox Piven and Richard Cloward also have argued that in Europe, economic class and education are not significant determinants of turnout, nor were they in nineteenth-century America. This suggests to them that the real problem is not individual attributes but institutional, legal, and administrative barriers, the contours of party mobilizing strategies, and party and candidate ideological appeals. "Apathy and lack of political skill are a *consequence,* not a *cause,* of the party structure and political culture," they argue. "The political system determines whether participation is predicated on class-related resources and attitudes."[17]

Voting turnout in the United States is sharply skewed by education, occupation, class, age,[18] and to some degree race and ethnicity, but not any longer by gender.[19] Table 1 reviews some voting turnout data[20] from the U.S. Census Bureau's Current Population Surveys (CPS) in presidential elections from 1964 to 2000, using 1964 as the base year.[21] It compares turnout between the top and bottom income quintiles and reports the ratio within each comparison as an *index of voting equality.*[22] Overall, for presidential elections, the ratio declines from .644 in 1964 to a low of .532 in 1996, and then edges up slightly to .546 in 2000.[23] By this measure the impact of low-income voters on election outcomes overall has declined relative to that of high-income voters over the past forty years.[24]

Political scientists have long noted that educational attainment is one of the best predictors of voting turnout. Raising educational level should be the best way to increase voter turnout. Steven J. Rosenstone and John

TABLE I
Presidential Turnout: Bottom and Top Income Quintiles and Voting Equality

Year	Turnout Bottom 5th	Change from 1964	Turnout Top 5th	Change from 1964	Index of Voting Equality
2000	39.1	−15	71.5	−12.5	.546
1996	38.7	−15.4	72.7	−11.3	.532
1992	42.0	−12.1	78.0	−6.0	.538
1988	42.2	−11.9	73.7	−10.3	.573
1984	44.7	−9.4	74.7	−9.3	.598
1980	45.5	−8.6	73.8	−10.2	.617
1976	46.7	−7.4	74.1	−9.9	.624
1972	49.5	−4.6	79.3	−4.7	.621
1968	55.3	+1.2	81.3	−2.7	.680
1964	54.1	—	84.0	—	.644

Mark Hansen report that all types of participation increase with education, because education imparts citizenship values and skills and makes it more likely that educated people, like the wealthy, will be in environments that have been socialized to follow and be involved in politics.[25] Levels of educational attainment have risen dramatically since the 1960s, so why hasn't the turnout gone up? According to Ruy Teixeira: because American politics is a high-cost, low-benefit affair. His most important example of high cost is that voter registration is up to the person rather than a state responsibility, as is common in Europe. The major low benefits include insufficient mobilization by the parties and a winner-take-all electoral structure that provides no incentive to vote in districts in which your candidate can't win. Turnout has declined rather than increased, Teixeira concludes, because the benefits of education have been offset by these other factors.[26]

Granted, voting turnout is an important problem in the United States. Isn't it true, however, that the United States has large numbers of voluntary organizations and massive numbers of people who are politically active in ways other than voting? Although the United States has more moderately active citizens than elsewhere, such "activists come disproportionately from the better educated and more affluent."[27] If we look at forms of political participation other than voting, the class-gap widens greatly. The well-off are twice as likely to sign a petition, attend a public meeting, or write a letter to a member of Congress than are the least advantaged. They are two and half times more likely to attempt to influence how others will vote, and they are ten times more likely to contribute money.[28] Race, ethnicity, and gender are also important factors regarding activist success in which white men are still typically the gatekeepers.[29] Emphasis on special interest politics abets this overall class skewing of activism. A democratic counterweight is needed. However, Teixeira argues, "Widespread nonvoting makes it less likely that electoral participation by ordinary citizens will be that counterweight."[30]

Rosenstone and Hansen argue that leaders now have "few incentives to attend to the needs of the disadvantaged."[31] Increasing the scope of conflict, on the other hand, would decrease the class bias.[32] In their view, low rates of participation reflect a *biased* political agenda and organization of politics, an institutional context for contemporary political inequality that squeezes out the poor and less educated.[33] This context is not as powerful in other democracies, where voting participation is far more egalitarian, partly a reflection of efforts to appeal to and mobilize more citizens, resulting in higher overall turnout. Notwithstanding major and extremely important advances in legal political equality, Rosenstone and Hansen conclude, "the economic inequalities . . . that prevail in the United States today are as large as the racial disparities in political participation that prevailed in the 1950s."[34]

By Invitation Only

The rise in political inequity has been abetted by important institutional changes within American politics and society. Union membership has been in decline since the 1950s and is now at its lowest point in six decades. Only about 9 percent of the private work force and 13.5 percent overall are enrolled in unions, compared to 35.7 percent and 32.5 percent, respectively, in 1953. Between 1999 and 2000 alone, union membership fell by 219,000, with 16.3 million workers remaining in unions, roughly the same number as in 1952 in spite of an increase in the workforce from 50 to 121 million persons over that time.[35]

While working-class interest associations, which have depended more on people power than money, have less input into the political process than before, the role of money in very expensive media-driven politics has grown enormously, the McCain-Feingold campaign-finance law notwithstanding. The newly emergent "527" organizations, allowing politicking outside the party or campaign without contribution limits, is an important problem. Exclusive focus on it, however, moves our attention away from the fact the McCain law *doubled* maximum individual contributions to candidates to $2,000, a sum far out of the reach of those most disadvantaged by the current bias of the political system. Meanwhile, political parties have been transformed, remaining important mobilizers of partisans, but doing so increasingly through the collection and use of money rather than organization in the neighborhoods.

While unions have been losing their voice, the groups left out of broader labor organizing of the fifties, women, minorities, environmentalists, have not been without recourse. The contemporary political scene is not dominated solely by the corporate lobbies. The number of lobbyists in Washington has grown dramatically and includes such groups as the Environmental Defense Fund, Common Cause, People for the American Way, American Association for the Advancement of Retired People, and a range of gun control, pro-choice, and gay and lesbian rights organizations. These liberal social-cause groups have in turn helped spawn a variety of social-conservative organizations, including the Eagle Forum and Concerned Women for America.

The focus of these lobbies is normally on single issues, and rather than emphasize widespread political mobilization, their objective is to raise money through direct mailings and negotiating compromises with other elite players. Even liberal interest groups, however, tend to be dominated by the affluent, with typical donors being well-off professionals or managers, those in the top one-fifth of income. As John Judis has put it, "Most of the wage earning classes don't give to these organizations and don't feel represented by them."[36] Even liberal groups such as the Children's Defense Fund have a membership base, not among the people they claim to represent, as the old National Welfare Rights Organization did, but among social workers.[37]

Political scientist Theda Skocpol emphasizes that these innumerable "public interest organizations" are "professionalized," largely run by their staffs, with leaders who are more sensitive to the concerns of outside donors than their membership base: "The thousands or (at times) millions of members claimed by such groups are more atomized subjects than socially interconnected participants." They don't know each other because there is no real participation involved. Instead, they get mailings with "fundraising appeals accompanied by newsletters, magazines, or carefully crafted questionnaires"; their only real involvement is to send checks "to keep the national staff afloat."[38]

Skocpol argues that this style represents an important change in America's civic life, toward instrumentally focused (or recreationally oriented) professionalized organizations, and away from organizations such as the American Legion, the Fraternal Order of Eagles, and the General Federation of Women's Clubs and others that no longer exist. These older-style organizations were broad based, had massive memberships that went across socioeconomic classes, and were oriented toward service and fraternity or sorority. Many of them also involved themselves in national politics and public affairs, a fact she believes raises serious questions about communitarian selective remembrances of older-style civic life as one resembling a mythical Jeffersonian ideal. She also disagrees with conservatives who use such mythology as a way to undercut the legitimacy of national government. "Contrary to conservative presumptions," she says, "I document that American civic voluntarism was never predominantly local and never flourished apart from national government and politics."[39] Large-scale, translocal membership groups had a long life, beginning in the 1820s and going into the 1960s. Such selective remembrances give an apolitical reading of America's past civic involvement, underplaying the role large civic groups played in national politics, thereby legitimating an apolitical model for how to solve what ails democracy today.

Skocpol also takes aim at liberals for failing to see the ways in which the rights movements emanating from the 1960s, although necessary and commendable and having achieved important goals, also had some *undemocratic* consequences. They

> also inadvertently helped to trigger a reorganization of national civic life, in which professionally managed associations and institutions proliferated while cross-class membership associations lost ground. In our time, civicly [*sic*] engaged Americans are organizing more but joining less. Solidarity across class lines has dwindled, even as racial and gender integration has increased. The professionally managed organizations that dominate American civic life today are, in important respects, less democratic and participatory than the pre-1960s membership federations they displaced.[40]

The impersonal appeals under the new civic regime and targeted activation of profiled members of socioeconomic and demographic groups, she claims, "limit the mobilization of most citizens into public life and encourage a fragmentation of social identities and trivial polarizations in public debates." Such "targeted activation," as Steven Schier argues, "arose as a rational response to a political environment characterized by party decline" and "a proliferation of organized interests, and new efficiencies in communication and campaign technologies."[41] The net effect, Skocpol notes, is to create "a mutually reinforcing—and deleterious—interlock of professionally managed associational and electoral activities."[42] Advocates need visibility and need to stand out in the cacophony of "causes" that seem to surround us. Selective activation, however, leaves out large numbers of Americans who either do not have the money to contribute, or who are not interested in the advocate's cause. The result of the very long-term transformation of the political party, and the more recent forty-year change in the nature of civic life, is to demobilize important segments of the public and to "trivially polarize" American politics over narrow single-issue arguments, even as these often stand in for larger cultural causes.

"Trivial" polarization, we would argue, however, encourages citizens to build rhetorical walls that can lead to profound polarization abetted by political demonology. Perhaps evidence of this escalation has been found by political scientists who suggest that elite polarization preceded mass polarization. Receptivity of the public to "trivial" polarization, however, still requires explanation that goes beyond the account Skocpol gives.

Throughout Part I we have endeavored to suggest some plausible explanations. Consider in light of our discussion of the politics of moral personae and America' moral paradox the following. Those who tend to be more economically insecure are often the most diverse in terms of ethnicity, race, and gender, and the least united and organized politically. These divisions become fertile ground for issues such as welfare, abortion, and busing to become wedge issues.[43] Whatever their validity as distinct concerns meriting attention, these issues too often become obsessive foci of politics and exacerbate the divisions, further disorganizing working people of modest means. The weaker they are as a group, the less the major interest groups and the Republican and Democratic parties will attend to their interests.

Given added economic pressures in an era of postindustrialism and globalization, the parties are less inclined than before to entertain policy proposals that challenge the sovereignty of the market over distributive issues. Nor do they seem to be willing to contemplate the massive expenditures required by the serious retraining of the less skilled and educated to make them truly competitive. The less the interests of those below the economic median are represented in policy proposals, however, the less incentive they have to vote, exacerbating their political weakness and in turn providing less incentive to the parties to address their concerns in the future. The political terrain then remains more open to those who focus on culturally and socially divisive politics as the smart way to attract those working people who do vote. Whom does it leave most vulnerable?

Three Sketches of Vulnerability

Target 1: Welfare Recipients

One group that has been an obvious target of much rancor over the years is welfare recipients. They are easy targets for a number of reasons, having to do with race and ethnicity, gender, lack of organization, lack of education, and other variables. They are vulnerable because they lack political power. President Clinton's signing of the welfare reform bill into law in 1996 was stark evidence that the coalition, both political and bureaucratic, that had defended the welfare system for the disadvantaged had completely broken down. With the movement of the center of political gravity to the right since the late 1960s, by 1996 defenders of welfare became reduced to the liberal wing of the Democratic Party.

Many who critically examine our welfare state emphasize their own version of "American exceptionalism," in which they recall the fact that America has had weak working-class movements and a small socialist presence. They often discuss the unique role race plays in American history and how, ironically as the first nation to adopt and maintain universal (white) male suffrage, early in our history we took away an easily identifiable issue around which to rally. There is more to this story.

In the United States more than in other major industrial nations, poverty is regarded a consequence of character flaws. In this view's earliest Protestant incarnations, the wealthy—and by implication the poor—were seen as chosen by God. But the wealthy also owed kindness to the poor, who in return had to learn to accept their lot. This created an ethic of charity as the way to ameliorate important social ills. This ethic has always framed debates over need in the United States.

To the extent it was practiced, charity was the main way of serving the needs of the poor throughout much of the nineteenth century. With the growth of industrialization and urbanization, individual charity work proved inadequate and, even before the New Deal, the state came to play a larger role.[44] Nonetheless, the charity model continued to affect the shape of the U.S. welfare state. Among the four original programs of Social Security, pensions, support for survivors, unemployment compensation, and welfare, the latter two were based on this model. Elaborate qualifications were set by the states with the implication that recipients were in need not of resources primarily but of better vocational skills or sounder personal characteristics.

The broad conclusion we draw is that severe economic crisis promoted the idea of universal social programs in the United States, but that the charity model continues to influence American policy. The implication of such policies is that individual attributes, not structured inequalities, are the cause of the need for help. In creating institutions based upon this model, cues are created in a multitude of ways, reminding us that the world is divided into better and worse people, measured by success in the market. Those who fail become easy targets and have few defenders.

Target 2: Prisoners

When President Clinton proclaimed in 1997 that the "era of big government is over," he may have missed the point that aspects of the welfare state were being replaced by the carceral state. Instead of "regulating the poor through paternalistic welfare," as Frances Fox Piven and Richard Cloward once famously put it,[45] both state and federal authorities are increasingly imprisoning them for long periods of time, for example, for nonviolent drug offenses. Has the war on poverty morphed via the drug war into a war on the poor, especially on minorities?

Alan Elsner and other analysts have documented numerous problems within our prison system, ranging from physical and psychological abuse, a culture of racism, another one of rape, serious health problems and lack of treatment, recidivism, enormous cost, and others. Elsner also shows a variety of ways in which the system is in denial—or just simply denies— what goes on inside prison walls.[46]

One particular problem that plagues criminal justice is a "war on drugs" which has increased in cost from $110 million in the early 1970s to $19.2 billion in President Bush's 2003 fiscal year budget.[47] Clinton's own drug czar, Barry McCaffrey, put the issue bluntly in a 1996 speech, saying "We have created an American *gulag*" with two-thirds of those "in the federal system there for drugs-related crimes."[48]

Not just anyone gets caught up in the drug wars. A 2001 government survey reported that "[r]ates of current illicit drug use among the major racial/ethnic groups in 2001 were 7.2 percent for whites, 6.4 percent for Hispanics and 7.4 percent for Blacks." Since blacks are roughly one-eighth of the population and use drugs at roughly the same rate as others, Elsner estimates, you would expect to find they make up around 12 percent of those arrested for drugs. Instead, African Americans make up 35 percent of arrests, 55 percent of convictions, and 74 percent of those imprisoned for drugs. "In Illinois," he says, "an African American man was 57 times more likely than a white man to be incarcerated for drugs."[49]

The extraordinarily high overall incarceration rates in the United States, the problems in our prisons, and the harshness and inequities in our drug war were not mentioned in the 2004 presidential election. Prisoners can't vote, of course. In many states, former felons can't, either. Nationally, some 4.7 million persons are disenfranchised in federal or state elections (approximately one-third are African American men), and in twelve states they can be permanently barred from voting. Florida is the most notorious example because of the election of 2000. Presently, 5 percent of Florida's voting-age but 10 percent of its African American population are ex-felons. It is virtually certain if more former felons had been allowed to vote and if people "*mistakenly*" removed from the voting rolls as ineligible felons (disproportionately minority) had not been removed, the Democrats would have won the state and the election. The constitutionality of Florida's permanent disenfranchisement law, which can be traced all the way back to 1868 when the state tried to limit political rights granted to blacks under Reconstruction, is working its way through the federal courts. In a class-action suit representing Florida's 600,000 ex-felons, *Johnson v. Bush,* plaintiffs are challenging Florida law as a violation of the Fourteenth Amendment (and on other constitutional grounds) and the Voting Rights Act of 1965.[50]

Even if all former felons were to have their political rights restored, for which polls show a surprising level of public support,[51] it is unlikely that our prison system will soon become a major national issue. In national politics at least talking about the prison system seems to be strictly off-limits. Well, almost.

In what Elsner rightly calls a "remarkable speech," the crucial fifth vote on the Supreme Court that upheld California's three strikes law spoke out. Justice Anthony Kennedy told the American Bar Association on August 9, 2003:

> Out of sight, out of mind is an unacceptable excuse for a prison system that incarcerates over two million human beings in the United States. . . . [T]he American Bar Association should . . . study these matters and . . . help start a new public discussion about the prison system.

Kennedy suggested specific policies, such as revising federal sentencing guidelines downward and ending federal mandatory minimum sentences. It made no sense, he said, to send a young man to prison for ten to fifteen years for possessing five grams of crack. Appropriate to our discussion of demonization and its sources, he told his audience:

> A people confident in its laws and institutions should not be ashamed of mercy. . . . I hope more lawyers involved in the pardon process will say to Chief Executives, "Mr. President," or "Your Excellency, the Governor, this young man has not served his full sentence, but he has served long enough. Give him what only you can give him. Give him another chance. Give him a priceless gift. Give him liberty."

Kennedy also told them:

> Embedded in democracy is the idea of progress. Democracy addresses injustice and corrects it. The progress is not automatic. It requires a sustained exercise of political will; and political will is shaped by rational public discourse."[52]

So far, the political will is absent. On the national stage, at least, Kennedy is one of the few exceptions that prove this rule.

Target 3: Aliens

Unlike welfare recipients and prisoners, foreigners have often been lionized in American political culture. We pride ourselves on the idea that "we are a nation of immigrants." As Bonnie Honig has shown, however, American political culture's very dependence on foreignness disposes it to be ambivalent with regard to foreigners: they, at the same time, both reinvigorate and unsettle the polity and its citizenry. Their worthiness for us, therefore, depends on whether they help us *restore* our own sense of nation.[53]

On September 11, 2001, nineteen foreigners literally blew up part of the nation's foundation. This event was not followed by widespread anti-Arab demagoguery, even as debate raged on whether Islam was a fundamentally violent and antidemocratic religion. President Bush called for tolerance. If there was any event that should have brought out a strong xenophobic moment in a people torn about foreignness, this surely was it. It did not happen among the public to any major degree.

Yet institutional machinery was put into gear in the war on terrorism that did target foreigners in general, and Arabs and Muslims in particular, and largely did so in secret. David Cole conservatively estimated the number of domestic detentions to be approximately five thousand persons, even though none were charged with involvement in September 11. The "centerpiece" of the preventive detention campaign has been immigration law: "At every opportunity since September 11, [Attorney General] Ashcroft has turned immigration law from an administrative mechanism for controlling entry and exit of foreign nationals into an excuse for holding suspicious persons without meeting the constitutional requirements that ordinarily apply to preventive detention."[54]

Cole argues that if the "balance between liberty and security" is made equitably without imposing extra burdens on any one group, one can have confidence that "the political process will achieve a proper balance." However:

> Since September 11, we have repeatedly done precisely the opposite, sacrificing the rights of a minority group—noncitizens, and especially Arab and Muslim noncitizens—in the name of the majority's security interests. The government has selectively subjected foreign nationals to interviews, registration, automatic detention, and deportation based on their Arab or Muslim national origin; detained thousands of them, here and abroad; tried many of them in secret, and refused to provide any trials or hearings whatsoever to others; interrogated them for months on end under highly coercive, incommunicado conditions and without access to lawyers; authorized their exclusion based on pure speech; made them deportable for wholly innocent political associations with disfavored groups; and authorized their indefinite detention on the attorney gen-

eral's say-so. These and other measures targeted at noncitizens and often defended either explicitly or implicitly by noting that they do not affect American citizens, have inspired relatively little protest from the public.[55]

Contrast this with the political reaction to initiatives that affect citizen liberties. When the "Terrorism Information and Prevention System" (TIPS) was proposed, in which millions of private citizens would be recruited to snoop on others, it was opposed by conservatives as well as by liberals. It was then-Republican Majority Leader Richard Armey, not a noted civil libertarian, who took the initiative to prevent its implementation in Homeland Security legislation. Similarly, the Pentagon's Total Information Awareness program, designed to do massive sweeps of private and public computer records for suspicious behavior, was blocked *only* regarding its application to citizens.[56]

Cole also reminds us that there are many instances throughout American history in which foreigners were specifically targeted, from the Alien (and Sedition) Acts of 1798, to the Palmer raids after World War I, to Japanese-American internment during World War II and its validation by the Supreme Court in *Korematsu v. U.S.* in 1944. Less well known by American citizens is that while the Alien Act was never enforced and soon expired, another law was put in motion at the time it was written, the Enemy Alien Act. This law, which still exists and has been upheld by the Supreme Court, authorizes the president during time of declared war to detain, expel, or restrict the freedom of any citizen, fourteen years of age and older, of a nation with which we are at war. Instead of requiring due process hearings, "the Act creates an irrebuttable presumption that enemy aliens are dangerous, based *solely* on their national identity."

In this overall context, Cole thinks, the story of the Alien and Sedition Acts has served as a "founding myth"—to wit, America made an early mistake regarding civil liberties but then quickly repudiated it. Yet this myth belies much of the government's historical treatment of aliens,[57] including racially selective immigration laws that excluded the Japanese and Chinese and later severely discriminated against Italians and other southern and eastern Europeans in favor of "whiter" Europeans from the north and west.

Cole warns us that restrictions of civil liberties are often first applied to noncitizens, and then later, when the circumstances become politically feasible, to citizens as well.[58] Perhaps the best example is the extension of antisubversion-style legislation from aliens to citizens just before and during the Cold War.

The war on terrorism to one side, foreigners do have important constitutional protections in America, but they lack important political rights and therefore important political powers. Even more importantly, the attacks by Al Qaeda in New York, Washington, and Pennsylvania cause citizens who fear both terrorism and being charged with abetting terrorism (e.g., citizens who are from the same ethnic groups as the accused) to be less likely to stand up for those who seem to be under a cloud of suspicion. They feel too vulnerable.

What does it mean to be an enemy alien during a war on terrorism? Alienage itself denotes that a person formerly resided in a foreign nation, and "enemy alien" signifies the notion that our country is at war against that nation. In a war on terror, however, an enemy alien can be from anywhere. Even as we profile certain groups, it is the proclivity to harm us that we are after. Violations of rights and dignity are easiest when they rely on undercurrents of race, ethnicity, and religion—dark, Arab, and Muslim. The "enemy alien," however, can take on another sinister form. She can be anyone, like the communists in the old days. He can be one of us. For each of us, how we fight this new war is extremely important. We, too, are vulnerable.

PART II

Demonization and Wars

5

Seeking the Enemy

Frequent recourse in our politics to a rhetoric of war against one's political opponents is symptomatic, some would argue, of a need for a more humane, all-embracing and engaging set of purposes that would bind our society together. The influential journalist E. J. Dionne makes an argument along these lines. He believes America has to move beyond assertions of particularistic interests to refashion a notion of civic virtue and civic republicanism to which all members of the public, whatever their affiliation, could subscribe. This was also the basis for the "new covenant" that Bill Clinton talked about in the early 1990s. It is the spine of the wave of communitarian political philosophy that became attractive to some political thinkers in the 1980s and 1990s.[1] We sympathize with these goals.

This overall concept of civic virtue, however, too often contains a romantic reading of republican history that, we think, leads us astray. The assumption of a singular moral center in the past and the desire to resume it in the future promotes an ideology of republicanism deficient on two counts. It is more intolerant toward those who feel harmed by the prevailing consensus, and it preempts the possibility that greater social unity might flow from value systems that are open to multiple sources of moral authority.

To imagine a pristine time before the fall is to assume a harmonious time that never existed. It fails to acknowledge how positing the idea of an all-inclusive, harmonious community leads one to conceptualize current problems and discontents as the consequence of a *willful* fall from grace. Every community and every individual needs ideals and standards by which to live their lives. To what degree, however, is the truth of dominant standards neatly self-evident? How difficult is it really to consistently apply them? How difficult is it especially to see disharmony steaming just below the surface?

Neither public nor even private life is sustainable or desirable without some politics of the common good. If acted out unreflectively, this desire can itself produce other harms. America is well situated to understand this result. Almost all Americans are "from away" and are descendants of vastly different ethnic and religious backgrounds. America has a complex history of diversity and repression and of tolerance. We have had everything from discrimination to "ethnic cleansing," a history we have learned from and can continue to learn from. A complex and "constructed" nation living in a world of increasing interdependence, however, can be an anxious nation. An anxious nation, no matter how powerful, can worry too much about who it is, and there have been times in our history when we have. One way to ease anxieties is overnarrowly to define who we are, and portray those who appear different as "outsiders," enemies of the common good regardless of any danger they may actually pose to our lives.

Democratic politics helps us avoid this danger through an open political process, representative bodies, democratic procedures, civil liberties, and a democratic ethos. Democracy also allows hidden questions to surface. Things can feel unsettled. We can combat this unease by effectively closing down discourse in the name of having discovered, in one way or another, the end of history. Or, we can decide that the primary goal of politics is not to "validate" one's way of life but to explore how we, as separate, strong, independent individuals, want to live together as a society.[2]

War as Metaphor

Our democratic process labors under a symptomatic rhetorical strain that contributes to a lack of civility in pursuit of political ends. Since at least the time of FDR, we have been inclined to fashion at the rhetorical level a "war" to solve major problems, whatever they happen to be. Roosevelt summoned us to a war against unemployment during the depths of the Depression; Lyndon Johnson declared a war on poverty; Presidents Reagan and Bush declared war on drugs. A rhetoric of war, when deployed by groups of citizens in ways that implicate other citizens as enemies, may be seen as both cause and consequence of an ever less vital democratic process.[3]

All political discourse must draw upon some metaphorical strands to tap the enthusiasm and commitments of its citizens. Nonetheless, as historian Michael Sherry points out in his work, *In the Shadow of War,* our disproportionate recourse to military imagery has unfortunate consequences.[4] Wars are fought against an enemy, usually with the goal of annihilating that enemy.

The rhetoric of war has also undergone a shift worth noting. During the 1930s the "average person" was not seen as being responsible for the Depression. In the 1960s President Johnson did not believe that poverty was caused by personal failure. The war on drugs, by contrast, largely sees extensive drug use as the simultaneous failure of many individual characters. The rhetoric of war now seems to focus more than before on the central role of individual character as cause of critical social ills.

One reason for this shift paradoxically may derive from the just assertion of group rights. While greater rights clearly were needed and to an important degree were established, their establishment encouraged a subtle shift in discourse. It became less culturally acceptable to talk and behave in overtly racist and sexist ways. However, defects and deviance previously thought emblematic of group "nature" were shifted to the personal responsibility of the individual, or of the group that is now understood as the sum total of free and equal citizens who happen to have similar ascriptive characteristics.

It seems, therefore, that in the post–civil rights era there has been a shift in the process of converting difference into otherness, from understandings grounded in purported physical distinctions of race and gender to a process rooted in assessment of individual character. A new kind of legitimacy attaches itself to holding individuals and groups responsible for behavior as if they were completely free and autonomous. Then the deviance or evil presumed to constitute the "other" can be seen as willful and responsible. If we all now are equal in opportunity, and equal in rights in a practical as well as theoretical sense (as some claim), why do some wind up where they do? Because of individual character. Racist rhetoric is supplanted by a new application of the old notion of "abstract individualism," in which all people are believed to be positioned fairly to become modern day Horatio Algers, pulling themselves up by the bootstraps, without any form of unearned educational, economic, or cultural support.

Without a doubt, much of this line of thinking leans and trades heavily on, and reinforces at a tacit level, older racist and sexist prejudices and stereotypes rooted in ideas about "nature." Indeed, an abstract view that conflates legal with real equality may lead to a quiet reinforcement of the old suspicion that natural differences persist, as one reads differential "achievement tests," employment figures, and housing patterns. Even when the focus is on the situation the individual is in, as in a "culture of poverty," the group of "free" citizens is often assigned most of the responsibility for choices that perpetuated this situation. In these ways, once the complete abolition of injustice can be rationalized as having been achieved, groups—through their individual members—can once again be held responsible for recalcitrant problems. Just as older constructions of race and gender used individual examples to shore up racist or sexist notions, contemporary examples of individual problems are probed less deeply for structural causes when they occur among members of groups that are quietly still presumed to have these flaws. Still, this shift in public discourse emphasizing individual character is worth noting for its egalitarian moment—that all are by nature equipped to be held fully responsible—and for the way it helps reconfigure demonization by focusing on individual character.

Paradoxically, the sense of moral purpose and the assertion of group rights that helped shift culpability to individual character have become the philosophical backdrop to the acrimony of the wars over values that often target these groups. In these wars, a person with a particular "values" profile is expected to play a predictable role in any moral drama.

The Enemy at Home

Domestic political warfare—especially civil wars or their rhetorical proxy culture wars—best illustrates the politics of demonization. Civil war is different from foreign war in that antagonists need to make the case that the opponent is an enemy, an "other" alien at odds with that society's way of life.[5] While a foreigner is inevitably "different" by virtue of his or her birthplace, a member of one's own society is thought to *become* "different" by factors such as character and choice of belief system. The threat of this "deviant" seems magnified because the person is held responsible for becoming different in spite of the fact she or he didn't really have to be that way. Sometimes in civil or cultural wars, the domestic dissident is made to appear worse by depicting him or her as having voluntarily embraced a foreign enemy. The reconstruction of a "brother" or "sister" into an "other" and then an "enemy" is strenuous, requiring motivation and psychological and political vigilance.[6] At the extreme, each side believes the other side is usurping the true values of the native land: "America: Love it or leave it."

In rigidly defining as evil and/or abnormal the purported character and code of the opposition and tying it to a type of political agenda, each side reflexively strengthens its own character, code, and agenda as unambiguously good and/or normal. Each side calcifies. For how can I be sure that you are completely wrong, evil, or deviant unless I have privileged access to knowing what's right, good, and normal? In attacking you for being how you are, I overdetermine who and what I am and elicit the same from you in reply. The more each of us persists, the further we go toward transforming former opponents into enemies.

Some of the most hurtful demonization in American history has occurred when Americans have not accepted the proposition that all are created equal, for example with regard to Native Americans, African Americans, and women. Full political and legal equality is a necessary condition for protection against demonization because difference cannot be as easily exploited when the targets have rights and can assert political powers heretofore denied. Nonetheless, full political and legal equality is an insufficient condition because it cannot guarantee power resources that are sufficient to bring about strong consequences against demonizers should full respect be denied.

The current debate over gay marriage and the proposed constitutional amendment to ban it illustrate these considerations and more. Gays are certainly better protected today because they have asserted their political and civil rights and gained social and economic powers in a variety of ways by organizing, voting, contributing to campaigns, holding office, carving out important niches in popular culture, and holding a proportionate share of economic resources. These powers, along with increased public tolerance, have borne fruit in a number of ways regarding rights. A recent example is in the historic Supreme Court case *Lawrence v. Texas,* in which laws banning same sex sodomy were declared unconstitutional under the right to privacy. The public is fairly evenly divided on the right to some form of legal recognition for gay couples, as well as on whether there should be a constitutional amendment banning gay marriage. A poll taken in May 2004 reported strong majorities opposed to introduction of "gay marriage" into the 2004 presidential election.[7] Strong majorities, however, consistently oppose legalization of gay marriage. Gays remain a minority, so a majority will likely continue to reject efforts to legislate gay marriage provisions. The most hopeful possibilities for gay advocates resides in some courts and in the difficulty of amending the federal constitution.[8]

But is it fair to characterize all opponents of gay marriage, by that fact, as demonizers? When George W. Bush or John Kerry opposed gay marriage in the 2004 campaign, each surely was making a statement about how he thinks gays and lesbians fit or don't fit into "normal" patterns of society worthy of state sanction. In implying that gay marriage is abnormal in this sense, are they demonizing gays? What are we to make of President Bush's use of respectful tones when speaking about gays, yet his proposal for a constitutional amendment during an election year to forbid states and the Congress from granting them marriage rights? Is he refraining from demonizing them himself, but for political advantage is he knowingly contributing to a climate in which others may more easily do so? These are not easy questions to answer. Even in the area of rights there needs to be—however passionate, intense, and hard fought—room for respectful disagreement. For disagreement to be respectful, each of us must take a sober look at our own motivations and intentions and at the validity of the positions we take and how they affect the well-being of others.

To more fully understand wars between values, however, we need to look beyond recent history, and further than the values themselves. We also need to look at the way modern humans frame values and the assumptions we bring to the process. This is perhaps especially true in unsettled social and economic times. When some citizens find their own lives insecure and feel deprived of voice and threatened by others, it becomes easier to see politics as a war in which unitary truth, represented by those who share our circumstances and views, is at ongoing war with those whose lifestyles and circumstances are very different and threaten the majority. However, as the 1960s culture wars have indicated and as their influence is still felt, such conflicts can occur even during times of relative affluence. Those who have different views and lifestyles are regarded at once as individually deviant or evil, personally responsible for their circumstances, and as the basic cause of our most important problems.

Seeking the Enemy

Modern demonization, we suggest, is connected to the modern quest to find a final and compelling source of truth and value in a world where God and traditional religion are no longer directly built into the structure of everyday life and discourse. In American culture this takes a particular form. Americans are the most religious people in the industrialized world.[9] At the same time, they have the strongest beliefs about the human ability and the right to manipulate the physical world. Overwhelming majorities of Americans report that they believe in God, even as they live their lives in very secular ways. One example is particularly telling. In spite of thoroughly relying on scientific discovery in almost all we do, contrary to all scientific evidence of the same methodological kind that builds cars, cell phones, and trips to the moon, polls reveal that half of Americans believe that God created persons in their present form within the last 10,000 years.[10] Given the choice between evolution and the biblical account of creation, 50 percent chose the biblical account compared to only 15 percent who believe the theory of evolution.[11]

Efforts to make sense of the world, however, always contain their own fundamentalist temptations, if William Connolly is right that humans have an existential "drive to establish commonalities and seal them in truth." For him this is as equally true for secular as for religious, rationalist as for spiritualist, progressive as orthodox worldviews. It is a temptation built into the modern human condition. From the perspective of lessening demonization, as we see it, the goal is first to understand this drive and loosen this seal.

Connolly specifically identifies six pressures at work upon us: we are born incomplete and must take on social form; we can only coordinate ourselves through social rules with moral and civil sanctions; in order to live in structured societies we must have delimited identities; because our capacity for conscious reflection is limited, we must rely on implicit rules and routines, or suffer "overload"; all of this occurs through the dense medium of language; "psychic disturbance . . . wells up when conventional character of socially established identities, implicit standards, and explicit norms is expressed."[12] Human beings, facing psychological and epistemic pressures to define their social and personal worlds in singular terms, encounter in nature—including their own physiological beings—a world not designed to accommodate such singularity. A human being therefore "encounters elements of resistance in itself to any specific form imposed upon it." Gaps and doubts arise, spurring endless efforts to provide reasons for reasons. Anxious efforts are made to stamp each new revision as final, self-evident, beyond challenge, creating a kind of "sickness" in the human being that "resides in its quest to reach the end of a trail which has no such terminus."[13]

Connolly acknowledges that this ontology of "resistance" is itself a presumption for which he can give no final justification. In this regard his thought does not differ from fundamentalist and rationalist opponents who also cannot ground their own standards of truth any more completely. But the lack of final grounding is fully acknowledged. The presumption of resistance is inspired in part by the recognition of the variety of ways human life is lived. Different ways of life spawn sets of fundamental interpretations of the world, which in retrospect turn out to be provisional as each sooner or later seems to run aground on internal contradictions from within as well as from pressures without. And this presumption of resistance grows out of and encourages a spark within each of us to experience the unexpected within our lives. Ironically, some religions may reflect this ontology of change and becoming as they express, in Connolly's words, "a yearning for that which has been sacrificed as well as sanctification of that which has been enabled."[14]

For empirical and theoretical reasons, we reject a categorization of views like Connolly's as a relativistic repudiation of moral and ethical postures. In our view, the claim that moral truth is relative to particular times and cultures exaggerates the degree of unity within those cultures, and underplays dissonance and resistance. In the modern world, it vastly underrates the extensive and rapid communication and intermingling among cultures. The perspective developed here actually valorizes those cultures and polities that adopt a reasonably problematic stance toward their own forms of order. We do so for the eminently *moral* reason that precisely such societies are the ones more likely, in a timely way, to become aware of the harms and damage their cultures are inflicting among themselves and outside. The pressures Connolly identifies and their consequences cannot be disentangled from our search for truth; indeed, they are among the reasons for our search.

Consider now what is involved in our search for "truth" as we look at the relationships between the following ideas: object, difference, morality, demonization, and discovery. As a being in the world, I fix the meaning of things. I objectify. I must do this to have an ontological center necessary for me to act as a subject in the world. But the fact that I, a subject, must do it means my objectification of the world cannot exhaust possible understandings of the world, nor my own experience. Part of the process of fixing the world is differentiating "objects" within it. I learn and apply linguistic rules to tell differences, including differences of morals. To situate ourselves and live in a world that is inevitably social (no language bearer is an island), we must be aware of moral notions.[15]

The potential for demons to lurk in our landscapes inheres in our need of objectification, differentiation, and judgment. Yet it is a historical question as to the kind of role they play in different societies and cultures at any particular time. Demons can be worshipped, feared, or hated; they can be evil or merely very powerful and dangerous. Demons can be external spirits to be warded off or placated, internal spirits that can be exorcised, intrinsic characteristics of particular groups or races, which in turn can be subjugated, enslaved or killed, or intrinsic characteristics of types of persons, who can be saved through love, cured through therapy, or, failing these, locked safely away. Political demonization as the wrongful framing of difference as evil or deviant otherness is always a prospect implicit in the structure of language and personal interaction in any modern political society. But it is a possibility that can be managed more or less effectively. One technique of management is to remain aware both of the reasons for the temptations and the costs to human discovery and a better life of giving in to them too easily and too often.[16]

Understanding existential sources of drives for absolutes is imperative, therefore, if we wish to move beyond the politics of moral personae. Otherwise, political positions that are designed to appeal to deep resentments can too easily become personalized wars in which each side feels its identity assaulted by an enemy whose character is intrinsic to the wrong perpetrated. Consequently, one must expose the ways these wrongs flow from aspects of the private life and character of the individual that heretofore had been thought to be beyond public scrutiny.

Humans, however, need a degree of certainty. Whether this brings with it a ritual need to demonize, and whether that need may be satisfied in more benign rather than more vicious forms, is less clear. History does not provide convincing grounds for optimism, although neither does it speak with one voice. The modern hope is that awareness of and reflection about pressures toward constructing oppressive regimes of alleged truths—while certainly not extinguishing the possibility of demonization —can make it less likely by making us wiser.

Our concern is with how the need to resolve doubts about the self in modern societies, which both prize the individual and the individual's control over her or his environment, including the individual, may create a tendency toward demonization that we can temper. Such demonization

does inhibit discovery, limits individualism, and can cause harm to the social fabric as well. The form of demonization we are considering, borne
in anxiety and fear, is done ritualistically but provides little worthwhile
ritual to deepen the moral basis of the society. All of these claims are contestable, of course, but these are our claims.

Serious dangers, however, do exist in the world, and enemies can be
quite real. An argument in favor of limiting demonizing rhetoric would
not only fall on deaf ears if it denied the real wrongs that are committed, it would by implication demonize those who want to protect themselves or warn us of danger. When real enemies exist they must be confronted, condemned, and, when necessary, defeated. Here we draw attention to a second sense in which modern people "seek the enemy," as
their identity needs, when viewing another person, slide from object, to
difference, to otherness, to construction of an implacable foe. Seeking
the enemy in this way may produce immediate harms and future real enemies.

What Foreignness Teaches Us

At the beginning of this book we discussed types of demonization in order
to draw distinctions between demonization in general and the politics of
moral personae in particular. As we have seen, however, the distinction
cannot always be sharply drawn. The most overt forms of classic demonization, such as racism, sexism, and even to some extent homophobia,
are for the most part at least publicly taboo, and the use of anticommu-
nism (but not antiterrorism) is less relevant today as a strategy for the demonization of political opponents.[17] Still, demonizers who don't rely on
pseudogenetics often find "evidence" of ostensible group characteristics
in the individual character and behavior of individuals inhabiting those
groups. If only "those people" would change their behavior, they claim to
be saying while trading on older stereotypes, "there would be no problems." Character plays a particularly important role in America with its
individualist culture, voluntarist ethos, religious focus on sin and redemption, changing ethnic profile, and somewhat shifting boundaries in
defining out-groups. But there is also another reason. The idea of individual consent is essential in the cultural narrative of America as an exceptional nation in world history. The fact that our rights are inherent,
that no person gives them to us, does not just make them "inalienable."

It gives the heavy responsibility of giving our democracy its legitimacy to *us*. It comes from our will and nowhere else.

There are many ways we can bear the load of democratic responsibility that is made even heavier than it would otherwise be in a liberal democracy because of our belief that we are "the chosen people." One is to believe that *our* rights come from God, and American exceptionalism is in part based upon this belief. Another tendency is to laugh at "good citizens" who seem to waste their time in doing civic duty. Another is to scoff at apathetic citizens for their thorough disregard of public issues that should be of great importance to everyone, but only seem to concern us. Rather than believe, laugh, or scoff, or in addition to them, we may resolve our doubts about our own responsibility by challenging the inherent worthiness of other individuals and the groups to which they belong.

It is here that the politics of moral personae and the general politics of demonization meet. For when I charge a leader with being evil or deviant, I ineluctably convert that citizen into an "alien," a member of a group foreign to my (our) inherent goodness. Isn't this, after all, what the "culture wars" of the last forty years have been about? *Conversion of such majesty, however, which can no longer be explicitly grounded in bloodlines, requires much information or at least many assumptions: about personality, character, affiliations, policy preferences, cultural proclivities, and ideology. All becomes fair game.* As I compile or assume what I need to know, I also create the profile of that other, evil, or deviant tribe to which the object of my rancor belongs. Clinton *is* the 1960s! It is precisely at these border crossings between purported individual and group character, and at the borders separating opposing groups, where one can find the richest stories regarding patterns of contemporary demonization.

One of the best examinations of the layers and textures of these crossings is Bonnie Honig's inquiry into the roles played by foreigners and foreignness in the American story, the temptations to demonize and demoralize them that flow, but go unnoticed, in the process of remoralizing the American narrative. In these times of terrorism, globalization, immigration, mass communication—border crossings, literal and figurative in unimaginable ways—Honig's work and this example merit attention in any study of demonization. But why does she think that in a nation of immigrants most democratic theorists misunderstand foreignness by reading the American story as a modern romance, a love story that must have a happy ending?

The modern romance she reviews is "the myth of an immigrant America" in the telling of the story of American exceptionalism.

> American exceptionalists, from Tocqueville to Hartz to Walzer, treat immigrants as the agents of founding and renewal for a regime in which membership is supposed to be uniquely consent based, individualist, rational, and voluntarist rather than inherited and organic. . . . [T]he future of American democracy depends not on the native born but on the recent arrival, not on someone with a past to build on but rather on someone who left his past behind. . . . The myth of an immigrant America depicts the foreigner as a supplement to the nation, an agent of national reenchantment that might rescue the regime from corruption and return it to its first principles.[18]

Writers may view America's first principles, she writes, as capitalist, communal, familial, or liberal, and variations on the myth exist within each of these domains. Immigrants may show us, for example, that the economic system is fair after all, and still rewards hard work; or they may display how community and family can exist in the face of American individualism and socioeconomic disruptions, or, by example, restore faith in traditional patriarchic families. Things don't always work out the way they should, however: the same immigrant who works hard and succeeds puts us out of jobs; the strong immigrant communities can look like ethnic enclaves; their family values threaten our greater gender equality.[19]

We are here most interested in the myth Honig describes as being contained within liberal consent theories, as they grapple in the modern context with the problem of consent posed by Rousseau. Because democracy cannot have an original lawgiver, the law is inherently alien. For it to become ours, then, we must will it so, and do so frequently. But how can such consent be affirmed in a mass heterogeneous society such as ours? Voting is clearly inadequate. Enter the immigrants who of their own free will leave behind their homes to choose America as their home, in a show of commitment a native born never needs to make.

This story of American exceptionalism casts the immigrant in the romantic lead that goes way back, to before the founding of the American republic. Yet, how can we then explain the xenophobia that has surely been a motif in American history? Is it inherent within the liberal and republican traditions, in which case these traditions are "flawed," or does it come from somewhere else? To answer this question, Honig examines the "multiple traditions" thesis of Rogers Smith. In Smith's account, various traditions compete for authority in America. While liberalism and republicanism, are egalitarian and consent based, others, such as racism, patriarchalism, and nativism, are inegalitarian and ascriptive. According to Honig, Smith's thesis allows him to claim, against critics of liberalism, that problems such as xenophobia may be internal to America but remain external to the core claim of liberalism. Once cleansed, American liberal democracy could become a fully humane regime based on consent. Thus the real romantic leads for Smith are those who protect liberalism and republicanism from, as he puts it, "ascriptive mythologies that can easily become demonologies."[20]

Honig argues, however, that Smith's efforts become themselves demonological in structure, in that he sets up ascriptive mythologies as "Girardian scapegoats," thereby protecting liberal democracy from further scrutiny. Instead, Honig thinks we need to ask, "Is foreignness a site at which certain anxieties of *democratic* self-rule are managed?"[21] If it is, with what consequences?

To answer, Honig believes we need to take a step back and away from the question that dominates foreignness discourse, namely, "How should we solve the problem of foreignness?" Instead, we should ask: "*What problems does foreignness solve for us?* Why do nations or democracies rely on the agency of foreignness at their vulnerable moments of (re)founding, at what cost and for what purpose?"[22] Looking at the question in this way, xenophobia in democratic societies may prove to be a consequence of seeking the very supplement that foreignness, the target of xenophobia, provides for the regime's legitimacy. Rather than simply placing blame on racists and xenophobes, this question asks liberal democracy to look at itself, to see if there is a "deeper logic at work" that helps explain what actually is a profound ambivalence within America to foreignness:

The co-presence in American political culture of xenophilia and xenophobia comes right out of America's fundamental liberal commitments, which map a normatively and materially privileged national citizenship onto an idealized immigrant trajectory to membership. This means that the undecidability of foreignness—the depiction of foreigners as good and bad for the nation—is partly driven by the logic of liberal, national consent, which, in the case of the United States, both produces and denies a fundamental dependence upon foreigners who are positioned symbolically so that they must and yet finally cannot fill the gaps of consent and legitimacy for us.[23]

Calls simply to become more inclusionist within the bounds of the liberal nation-state cannot set this logic aside. For example, Honig believes that Michael Walzer's plea to see immigrant and ethnic communities as vehicles to moderate the major corruption within liberalism of excessive individualism also invites further suspicion of them as foreign enclaves opposed to American values. "The communitarian xenophilic deployment of foreignness *on behalf of a national project*," she concludes, "itself plays into the hands of and, indeed helps to feed this xenophobic response." Honig's point is that accounts such as Smith's or Walzer's miss the ways in which the enormous pressures built into "consent" as the foundational legitimation generates unanticipated resentments. Liberal democracy within the narrative of American exceptionalism, she believes, itself engenders "ambivalence" toward foreigners:

> The foreigner who shores up and reinvigorates the regime also unsettles it at the same time. Since the presumed test of both a good and a bad foreigner is the measure of her contribution to the restoration of the nation rather than, say, to the nation's transformation or attenuation, nationalist xenophilia tends to feed and (re)produce nationalist xenophobia as its partner.[24]

Honig uses naturalization as a prime example of how immigrants become agents of renewal within American exceptionalism by reassuring natural-born citizens, who never need *choose* to become Americans, that our nation is uniquely based on consent. This rite returns us to first principles, reminds us that we rationally and freely choose our faith in our democratic creed, perhaps even gives natural-born citizens an opportunity to choose the regime empathetically as they watch or read about the ceremonies periodically reported in the media. With the "embrace" between new citizen and state, the naturalization ceremony reassures us that we the citizens consent. We remain in a position to choose the "law" freely, and therefore it is *we* who come before it. This is especially important in Honig's account because she believes that one of the paradoxes for the idea of the founding of a democracy, and therefore crucial for its legitimacy in the eyes of its public, is that the law remains alien; someone has to "give" the law and yet "we the people" must come before the law. The naturalization rite also diverts attention both from historical violence and contemporary injustice, each of which raises questions about the unvarnished idea that we are a consent-based republic. All told, it "reperforms the origin of the regime *as* an act of consent."[25]

Reaffirmation of the consensual basis of our democracy, however, causes problems of its own. For in relying so heavily on foreigners it puts enormous symbolic power into their hands in ways that can breed resentment toward them, especially by raising questions in us. Some foreigners, legal as well as illegal, don't consent to becoming citizens. In what ways, however, do we who were born here choose this regime over others, rather than pledge allegiance to the only regime we know, just as we might in a monarchy or dictatorship? Think how good the foreigner looks when she is sworn into citizenship; now compare her to many of us who seem to shun basics such as voting or serving on juries. Think how much we resent the foreigner who takes what we have without consenting to the regime (the legal immigrant who does not become a citizen), and even more so the bad foreigner (the illegal immigrant) who takes without even asking our consent to be here. In ways such as this, Honig believes, the myth of American exceptionalism leaves Americans with "a quite *anxious* dependence upon the kindness of strangers,"[26] with consequences relevant to the study of demonization.

If we can't end this dependency, given the paradox of consent within liberal democracy, are there ways to better negotiate it? Honig believes there are, starting by changing our genre from modern to gothic romance, thereby appreciating that the love object may portend danger, and where the ending is not known nor are the protagonists ("us" and "them," "you" and "me") fully knowable. It is possible, Honig writes, for one to "be passionately attached to something—a nation, a people, a principle —and be deeply and justifiably (and even therefore!) afraid of it at the same time."[27] This alternative sensibility does not solve the problems we face, nor does it erase the paradoxes, but it makes it more likely that we will resist rewriting paradoxes into the antagonistic problematic of "us" versus "them." This kind of sensibility gives us a better chance to understand that patterns of solidarity and kinship "always exclude as one of their enabling conditions."[28] It gives us the best chance to do good, while doing least harm.

6

Terror, Evil, and
the New Cold War

The great power of terrorism is obvious. It terrorizes. It creates an unpredictability of horror, absolute insecurity from moment to moment and in every place. It makes everyone always vulnerable and thereby undermines the basic conditions of civilized life. To call terrorists evil is *not* to demonize them. Terrorism *is* evil and its perpetrators deserve the strongest condemnation. They *are* "evildoers," although as we will see, they are sometimes our allies.

Fighting terrorism is therefore one of the most important responsibilities leaders and citizens have, freeing them, even obligating them, to consider the use of all the tools, techniques, and ideas at their disposal. They must of course weigh these against other important ideas and values such as liberty, because Benjamin Franklin was surely right that security should never be our only concern. Still, terrorism puts a premium on all manner of things we would normally never consider. Fighting against terrorism is one of those fights we engage in for survival.

To the degree we feel the power and weight of this responsibility, we should consider the care with which a "war on terrorism" must be fought. If the charge that terrorism is evil has a core, it is surely that innocent people, those far removed from any real or imagined grievance, become vulnerable and expendable for the sake of the terrorists' purposes, even to the point of demonizing them as the embodiment of all that is wicked—blaming the victim. Therefore, *we* want to be as sure as humanly possible that our broad mandate for war against this sort of thing in fact targets the evil we seek to overcome. For using such a mandate to target the innocent, whether it is done out of malice, laziness, selfishness, or ineptitude, is doing something very bad.

To charge someone with being a terrorist or with abetting terrorism is to say this person has done evil and to imply he or she may *be* evil. We distinguish between doing evil and being evil because to evaluate an act, however difficult, can in principle be definitive to a degree that judging other humans rarely is. Just as we can judge people as good or even saintly by their deeds, we can also judge them as intrinsically evil, but should rarely do so. The "devil may get in us," though few of us are actually devils. These principles are long established in religion, for example. Americans are familiar with ideas and practices such as the Catholic confessional and the notions of personal salvation and redemption, even, among some Christians of being "born again." In law we punish people for an act but may mitigate their sentence if they show signs of reform.

To wrongly and especially falsely and deliberately charge someone with evil, or abetting evil, is to engage in the most reprehensible form of demonization. If there ever was a time in American history that we need to take this claim seriously it is now.

What marks terrorism as evil? Let's take a look first at what terrorism is, and its connection to evil. Then we will consider evil itself to find some answers on how to fight a "war on terrorism" as an actual war against terrorists.

Deliver Us from Evil

Until the nineteenth century and the French Revolution, the almost exclusive justification for terrorism was religion. Important examples include the *zealots* in Judea who murdered Romans and their Jewish collaborators; *thugs* in India engaged in ritual murder to serve the Hindu goddess Kali; and *assassins* or radical Shi'a in the Middle East who fought to repel the Crusaders. The French Revolution is one of the only examples of a regime in power that positively appraised terrorism, but it is far from the only example of state-sponsored terrorism. For much of the last fifty years we have been most concerned with political, or ethno-separatist terrorism, including the role of states in sponsoring such groups, particularly during the Cold War.

What do terrorists believe they are doing? While some students of terrorism believe terrorists have gone through a process of psychological detachment from morality, others focus on their motivations, finding a kind of rationality to their behavior.[1] Martha Crenshaw, for example, believes that terrorists use terrorism as a tactic and are trying to achieve objectives. By and large, they should not be viewed either as "crazy" or "irrational." If she's right, their rationale for terror is another reason the term "evil" may apply to them.

Terrorists often attack targets in order to augment their political position, and they employ tactics consistent with their goals and beliefs. They are most concerned with the problem of legitimation. Though the violence may be characterized as wanton, the terrorist is purposeful. As Jerry Adams of the Irish Sinn Fein once put it:

> Rightly or wrongly, I am an IRA Volunteer. . . . I take a course of action as a means to bringing about a situation in which I believe the people of my country will prosper. . . . The course I take involves the use of physical force, but only if I achieve the situation where my people can genuinely prosper can my course of action be seen, by me, to have been justified.[2]

Along with their hatred and the willingness to kill innocent people, therefore, terrorists employ tactics and strategies and have audiences and hold beliefs, each of which constrains them. Bruce Hoffman, a terrorism expert at RAND, has argued:

> Even when terrorists' actions are not as deliberate or discriminating, and when their purpose is in fact to kill innocent civilians, the target is still regarded as "justified" because it represents the terrorists' defined "enemy." Although incidents may be quantitatively different in the volume of death or destruction caused, they are still qualitatively identical in that a widely known "enemy" is being specifically targeted. This distinction is often accepted by the terrorists' constituents and at times by the international community as well.[3]

Even before 9/11, religion-based terrorism had become a major source of concern. In that light, does the above characterization of the "rationality" of terrorism need to be qualified?

Writing several years before 9/11, Bruce Hoffman argued that the reasons religious terrorism is so much more destructive of life "lies in the radically different value systems, mechanisms of legitimization and justification, concepts of morality, and world-view embraced by the religious terrorist, compared with his secular counterpart." Secular terrorists may of course act out of revenge or other personal motivation, but for the religious terrorist violence and even killing is "first and foremost" either a sacramental act or a religious duty compelled by theology. The constituencies are also different. For the religious terrorists, they (and of course God) are their own constituency providing at once fewer constraints on action and a virtually limitless pool of targets. Thus people outside the chosen community are demonized by that fact, as some variation of the "children of Satan." Finally, the degree of alienation is greater in religious terrorists, as they seek not to correct or change the system but to fundamentally change the "existing order."[4]

Do legal definitions of terrorism help us understand its relation to purported evil? They do, but not in the way one would think. Consider these examples. For the FBI, it is

the unlawful use of force or violence against persons or property to intimidate or coerce a Government, the civilian population, or any segment thereof, in furtherance of political or social objectives.[5]

For the State Department:

The term "terrorism" means premeditated, politically motivated violence perpetrated against noncombatant targets by sub-national groups or clandestine agents, usually intended to influence an audience. The term "international terrorism" means terrorism involving citizens or the territory of more than one country. The term "terrorist group" means any group practicing, or that has significant subgroups that practice international terrorism.

For the Defense Department:

Terrorism is the unlawful use or threatened use of force or violence against individuals or property to coerce or intimidate governments or societies, often to achieve political, religious, or ideological objectives.

For the Defense Intelligence Agency:

Terrorism is premeditated, political violence perpetrated against noncombatant targets by subnational groups or clandestine state agents, usually to influence an audience.

The first thing to note is that these are instrumental definitions. They stipulate a category of activity in order, often, to make it punishable by law or by other forms of state action. However much they try to capture a sense of immorality, by their nature they are definitions relevant to, but inherently incomplete with regard to, considerations of morality, and inherently open to being contraindicated under scrutiny. The Defense Department and FBI definitions would implicate the Boston Tea Party participants as terrorists. So would the others if violence against noncombatant targets were defined to include violence against property. But even when we do not construe them this way, the actions of other American patriots might fall under these definitions. This of course simply raises the question: When and what kind of revolutionary violence is justified?

These examples do not point to hypocrisy within the law but rather the inadequacy of legal definitions in making definitive moral judgments. In moral terms, distinctions between states and nonstate actors has virtually no meaning without giving deep consideration to the nature of each group, its purposes, and the actions perpetrated. Some political theorists in the liberal individualist tradition, such as George Kateb, argue that states by their nature are actually more likely to engage in what he calls political evil, which includes a broader array of evils than terrorism, than are smaller groups or individuals. What do these definitions have to say, for example, about the routine use of terror by all states involved in World War II, from the Italians in Ethiopia, to the Japanese in China, to the Germans in Europe, the Americans and British in Germany, and, of course, the Americans finally in Japan? For all of these combatant states, noncombatant civilians were fair game. Why? To terrorize and demoralize them was one weapon in getting their leaders to surrender. How could this be countenanced morally? By claiming there was a greater good at stake, by demonizing the enemy population, or by ordering the acts from the distance offered by abstraction, either physically or emotionally. Perhaps all of these are not very different things.

Sometimes there are plain contradictions. According to Jonathan R. White, "Under the legal guidelines of the United States . . . *some groups can be labeled as terrorists, while other groups engaged in the same activities may be described as legitimate revolutionaries.*"[6] We only need remember Ronald Reagan's "freedom fighters" against godless communism in Afghanistan and Jimmy Carter's national security adviser Zbigniew Brzezinski's continuing defense of that policy. All things considered, it was said to achieve the greater good of having done lesser evils to get rid of "the Evil Empire," as Ronald Reagan famously called the Soviet Union.

Surely the United Nations can do better? For the United Nations:

> A TERRORIST is any person who, acting independently of the specific recognition of a country, or as a single person, or as part of a group not recognized as an official part or division of a nation, acts to destroy or to injure civilians or destroy or damage property belonging to civilians or to governments in order to effect some political goal. TERRORISM is the act of destroying or injuring civilian lives or the act of destroying or damaging civilian or government property without the expressly chartered permission of a specific government, thus, by individuals or groups acting independently or governments on their own accord and belief, in the attempt to effect some political goal.

That solves the problem, right? If your political violence against civilians, governments, or their property is not sanctioned by a state, you're a terrorist. From a moral point of view, this definition is as limited as those of the American government. But why this failure to encode in law the moral depravity that most believe terrorism entails?

As Christ (and yes, Gandhi and Martin Luther King Jr.) well understood, there is always a law higher than that of the government or even that of religious institutions. That is why civil disobedience is always a moral possibility and sometimes a moral obligation. That is also why, whatever the rationale from a legal point of view, drawing a line in the sand between the state and terrorism simply won't do morally. Some would argue a point worth some deference—that some states actually represent the best interests of society and the will of the people, and that they carry out central functions of security without which civilized life cannot go on. Even if a supermajority of citizens wills an act, it does not absolve from moral review the decision they made. As for the other considerations, all are exactly the kind that requires specific inquiry of the type which instrumentally oriented legal definitions severely limit.

It seems to us that we are left with variations on several options. Either we *define* terrorism instrumentally to achieve a specific purpose, or we *stipulate* its relation to moral notions and work out in each instance whether something we wish to call terrorism has occurred. Or we opt for a combination that is inherently subject to the possibility of hypocritical results, but which still may serve some valid purposes. Here we would be defining terrorism for practical legal purposes in one way, and stipulating its relation to morality in another. This is in fact what we do. We fix in law the definition of terrorism even as we know that the state, as the sole institution that can legitimately make and enforce the law, is in principle able to escape the legal but not moral charge.

What we *cannot* do from a moral point of view, but often do anyway, is define terrorism instrumentally, selectively apply it, and then claim for that application the status of moral certainty. That is a setup for hypocrisy of not just any sort, but of *precisely the sort that strengthens terrorism by undermining the moral stature of those who claim to oppose it and, thereby, the moral claim against terrorism itself.*

Many experts on terrorism have tried to come up with their own definitions, often because they advise on security matters. Brian Jenkins calls it simply an effort to bring about political change through the use or threatened use of force. Walter Laqueur says it is the use of illegitimate force against innocent people to achieve a political objective.[7] Each recognizes the limits of his definition, and Laqueur believes we must live with these limits because, if we get more specific, different people simply will define terrorism in different ways. He is right, of course, *if we are seeking an instrumental definition with moral reach.* What, however, if rather than focusing on a usable definition for governmental purposes we think through the problem from the view of the relevant moral stipulations? And then we insist that we, and our leaders, consign to ourselves the responsibility in every case to use the term "terrorism" only when, and whenever, these stipulations are met? In other words, what if we insist always in democratic politics on a moral supplement to the law?

In practice, leaders normally do not talk about terrorism in legal terms, but if they choose to use coercive power the law backs them up. Rather, they "define" this evil against their perceptions of our nation's good and interests. When President Bush seeks out "evildoers," he rightly looks at bin Laden and to post-1991 Saddam Hussein, but not to pre-1991 Hussein and to Vladimir Putin and the Russian republic's atrocities in Chechnya. The president said he looked Putin in the eye and declared him a "good man." Was Hussein a "good man" when he fought our enemy Iran in the 1980s, for example in 1983 when Donald Rumsfeld shook his hand? Or do these statements come down to the familiar argument that, all things considered, state terrorism of Russia in Chechnya is outweighed by the need to defeat Islamic fundamentalists there and elsewhere, and that Russia is of geo-strategic importance? But to introduce such self-regarding considerations is to fatally weaken the dualistic ideology of universal good and evil to which President Bush seems both genuinely committed in religious terms, and shrewdly knows how to deploy politically.

While she does not solve definitional problems, Martha Crenshaw comes up with an interesting variation. She thinks that in order to define terrorism you must consider three things: the methods used, who and what were the targets, and, intriguingly, the likelihood of success. (She also believes we should not confuse revolutionary violence with terrorism.) In her view, terrorism is violence aimed at innocent targets, which is socially and politically unacceptable, and has the purpose of achieving a psychological effect.[8] Jonathan White thinks this definition still leaves two problems unsolved: those who have "the political power to define 'legitimacy'" also have "the power to define terrorism." Moreover, her "analytical definition has not moved far from the simple definition."[9]

While White's first point is plausible, it is beside Crenshaw's point, because she is not so much "defining" in an instrumental sense as stipulating conditions that need to be established before we can say that terrorism has occurred. That is why White's second point is wrong. Crenshaw is getting back to the core by asking question such as these: Who is being targeted: the military or innocent civilians? What methods are being used: attacking utility lines or dispersing nerve gas into crowded subways? What is the reasonable likelihood that even violence done for the most noble of goals, which after all remains violence, has a reasonable chance of succeeding in bringing about a worthwhile goal? For if it doesn't, people will still be dead and the retribution may produce additional harms.

Does it matter who is targeted? Is it morally acceptable to harm a general but not a private, or a policeman but not an elected official, or an elected official but not a businessperson, or a businessperson but not food service workers such as those killed in the Windows on the World restaurant in the World Trade Center?[10] If it does not matter, can revolutionary violence ever be justified?

Questions of the sort Crenshaw raises can and should be asked and they should be answered, but, as she notes, terrorism does have a core meaning. Most of us embrace this core. It is explicit or implicit in many of the definitions above. Terrorism is the targeting and harming of innocents. If the harm is great, intentionally doing so is to do evil.

Thinking about terrorism in this way centers but does not settle the contestability of the use of the term. But why not? One practical reason is that political institutions and especially great powers have always defined terrorism in ways that suit their purposes. Political scientist Michael Stohl makes the point that "by convention" and "only by convention" a great power uses "coercive diplomacy" which turns out to be "the threat and often the use of violence for what would be described as terroristic purposes" were it not being done by a great power.[11] Below this, however, is a deeper reason that may even partly explain, but not absolve, "hypocritical" state use of the idea. Tied as it is to critical moral notions of harming innocents and breeding fear in ways that undermine civilization, terrorism as a concept has an inherent contestability. Harms and lesser evils will always be weighed and the term "terrorism" will be deployed to denote *judgments* about unacceptable violence. That is why we are not as hopeful as Noam Chomsky that were there the will to employ plain definitions in rigorously consistent ways (which he does not believe now exists), "inconsistency" in the application of the term by states or individuals could be unproblematically stopped. But we do think it would produce better moral results, better treatment of people by states, and put more pressure on states and individuals not to be hypocrites.

Can terrorism ever be the lesser of evils? Ronald Reagan did not think that the thousands who perished as a result of U.S. aid to the contras seeking to overthrow the Sandinistas in the 1980s in Nicaragua was caused by acts of terrorism, but if he had accepted the World Court's 1986 decision that U.S. support was illegal (or matched contra behavior against any of the U.S. government definitions listed above), might he still have argued that U.S. support was worth it, that communism was the greater evil? He wouldn't, of course, make such concessions, but *could* he have and morally continued to believe U.S. support justified? The film *The Battle of Algiers* illustrates this type of question in another way. It points to a cycle of violence leading to Algerian terrorism. Terrorism was not the first instinct of the rebels, but they nevertheless targeted bars frequented by innocent French teenagers, and some were killed. Since in the end the French were forced out of Algeria, was French colonial rule the greater evil that justified the use of (the evil of) terrorism that contributed to ending the rule? (Reagan's arming the Muhajadeen in Afghanistan or his collaborating with Saddam Hussein were lesser evils?) Were there other ways the same end could have been achieved by the Algerian rebels? Might one argue that terrorism is always wrong but not always evil? We can go on and on, but not without end.

The precise point is to raise a higher standard of discourse in the use of "terrorism" than our leaders and many of us now employ. Demanding this standard should not be foreign to us; doing so is appropriate to all serious moral judgments, including this one. It is an exacting requirement, and that's exactly the point. When we say "terrorist" we are explicitly saying "evil" and we must be ready to fully outline and rigorously defend the charge. We must also insist that others do the same. That is why, in spite of all the evil of Saddam Hussein, we think starting the war in Iraq under the false pretenses we discuss below was morally indefensible (even if history adjusts the moral balance), a charge to which we will later return.

Lead Us Not into Temptation

In an address to Congress on September 20, 2001, President George W. Bush asked: "Why do they hate us?" His answer was ready: because of our freedom. Speaking from the cross, his favorite philosopher says in Luke 23:34, "Forgive them Father; for they know not what they do." Christ's plea and Bush's rhetorical question, each uttered in the face of horrible evil, were so very different. Can they be reconciled, or does Bush need a new philosopher? The work of political philosopher George Kateb indicates he probably does, although it is unlikely to be Kateb.

Kateb believes, like Bush (and us), that there are some actions or systems that are so hideous that they deserve the "utmost condemnation." "If they are not wrong, nothing is wrong," Kateb says. "Evil is the worst wrong." Unlike Bush, however, he believes the term should be used "as sparingly as the facts allow." In Kateb's moral world, but not Bush's, opposition to a president's preferred way of responding to terrorism ("you're either with us or against us") cannot by that fact alone be grounds to implicate someone in that "worst wrong." In fact, Kateb's core argument is that in the process of creating government to protect citizens from wickedness and evil in everyday life, we make them "parties to evil on a large scale." The very abstractness (and scale of power) that comprises the actions of governments, leaders, and followers makes them more likely to do evil that is worse than that of individuals. Unlike Bush, Kateb not only claims not to trust government's consolidation of coercive power, he actually doesn't trust it.[12]

Kateb's fundamental assumption is that the worst wrongs therefore are likely to be political evil of the kind we witnessed in the twentieth century. In a way, that would buttress Bush's position, Kateb thinks Christ could not have been contemplating such evil when he taught us to love our enemies in spite of the evil they do to us. To use Kateb's reasoning, arguably, on 9/11 Bush was responding to a level of evil Christ literally could not imagine.[13] Bush himself, however, cannot avail himself of this view because for him there was no way that Christ could not have known.

Kateb worries that dualisms of good and evil, allied to state power as they often are, become an invitation to the worst sort of evil. For Kateb views political evil not as the "wickedness" of individuals multiplied by great numbers but rather as a product of susceptibilities and conditions brought into play when power is concentrated for the sake of social order, abetted by human frailties.[14] Group identity and ideology play a central role.

> I think that we will find that political evil on a large scale is instigated when the normal abstract mentality of power holders is inflamed by an ideology that simultaneously inflames group identity (in leaders and people) and ties that identity to a moral or transmoral purpose. Inflamed identity pursues its purposes without regard to moral limits: I mean for individual human beings, for what we now call human rights. And where evil is done while resisting it (and hence not instigated, properly speaking), the resistance often takes on the qualities of what is resisted.[15]

This is not an accusation by Kateb but a warning, for all of us "love the supposed clarification that dualism gives life." In turn, dualistic ideologies intensify group self-love in ways that are abstract and dangerous, as dualism is the driving force within most "ideologies that help to initiate (as well as maintain) evil on a large scale." *They* are uncivilized, lower, impure, or evil. *We* are good, or even better than good. The better we conceive ourselves to be, the greater the danger *they* pose to *our* civilized life. Kateb writes:

> It may be that evils on the greatest scale come about when governments or political groups believe and persuade people to believe that there is evil worse than moral evil, or good greater than moral goodness, and act with a total lack of scrupulousness on that belief.[16]

Isn't that, after all, what the Ayatollah calling us the "Great Satan" meant, that we were worse than *simply* being morally evil. Whatever bin Laden's strategic and tactical goals, wasn't it precisely this kind of belief that fueled his crimes against Americans and against humanity? Writing ten years before 9/11, Kateb was warning us all.

To understand how evil occurs on a large scale, Kateb believes we need to look not to the innate goodness or evil of individuals or even of societies, but at the goals of leaders that inspire or instigate evil and the vulnerabilities and feelings of the followers who are necessary in the commission of evil or at least allowing evil on a large scale. The role of leaders is particularly dangerous because they "are vocationally impelled to create the objects that create the passions." That's how they organize and mobilize people, and govern. Taking all of his considerations together, for Kateb, "the politics of evil is only the hideous exaggeration of normal politics and it is not best understood as the exaggeration of everyday evil."[17]

William Connolly gives an account of the problem of evil in ways that resonate with Kateb's sensibilities. He shares Kateb's concern about a totalizing dualistic ideology and the temptation for leaders and followers to demonize, but, unlike Kateb, he does not focus on the danger of evil immanent in the abstract relations that must accompany large-scale organization. Although Connolly is wary of the temptation to demonize that is inherent in nationalism, for him the primary susceptibility to evil by governments and groups is not as radically distinguishable from that of individuals as Kateb imagines. Kateb's distinction between the inherent dangers in the abstractness of government action and the value of face-to-face encounters in warding off evil would be an important but not compelling distinction for him between individual and governmental evil. Consequently, Connolly's view raises somewhat different concerns about human nature than Kateb's, and it holds out greater hope that democratic politics, imbued with a pluralized and cosmopolitan ethos, can achieve valuable goals.

Connolly describes the fundamental aspect of the problem of evil as flowing from the desire to believe God exists *and* is omnipotent and good. To have faith in such a God, he believes, one must come to terms with responsibility for the bad things that happen to people in life, especially the perpetration of evil by creatures made in God's image. To have faith, responsibility for evil must be extruded from God. Take the example of Augustine. Connolly sees the priest pressed by his own desire to believe in an omnipotent and benevolent God. Augustine's view of God, once "set in stone" through such beliefs and actions as casting aside other religions as forms of heresy, discovers that "primacy of the will emerges as the best means to create the gap between god and evil." The human being is responsible and "the notion of will becomes indispensable to both the faith and the self-identity of the faithful. . . . [A]ny position that might compromise the conviction of its universal necessity or intrinsic truth becomes a threat to the internal integrity of one's faith and identity."[18]

For Connolly the first problem of evil leads therefore to the second less recognized one:

> The second problem of evil is the evil that flows from the attempt to establish security of identity for any individual or group by defining the other that exposes sore spots in one's identity as evil or irrational. The second problem of evil is *structural* in that it flows from defining characteristics of a doctrine as it unravels the import of its own conceptions of divinity, identity, evil, and responsibility; but it is a *temptation* rather than a necessity because it is juxtaposed to other interior elements— such as in Augustine, the orientation to mystery, a certain presumption in favor of leaving judgment to his god that could be drawn upon to disrupt or curtail it. It is a temptation rather than an implication, and a structural temptation rather than simply a psychological disposition.

Since humans probably cannot and surely should not live without some form of identity, it is "how an identity is experienced and how it defines itself with respect to different identities that is crucial to engagement with the second problem of evil."[19]

Although Connolly's arguments seem to be addressed here to religious faith, he also sees their imperative affecting secular dispositions (which themselves have unacknowledged roots in the religious traditions he discusses), for example, faith in nonreligious beliefs, such as in progress, normalcy, economic growth, rationality, and technology. The connection he seeks to explore is between faith and identity, not undermining either, so much as to unsettle them to make us aware of the *structural temptation to allow our needs for identity to outstrip our other interests*. Those other interests can be material, social, or moral, and while we here distinguish them from identity interests, they are inevitably implicated in the formation and reformation of identity.

For Christ, if one can fight war—including a "war against terrorism" —at all, one should show no self-preference in the admonition not to use violence. For Kateb, such a war runs the grave risk of itself leading to *po-*

litical evil of the sort large-scale organizations, by their nature, are likely to engage in. For Connolly, the danger is in becoming an *ontopolitical extremist* in the politics of being—the human's very real need to establish a place in the world, to have an identity.

George W. Bush's prosecution of the "war against terrorism," measured against each of these accounts, shows signs of giving in to the temptations each of the above cautions against. Moral leadership that is also strong leadership under the duress of terrorism will require the greatest care, a refined moral touch, even an instinctual awareness of human vulnerabilities. These vulnerabilities are inherent in abstract political power and everyday ontopolitics, in our desire to develop and deploy radically dualistic ideologies, and in all the temptations to do evil in combating evil when violence must be employed.

What Is a War on Terrorism?

President Bush made a fateful and deliberate decision to declare war on terror rather than limiting his declaration to Al Qaeda. This decision created the trap of the war in Iraq into which the American Congress and the public fell. In choosing to fight the terrorism war in this way, Bush also reflected and replicated some of the worst impulses of the culture wars that have riven our nation since the 1960s. What appears to be the deliberate confusion of Iraq with Al Qaeda was based on the kind of Manichean rhetoric all too common in our culture wars and served to reinforce those deep divisions. All evil must emanate from one source. "Let's roll." Rather than seizing upon the opportunity of the 9/11 horror to salve the nation's wounds caused by polarization, he used it to try to bring the nation along to his purposes and ways. In doing so he became one of the most polarizing figures in modern American history.

Like other conventional wars, and unlike culture wars, this war was a response to an unprovoked deadly physical attack. In this sense it is close to our traditional notions of war. Yet, like wars in our culture over drugs, crime, and poverty, Bush chose and the Congress endorsed as our enemy an amorphous thing, one whose very definition is often contested and whose application to living persons is often determined by power.

Who are terrorists and what motivates them? Terrorists can be engaging in retribution for previous harms; they can be militarily weak, using terror as a tactic that packs the most punch; they can be crafty operators using an immoral tactic for a specific tactical advantage or to win a clearly defined goal; or they can be religious fanatics engaging in a quasi-sacramental act. Can terrorists be redeemed? Nelson Mandela, once considered a terrorist by the U.S. government, has since 1994 been revered by it. States engage in terrorism, as has our own at times, and modern conventional warfare often relies on terror. Anyone, it seems, can be a terrorist (even good persons and good states?), and for any cause.

By directing *this* war against such a *thing,* have we constructed a way of thinking whose open-ended character creates mutually reinforcing pernicious conditions that close down debate in ways that may harm us? For rhetorical purposes, do we lump all kinds of actions and people together, in ways we cannot and do not really want to sustain? Might this make us susceptible to future attacks by those who so far bear no responsibility for harming us? Does it avert our eyes from abuses by newly found friends in Russia or China, for example, who have self-interest in supporting our war? We used to be publicly far more concerned, for example, about China's repression of what it claims to be "its religious extremist forces" and "violent terrorists" in its northwest majority Turkic province of Xinjiang.[20]

Worst of all for us, it threatens to close off space for discussion on how to fight terrorism in particular, precisely because of the stifling of debate fostered by the ideological mobilization for a war without end against a hard-to-know thing. As a result, by extending the rhetoric of a war against terrorism into war against Iraq we have increased the threat of terrorism directed by Islamic fundamentalists against us. Indeed, Bruce Hoffman recently suggested that "Iraq has become a cause célèbre for radical jihadists the way that Afghanistan did a decade and a half ago." It has "a lot of the same conditions that allowed Afghanistan to become a hub for terrorists."[21]

By thinking of our enemy as a "thing" we also create a climate in which all political protest can be chilled. For example, Section 802 of the USA Patriot Act, according to Nancy Chang of the Center for Constitutional Rights, creates "a federal crime of 'domestic terrorism' that broadly extends to 'acts dangerous to human life that are a violation of the criminal laws' if they 'appear to be intended . . . to influence the policy of a government by intimidation or coercion,' and if they 'occur primarily within the territorial jurisdiction of the United States.'" Chang believes this law "is likely to be read by federal law enforcement agencies as licensing the investigation and surveillance of political activists and organizations that protest government policies, and by prosecutors as licensing the criminalization of legitimate political dissent." Confrontational protests, she argues, could easily be construed to fit this charge.[22]

A war on terrorism is also a way of speaking that trades on the idea that wars are winnable, which in turn is based historically on the idea of winning territory. "War on terrorism" is an open-ended term that does not define who the enemy is, however, making it hard to know *how* to know if we have won. Perhaps for this reason, we have sought to territorialize the war, as President Bush appropriately did by attacking Al Qaeda's training camps in Afghanistan. But he did so egregiously with the war in Iraq, conceptualizing it in his overall preemptive war strategy and turning the war into pure dualist ideology by claiming that if a nation is not with us they're against us. He has not and could not really carry out this threat. Therefore, even as we declare this to be a "new kind of war," we seem to lean quite heavily on old ideas about what wars are and how they are to be won. Perhaps we would have been better off doing something more like Rudy Giuliani did when he was a prosecutor. Rather than declare war against crime in New York, he declared war against organized crime, meaning specific Mafia families—war that, in principle at least, you can win.

These are also some of the traps of the careless use of the rhetoric of war itself. The problem is not that war is the antithesis of peace. War creates conditions antithetical to political dialogue both within the United States and between the U.S. government and its citizens and other governments and their peoples. A healthy democratic process allows us to express discontents, encourages us to acknowledge the discontent of others, and enables people with real differences a better chance to prosper together.

A War against Evil

President Bush may be driven by an underlying Christian fundamentalism more than any previous U.S. president. Fundamentalist eschatology envisages a final struggle between good and evil. Only the active and determined leadership of a benevolent leader and nation can save the world from the chaos and destruction this evil is poised to inflict. Perhaps the *Guardian,* based in Great Britain, is right when it answered a question it posed to itself: "Why then has the Bush administration consistently tried to make a connection between Iraq and al-Qaida? The answer lies in the administration's quasi-theological conviction that such a connection must exist. . . . Bob Woodward makes this point abundantly clear in his recent book. . . . Directly after the September 11 attacks, Paul Wolfowitz, the chief architect of the administration's get-tough policy on Iraq, told the cabinet: 'There was a 10% to 50% chance Saddam was involved.'"[23]

Fundamentalist presumptions of a secular kind are also reflected in neoconservative narratives that bear on the "war on terrorism" and the war in Iraq. Neoconservatives such as Paul Wolfowitz and Richard Perle began with a historical perspective on the Cold War that has, according to John Patrick Diggins, nowhere been more disastrous than in the Middle East. They assumed that opposition to the United States originates in a sovereign and exceedingly powerful source, the former Soviet Union. They took the fall of the Shah of Iran as a sign of future Soviet expansion. Anyone who opposed Iran was therefore seen as good (for us at least), so the United States was willing to help Saddam Hussein, Iran's foe. More broadly, in their interpretation of the Cold War, neoconservatives assumed that only *they*, and not even conservative Republicans, were really willing to stand up to the Soviets, and that only a massive military buildup played a major role in ending the Cold War and the breakdown of the Soviet Union. This claim is disputed by Anatoli Dobrinin, former Soviet ambassador to the United Nations.[24] Treating the Soviet Union as the source of all-evil throughout the world created severe problems, however, including a misunderstanding of dissent and even of revolution in many areas over many years. Some of the consequences of this misinterpretation—for example, the Taliban (whom our Cold War ally, Pakistan, helped set up) and Al Qaeda (some of whom we supported) in Afghanistan, as well as our earlier support of the Shah in Iran—came back to haunt the United States in the form of fundamentalist regimes that view us with as much suspicion as we regarded the Soviets.[25]

If the Bush administration's "war on terror" is a new kind of war, therefore, it is also indebted to the tropes and miscalculations of the Cold War. Not unlike the broad brush used to paint a worldwide communist menace, the president now famously located other, related sources of evil —an "axis of evil" of Iran, North Korea, and of course Iraq—to be targeted in a broadened "war" whose aim extends well beyond destroying those who harmed us. Thus, the war against Al Qaeda and its missionaries of death within a short period of time transformed itself into a war against Iraq, threats against several other states, and greater surveillance at home. It became a far broader war against an evil that, like communism, is capable of living among us as well as at known foreign addresses. Consider the president's own words in his famous "axis of evil" State of the Union address to Congress and the American people on January 29, 2002:

What we have found in Afghanistan confirms that, far from ending there, our war against terror is only beginning. . . . Thousands of dangerous killers, schooled in the methods of murder, often supported by outlaw regimes, are now spread throughout the world like ticking time bombs, set to go off without warning.

. . . These enemies view the entire world as a battlefield, and we must pursue them wherever they are. . . .

Our nation will [pursue] two great objectives. First, we will shut down terrorist camps, disrupt terrorist plans, and bring terrorists to justice. And, second, we must prevent the terrorists and regimes who seek chemical, biological or nuclear weapons from threatening the United States and the world.

. . . camps still exist in at least a dozen countries. A terrorist underworld—including groups like Hamas, Hezbollah, Islamic Jihad, Jaish-i-Mohammed—operates in remote jungles and deserts, and hides in the centers of large cities. . . .

My hope is that all nations will heed our call, and eliminate the terrorist parasites who threaten their countries and our own. Many nations are acting forcefully. . . .

But some governments will be timid in the face of terror. And make no mistake about it: If they do not act, America will.

Our second goal is to prevent regimes that sponsor terror from threatening America or our friends and allies with weapons of mass destruction. Some of these regimes have been pretty quiet since September the 11th. But we know their true nature. North Korea is a regime arming with missiles and weapons of mass destruction, while starving its citizens.

Iran aggressively pursues these weapons and exports terror, while an unelected few repress the Iranian people's hope for freedom.

Iraq continues to flaunt its hostility toward America and to support terror. The Iraqi regime has plotted to develop anthrax, and nerve gas, and nuclear weapons for over a decade. This is a regime that has already used poison gas to murder thousands of its own citizens—leaving the bodies of mothers huddled over their dead children. This is a regime that agreed to international inspections—then kicked out the inspectors. This is a regime that has something to hide from the civilized world.

States like these, and their terrorist allies, constitute an *axis of evil,* arming to threaten the peace of the world. By seeking weapons of mass destruction, these regimes pose a grave and growing danger. They could provide these arms to terrorists, giving them the means to match their hatred. They could attack our allies or attempt to blackmail the United States. In any of these cases, the price of indifference would be catastrophic.

We will work closely with our coalition to deny terrorists and their state sponsors the materials, technology, and expertise to make and deliver weapons of mass destruction. We will develop and deploy effective missile defenses to protect America and our allies from sudden attack. . . .

We'll be deliberate, yet time is not on our side. I will not wait on events, while dangers gather. I will not stand by, as peril draws closer and closer. The United States of America will not permit the world's most dangerous regimes to threaten us with the world's most destructive weapons.

Our war on terror is well begun, but it is only begun. This campaign may not be finished on our watch—yet it must be and it will be waged on our watch.

We can't stop short. If we stop now—leaving terror camps intact and terror states unchecked—our sense of security would be false and temporary. History has called America and our allies to action, and it is both our responsibility and our privilege to fight freedom's fight.

The first thing to say about this speech is that it is, on the model of many speeches given by leaders, a rally cry to action. In that sense the strong and stirring rhetoric may be compared to other "day of infamy"-style speeches.

The real issues are the intentions within the rhetoric and the uses to which the speech is put. Recall Kateb's concern that the vocation of leadership often drives leaders to create dualistic categories in order to accomplish the work of large organizations. This for Kateb is always a worry. Is it especially worrisome here? We think it is.

Consider the nature of the war. The first thing to note is *speed*. And not just speed of action but speed of decision in determining who our enemies are, what their connections are to each other, and in lining up new allies and new enemies. And speed in going after all who oppose us. Everything is spinning so fast, we can allow no doubt, we must move, and then move even faster.

Next, the war is just beginning. And the entire world is the battlefield. It is fast, long, and big, this war. What are its objectives?

First, to "shut down terrorist camps, disrupt terrorist plans, and bring terrorists to justice." This is a goal we, along with an overwhelming majority of the American public, endorse, but we wonder why he selectively includes organizations that have not attacked Americans, such as Hamas, while leaving out certain others with likely ties to Al Qaeda such as those in Xinjiang (some of whom are actually in Guantanamo) and Chechnya. (Also, while he mentions Islamic terrorism, he ignores Hindus who have killed hundreds of Muslims in India.) To include them would raise questions about the unambiguous moral evil of terrorism as a unitary entity. For, in other contexts, we have publicly and properly chastised Russia and China for the very oppressions that we believed helped bring about terrorism in those regions, and are documented in annual State Department Human Rights Reports. If we bring these considerations back into the picture, however, we raise the troubling issue of whether terrorism has any causes extrinsic to certain individual or group characteristics or religious attitudes.

"Our second goal," Bush pronounced, "is to prevent regimes that sponsor terror from threatening America or our friends and allies with weapons of mass destruction." We know the "true nature" of these regimes, he claimed, and then famously listed North Korea, Iran, and Iraq and labeled them the "axis of evil."

Ironically, for all the claims that our invasion of Iraq scared Libya into giving up a weapons program we didn't know it had, Bush's assertion has weakened our hand in dealing with Iran and, especially, with North Korea. The conflict with North Korea has been far more dangerous (we came close to war in 1994) than that with Iraq could have conceivably been thought to be by any reasonable estimate. In 2003 Iraq was still militarily devastated by the Gulf War (how long was it before the president was able to land on the *Abraham Lincoln* to proclaim "Mission Accomplished"?), prostrate from over a decade of harsh sanctions, and under close military surveillance. It had limited sovereignty in the north and had endured what turns out to have been fairly thorough U.N. inspections.

In spite of Iraq's weakness and our ability, rightly, to completely contain it, Iraq "flaunted its hostility" toward us. It is hard to imagine what that can mean considering Iraq's utterly anemic condition. It continued to "support terror." It was a regime of terror, but that was not Bush's point. What kind of terror did Iraq continue to support, and what did that have to do not only with 9/11 but with us? Bush now admits there was never any link between Iraq and 9/11. That he traded upon this linkage in building support for war is indisputable.

Before the war, American and British intelligence experts had downplayed or denied connections between Iraq and Al Qaeda. Regarding Secretary of State Colin Powell's prewar presentation to the United Nations Security Council, Phyllis Bennis, from the Institute for Policy Studies, commented that Powell "segued disingenuously from the accurate and frightening information about what the al Zarqawi network could actually do with biochemical materials to the not-so-accurate claim about its link with Iraq—which is tenuous and unproven at best." On June 16, 2004, the staff of the National Commission on Terrorist Attacks on the United States (the "9/11 Commission"), which was established by Congress in spite of the opposition of President Bush (although he signed the enabling legislation), drew the following conclusions:

> Bin Laden is said to have requested space to establish training camps, as well as assistance in procuring weapons, but Iraq apparently never responded. . . . [Despite reports of contacts in the 1990s] they do not appear to have resulted in a collaborative relationship. . . . We have no credible evidence that Iraq and Al Qaeda cooperated on attacks against the United States. (p. 5)

The White House responded by saying the commission staff report did not contradict what President Bush and Vice President Cheney had been saying all along. According to Dan Bartlett, director of White House communications, "It is not inconsistent for Iraq to have ties with Al Qaeda and not to have been involved in 9/11 or other *potential plots* against America."[26] President Bush put it this way the next day at a Cabinet meeting: "The reason I keep insisting that there was a relationship between Iraq and Saddam and Al Qaeda" is "because there was a relationship between Iraq and Al Qaeda." He further claimed: "This administration never said that the 9/11 attacks were orchestrated between Saddam and Al Qaeda. We did say there were numerous contacts between Saddam Hussein and Al Qaeda. For example, Iraqi intelligence officers met with bin Laden, the head of Al Qaeda, in the Sudan. There's numerous contacts between the two," and Saddam had been "a threat" and "sworn enemy to the United States of America."[27] That night, Vice President Cheney said the "evidence was overwhelming" and that he "probably" had information that the 9/11 Commission had not seen. Commission chairs Thomas Kean and Lee Hamilton immediately called on the Vice President to turn over the information.[28]

Perhaps the claim by President Bush most remarkable for its lack of irony or sense of history is this: "This is a regime that already has used poison gas to murder thousands of its own citizens—leaving the bodies of mothers huddled over their dead children." This of course happened when the Reagan/Bush administration was collaborating with Iraq as it fought against the "evil" of Iran. President George H. W. Bush had used similar language to build support for the first Gulf War.

This "axis of evil" speech was designed to conflate three different nations, various terrorist organizations, and each group with the other, and blend them into an enormously powerful and singular motivational state, character profile, ideology, and alliance of evil aimed at every American and every friend of America throughout the world. Its Manichean scope was breathtaking. It laid out sweeping purposes that could not have been accomplished—if for no other reason the fact that North Korea is on China's border, within cannon shot of Seoul, and only a short missile launch from Japan. Unlike Iraq, it probably does have nuclear weapons and may have an army ready to fight.

The greatest damage done with this speech was the declaration of a war on something that cannot be specified in the way an enemy needs to be specified. Our personal views aside, however, Bush's speech was a success, as was the war propaganda campaign that followed it. The public did support the war, although in time the realities have damaged that support. Incredibly, a Harris poll as late as June 2004 found that 69 percent of Americans think Saddam Hussein "was supporting the terrorist organization Al Qaeda, which attacked the United States on September 11, 2001." Only 22 percent said no (see table 2). We offer a few reflections.

The most common explanation, especially given by liberals and the left, for public ignorance regarding the connection between Iraq and 9/11 is that the media failed us in its responsibility, or worse, helped orches-

TABLE 2
The Harris Poll, June 8–15, 2004. (N = 991 adults nationwide. MoE ± 3.)

"*Do you believe that Saddam Hussein was supporting the terrorist organization Al Qaeda, which attacked the United States on September 11, 2001?*"

	Yes	No	Unsure
June 8–15, 2004	69%	22%	9%

"*Do you think the invasion of Iraq strengthened or weakened the war on terrorism?*"

	Strengthened	Weakened	Unsure
June 8–15, 2004	52%	38%	10%

"*Do you think the invasion of Iraq has helped to protect the United States from another terrorist attack or not?*"

	Has	Has Not	Unsure
June 8–15, 2004	41%	52%	7%

trate the rush to war. They were "embedded" in more ways than one. Whatever the failure of the media may have been, it is important for us to think through why so many people were willing—and *needed*—to believe in the idea that a strong connection existed. Certainly the gravity of the attack is one explanation for this need. The need for a tangible enemy after such an unsettling experience and feeling of vulnerability is another. Perhaps the simple need was to do something more to show *they* can't get away with such a horrible thing. Evil also seems most compelling and comprehensible to most of us when it is both personal and connected to a place. Such an evil is powerful, yet excisable because we know where it is.

All of these needs, however, are most likely to take the strongest hold when they mature in a political culture that embodies puritan moments of righteousness and entitlement, in which the politics of moral personae and other forms of demonization still have purchase. Put into the mix the fact we were responding to a deadly and inhuman attack, and place all of it on a foundation of political polarization and partisanship. Thus the nation is attacked and the public and its leaders rally around the president. The president develops his policy to respond, and the opposition is cautiously supportive. The president overreaches and the opposition is afraid to strongly criticize, *for to do so is to invite the president and his party and others to use all the tools of polarization from the culture wars to marginalize, depatriotize, and otherwise demonize the opponents of the war.* We cannot be sure, of course, about individual legislators who voted for the war-authorizing resolution. Some undoubtedly believed at the time that the war was being fought properly on the exact grounds Bush laid out for it. Most believed Saddam Hussein to be a genuinely evil man; who could disagree with *that?* Fear of political demonization of those who might have otherwise been more thoughtful undoubtedly played an important role. It provides yet another example of how demonization is destructive of democracy, especially important to remember as we struggle to find a way out of the morass of the new terrorism we helped inflame in Iraq.[29]

What Is an Axis of Evil, Anyway?

Dividing the world neatly into good and evil states may produce a comforting level of moral outrage and strategic clarity for left and right, but it can also contribute to insensitivity to nuances and cruelties that ultimately undermine our security. Tropes may not themselves break bones, but inappropriate ones, left unanswered, can cause immense damage.

George Bush's lexicon of an "axis of evil" willfully ignored the complex histories of Iran and Iraq and their interrelationship, including profound religious differences and an extremely brutal war. Indeed, in 1991 during the Gulf War, President George H. W. Bush decided not to push on to Baghdad at least in part because his advisers warned him that Iraq was still needed to offset Iran, and there was a fear of civil war. Including communist North Korea in the "axis of evil" with these two Moslem peoples is more puzzling still. Saddam Hussein and Kim Il Sung and his son Kim Jong Il and their acolytes surely have done evil things, but in what sense is this an *axis* of evil?

To be an axis in the historical sense there must be a significant ideological and working relationship between allies. Thus, when fascist Japan attacked Pearl Harbor, its Axis allies, fascist Nazi Germany and Italy, declared war on the United States. That was an *axis*. To identify specific world centers of egregious "evil," President Bush must show that "evildoers" located in them are doing or planning things that go beyond the pale of the "normal" evil human behavior of the kind *we* largely ignored, for example in Rwanda or the Congo, or countenanced and even encouraged, such as Iraq's role in its war with Iran from 1981 to 1988."[30]

To frame an idea as morally precise as an "axis of evil," one has a moral obligation to show more than individual acts or patterns of evil. One must demonstrate that there are centers of singularly immoral behavior, tied together in a coherent way that goes beyond the label of evil itself. Stalin and Hitler were evil. No one in his or her right mind would call them an axis.

President Bush and his advisers believe, nevertheless, that in this case the evil he sees in the accused states is sufficient alone to connect the new axis: after all, the fear is, they each have the desire to obtain and use weapons of mass destruction and their delivery systems, or to deliver them to terrorists. Even if he is right, similar evil characteristics in each of these states would not make them an axis. But the rhetoric of "axis" allowed him to expand the war against Al Qaeda into a war against terror*ism* in a technological age. Tehran and P'yongyang (and formerly Baghdad) are the temporary headquarters of the new, amorphous, and pervasive enemy.

The specter of an "axis of evil" can serve multiple purposes, some less lofty than others, just as the specter of communism once did. Of foremost importance, it simplifies the world in such a way as to try to make intelligible, under a single rubric, policies that may actually have disparate causes and reasons for existence. For example, an "axis of evil" that includes North Korea may have broadened the public's fear of the danger from Iraq, helping justify the attack, while still tapping and expanding vague currents of a "civilizational" war[31] without being quite as vulnerable to charges of harboring antipathy toward Islam. Nonetheless, Bush's rhetoric is subtly parasitic upon the satanic images that are so ably tapped in Joseph Conrad's *Heart of Darkness*.

West versus East has lost much of its original meaning. Iraq and even Iran are complex mixes of secular and absolutist religious and political currents. Their fundamentalists have an agenda that may be exacerbated and even shaped by U.S. policy, but divisions within the Islamic world long predate the central role of the United States in that world. Roxanne Euben points out that the Egyptian Islamic Jihad has historically been more interested in toppling modernist Arab regimes than in attacking American interests. The term *jihad* itself carries an ambiguous legacy in the Islamic faith. Euben points out that even those voices that justify violence invoke a set of specific rules about who can be fought, when, and by what means.[32] The "West" is indebted to the role of the "Orient" in preserving its own great mathematical and philosophical traditions. And modern western secular culture is not without its own fundamentalist political fanatics.

Because "axis of evil" is such a strong moral condemnation, those who would employ it have a responsibility not to use it as a cloak for things they would like to do anyway. It is a political idea that should be used with far greater care.

Michael Rogin's work would likely place rhetorical excesses such as these in what he has called the "countersubversive tradition" in which American demonology "splits the world in two, attributing magical, pervasive power to a conspiratorial center of evil." While Rogin acknowledges that political demonology occurs outside of the United States, here it has a distinct form:

> American countersubversion has taken its shape from the pervasiveness of propertied individualism in our political culture, the expansionist character of our history; and the definition of American identity against racial, ethnic, class and gender aliens.[33]

While Rogin's arguments have some merit, we would suggest that tendencies toward political demonization can be found across the political spectrum, including among critics of the very system Rogin describes and faults. In saying this we do not suggest that all players begin on an equal footing or that some are not far more harmed than others in its application. But denying these tendencies will at once deny critics a better hearing, and more importantly leave a gaping lacuna in their thought.

As the war in Iraq raged in the spring of 2003, *New York Times* award-winning war correspondent Christopher Hedges published a new book about war. Though written before the start of the war, Hedges's work may help us understand why Americans were susceptible to the administration's claims about Iraq. In *War Is a Force That Gives Us Meaning*, Hedges points out that modern wars often affirm the virtue of the nation-state. He recognizes that in a world in which God and an afterlife have a less secure presence than they once did, in a culture that rates at the top among modern nations in religious belief but remains highly competitive and commercial, nationalism may help to fill a void:

> Lurking beneath the surface of every society, including our own, is the passionate yearning for a nationalist cause that exalts us, the kind that war alone is able to deliver. It reduces and at times erases the anxiety of individual consciousness.[34]

The Iraq war was not made possible by this yearning alone. All of our susceptibilities and vulnerabilities together, thrown into our domestic political wars and punctuated by a truly inhuman attack, made it plausible enough for us to go along with it. It was a war of choice and we helped choose.

7

Terror Wars and Culture Wars

With success in the war on terror being elusive and hard to define, what better way to ease the doubts and anxieties implicit in the war than to merge that war with the ongoing culture wars? Take the drug war, for example. Commencing with the 2002 Super Bowl, the Bush administration has striven to convince us that the purchase of illegal drugs is more than an act of personal irresponsibility. As one of the ads put it: "Where do terrorists get their money? If you buy drugs, it might come from you." The charge may be rhetorically effective, but the logic is fuzzy and hard to document.

The effort to merge these wars discursively may be a smart strategy for garnering support for selected allies and certain values, but it is a form of political manipulation that trades on the public's revulsion of the attack on the World Trade Center. It would remain manipulative even if it helped gain support for measures that later could be shown to produce legitimate public health or safety needs.

Terrorists have benefited from the sale of certain illicit drugs, but so have many of our "friends" in the war against terror. The FARC (or Fuerzas Armadas Revolucionarias de Colombia) in Colombia profits from cocaine sales, but, as National Public Radio has reported, right-wing paramilitary groups, often associated with the Colombian government, have even more long-standing connections to the drug market. In fact, since the fall of the harshly repressive Taliban regime, by 2002 opium production jumped in Afghanistan to 76 percent of the world's total.[1] Between 2003 and 2004 alone opium production grew 73 *percent*.[2] The Karzai government, which the United States strongly supports, has turned a blind eye toward its farmers' opium production in the hope that revenues from this cash crop will still criticism of the government. Perhaps the greatest irony here is that the hateful Taliban was perhaps one of history's greatest enforcers of a zero tolerance policy toward drugs.

The administration's public relations campaign also makes no distinctions among drugs. Opium or cocaine sales may line foreign pockets, including those of terrorists, but for other drugs, such as marijuana, the drug/terror connection is virtually impossible to sustain.

Some analysts go so far to argue that, if the war on terrorism were our top priority, it might make sense to ease rather than tighten drug laws. For example, Geov Parish points out: "The effort to eradicate certain popular drugs . . . has literally created, and perpetuated, the very black market now accused of being a source of cash for al Qaeda's jihad. Ending drug prohibitions would do far more to thwart terrorism than the War on Drugs ever could."[3] Rehabilitation and drug education, as RAND Corporation studies have indicated, are better ways to reduce drug demand and foster public health than the police actions and foreign interdictions that help radically drive up drug prices and profitability. The analogy, of course, is to the benefits that the criminalizing of alcohol production accrued to bootleggers and the mob. Even if we are to remain committed to our war on drugs, why wouldn't we pour money into such proven ways to lessen suffering, reduce drug demand, and consequently the profitability of the illicit drug trade? To answer this question, a fuller discussion of the political and cultural wars of the last forty years is in order.

It should not surprise anyone that Saudi crown prince Abdullah, eager to take the heat off his nation's connections to terrorism, has recently joined the chorus of those blaming the United States for illegal drug purchases. Without western and Japanese dependence on foreign oil, the millions of dollars channeled from Saudi Arabia to terrorists would have been much harder to come by.[4] Indeed, it is certain that our troops would never have been stationed on the Arabian peninsula in the first place (the premiere grievance cited by Osama bin Laden in his 1996 *fatwa*),[5] and Muslim resentments toward us would likely have lessened, although hardly eliminated. If we want to coldly calculate the best route toward undermining a major economic and political foundation of Middle Eastern terrorism, the oil dependence of the West and Japan would be a better vice to target than drugs.

Terrorists provide images of a horrifying foreign enemy, perhaps now in our midst, while dope pushers and addicts are familiar scary urban figures at home. Taking these two images together serves several purposes. It extends the axis of evil from foreign capitals to suicide bombers, to drug runners and users, pulling together disparate problems and threats under the idea that evil itself is the source of all these troubles. In this way, it extends the Manichean logic of the new Cold War. It serves the more practical political purpose of giving those committed to the old culture wars more ammunition with which to fight the drug war they fear has flagged in the public's consciousness. It also gives the public a new tangible face of the terrorist enemy, waiting on the corner, or in the self, to be conquered.

The urge to affirm the truth of core values requires an enemy that can unite large numbers of our citizens. The ideal demon to cement a sense of absolute moral probity must be plausible enough to arouse a sense of real threat to a wide sector of the population, yet it must also be one against whom tangible progress can be made. Merging of the drug and terror wars provides drug and new Cold Warriors a new incentive to present to skeptics. Recreational drugs can be portrayed as more evil if they are viewed as promotions of and revenue for people like bin Laden.

Unfortunately, merging these wars is not without risks. Each war has already been an occasion for threats to our civil liberties. Should we actually prosecute them together, the threat could deepen all out of any proportion to legitimate security needs. Worse, should we actually come to believe the implication of our rhetoric, that drugs and terror have a common source in generalized "evil," we will confuse ourselves both on how best to fight terrorism and how best to prevent drug addiction.

Left Fundamentalism

The Bush administration's conflation of drug and terror wars may be partly driven by fundamentalism, but it is hardly alone in this regard. Some on the left have their own version: eager to gain new profits for the oil companies that have him and his vice president in their hip pocket, and to get political rewards for himself, the president fabricated a scenario of "weapons of mass distraction" and misled both Congress and the American people into a war effort that left the nation in a quagmire.

As appealing as this version or its variations may be to critics of the administration, it has several limitations. Even if we assume that the president was engaged in a calculated lie, we need to explain why so many citizens bought into it. Analysis suggesting that a consolidated and compliant media collaborated in the lie, either consciously or unconsciously, will not suffice. Just why did so many of us, and our representatives, seem eager to believe that Saddam harbored weapons that would soon be targeted at us and had also collaborated in the events of September 11?

Matthew Rothschild, a careful critic of leftist perspectives on terror, raises a similar concern about fundamentalism on the left:

> Almost every time I've spoken in public since September 11, I've heard variations of the following theme: Bush not only knew about the attacks, but wanted the United States to be attacked so that he could (and here you can take your pick): a) Increase his popularity by waging war; b) Justify an increase in Pentagon spending; c) Boost the profits of the Carlyle Group, a private military investment group that includes Bush's father, among other heavyweights.[6]

At the fringe, some even contended that "we" got what we deserved. Such rhetoric is inherently immoral. Terrorism is morally wrong because it abstracts innocent lives into targets. Without doing the actual killing, this brand of fringe retribution does so as well.

A Political Economy of Terror?

Many traditional liberal and radical thinkers and even some conservatives suggest that improving economic fortunes can successfully build bonds across ethnic and national boundaries. Yet such bonds are far from inevitable even with the promise of prosperity. Citing poverty as a catalyst for terror can also be misleading. Rejecting moralist accounts that terrorists are utterly different from others, proponents of this view sometimes assume that, down deep, those susceptible to the appeals of terrorist organizers are "just like us" in what they presume to be our economistic motivations.

The reality is more complicated. Princeton economist Alan Krueger and Jitka Maleckova, a Middle East specialist in Prague, did a study for the National Bureau of Economic Research that analyzed the backgrounds of Hezbollah militants killed during the late 1980s and early 1990s. These fighters were more likely than the average resident to be above the poverty line and to have enjoyed a secondary or higher education. The authors also cited opinion polls taken in Palestine that show the poor are not more likely to support terrorist attacks.[7]

In a thoughtful commentary on the Krueger-Maleckova study, *Washington Post* columnist Sebastian Mallaby points out, however, that even if poverty does not directly cause terror, it plays an important indirect role. Widespread poverty is often accompanied by political chaos, upon which terrorist cells can thrive. And in such societies, terrorist cells often provide the best avenues of educational and social mobility.[8]

Mallaby's suggestion takes us in a fruitful direction. Dissident intellectuals always play important roles in political transformation. Political chaos does more than provide space for violent political cells. Dissidents witness the suffering and dispersion of their people, especially in nations where Islamic militants have had little political voice. Discourse across and within national and ethnic boundaries are too often difficult. Government, and quasi-public and private corporations dominate the media. Lacking a voice within their larger society, seeing the hardships of their own people, and facing no internal challenge to their own verities, some of the most educated and affluent may come to regard their own truths as immortal, all embracing, and worth dying and killing for.

Our own politics of energy, often trapped as it is within our culture war, may make us insensitive to popular foreign aspirations, including democratic ones. "Moderate" regimes often turn out to be ones, like Saudi Arabia, that are undemocratic and repressive. The strong policy bias toward policies adopted by the Likud party in the Israeli government also needs rethinking. Energy and foreign policy are intertwined, each related to the impetus of Islamic extremism directed at the United States. Nonetheless, to excuse terror is morally wrong: the United States is not the author of all of the world's progress, but neither is it the cause of all the world's evil, as some seem to need to believe.

Manichean rhetoric serves a purpose for some liberals and some on the left, but it takes a toll. Activist peace-and-justice groups that feel isolated within our politics can gain a degree of compensatory revenge and comfort by labeling and enumerating the sins of the mainstream. Nonetheless, such rhetoric leaves activists unprepared to address and acknowledge the obvious acts of violence perpetrated by the bin Ladens of the world, and the exploitation extracted by them. Worse, these groups design explanations of war that share a fundamental depth similarity with their opponents: war begins with one or a few evil and manipulative men; if only we could get rid of those evildoers; if only *we* could win the culture war.

Patriotism and Culture Wars

We will always have fundamentalists with us, but how do we reduce the odds of their killing in the name of their truths? Soon after bin Laden callously celebrated September 11, Jerry Falwell and Pat Robertson gossiped on TV that his victory was God's punishment for the perversions of our secular society. In addition to secularists, Falwell listed "the pagans and the abortionists and the feminists and the gays." Why else would God have opened up America's skies and left us vulnerable to attack? What could these two politically astute men have been thinking to say such politically self-damaging things on national TV?

Perhaps they should follow the gospel according to the film *Moonstruck,* when the mother (Olympia Dukakis) turns to her daughter (Cher) and pleads: "Loretta, reflect on your life." Upon reflection they might see that the social world may for us ultimately not be fully known or even knowable. Perhaps one posture with regard to all fundamentalisms is to entertain the possibility that understanding the world may always exceed our grasp. Terrorists are like us, and Robertson and Falwell are like us, not in the sense that they harbor similar motives or have the same moral structure, so much as that all of us must live with our own inner demons. All of us die and must find reasons for our death and life. We harbor musings, fantasies, and fears that often exceed our most carefully formulated ideals and expectations. Part of the answer to terror, or to fundamentalism of whatever stripe, lies in developing the kind of democratic politics most willing to engage the possibility that groups, or even "society" itself, may have cherished ideals that wittingly or not entail injustices for others. To ask why Robertson and Falwell needed to say what they did is not to ask a psychological question: it is a deeply moral question. And it is the kind of question we each need to ask ourselves.

Our security demands self-defense as well as punishing—even killing or otherwise eliminating—those who would impose their worldview on us. It also means rethinking the U.S. economic and political role in the world, perhaps now made more possible by forthright neoconservative theories of unabashed American global domination. Our security also requires a willingness to think outside the kind of dichotomies that have guided us since the Cold War and before. To take one example, we could take cross-cultural education far more seriously. Former senator Paul Simon pointed out: "Only 1 percent of our students ever study abroad, and two-thirds of them go to Western Europe. In the United States we can go from grade school to getting a Ph.D. without having a year of a foreign language, and that adds to our insularity." Even the CIA had too few operatives familiar with the cultures and languages of the Middle East before 9/11. Destructive and self-defeating Manichean views encourage and are encouraged by such educational neglect.

For many years, sports fans heard our national anthem only when they were actually in the stadiums. Today, televised games often begin with honor guards and elaborate renditions of both the national anthem and "America the Beautiful." A recent Advertising Council campaign also repeats the familiar line: "I am an American." The voices and faces in this ad democratically reflect the race, nationality, age, and gender classifications in our official census. As this nation moves toward a war of indefinite scope and duration, it is a good time to ask: What is it to be an American?

It is important to think more about patriotism in ways that affirm what is best in our heritage. If love of country becomes reduced to commitment to a stifling set of postures and policies, patriotism can be self-destructive. It becomes more a security blanket than a stance toward society that engenders security. "Patriots" of this type submerge inner doubts and anxieties by immersing themselves in a mass cause and defining all dissidents as not only wrong but inherently dangerous. But our society too pays the price.

Some who witness and reject the invocation of patriotism in defense of immoral policies have themselves jumped to two other problematic conclusions. In a Manichean desire to find the United States guilty of being the root of all evil, one group finds a new patriotic home among America's opponents. A few of our generation's Vietnam War dissenters, for example, flew Vietcong flags while in deep denial of the atrocities the Vietcong had committed. Such denial, neglect, or outright hypocrisy regarding inconvenient moral facts robs them of more than credibility. In treating all "Third World" targets of U.S. aggression as without choices, power, and responsibility—as mere victims—they encourage moral passivity that justifies a turn to Leninist-style organizations that further block political dialogue.

Others appalled by mainstream patriotism's excesses turn to international law and its tribunals as the fitting successor to the nation-state. International law can play a vital role in addressing violence among states, but any law always reflects to some extent imbalances of power and congealed prejudices. Law needs the supplement of active politics within and between nations.

Patriotism properly conceived is important to such politics. For us, many of the public commemorations of September 11, while grasped by a few to ratchet up chauvinism, and by some for political advantage,[9] displayed a will to affirm and preserve life for all, even complete strangers, amid tragedy. They reminded us of the great Protestant theologian Reinhold Niebuhr's claim that God does not will all, but wills that we make the best of all. These celebrations reflect in part historic American struggles to grant opportunities for voice and individuality. Our pantheon of patriotic heroes includes, but is not limited to, figures such as Abraham Lincoln, who, as a young member of Congress, opposed the Mexican War. It also includes Henry David Thoreau, whose reflections on civil disobedience have inspired generations of activist critics of received opinion. Many post–September 11 memorials for those who died featured the great civil rights song "We Shall Overcome." Now a sanctifying hymn, it was once a song of protest by those slandered as "unpatriotic," even Communists.

Official patriotic celebrations are sometimes designed only to remind us that here rights for all represent the inevitable course of history. Yet U.S. history may be better understood as one of democratic struggle. To the extent we are a beacon of freedom and democracy, it is because struggles had a chance to succeed and often enough did. If we are to remain a beacon, it is more necessary than ever to remember and commend these struggles. Even the multicultural face of what remains homogenized American advertising today is a testimony to decades of struggle by minorities and reform leaders to gain a place in our economy and politics.

Democracy can itself fall victim to destructive fits of collective and self-justifying illusions, but democracy is the best answer to these illusions. The democratic celebration of individual voice can also demand that we learn to get along with creeds, ethnicities, and races that we once did not count as "American." As Walt Whitman recognized, democracy also encourages a willingness to hear and explore the multitude of subterranean voices, currents, and lifestyles that inevitably arise in response to mainstream culture and practices. Such openness and exploration is vital if we are not only to survive but also to thrive intellectually and emotionally.

At its best, American democracy has continually negotiated and revised procedures and policies that allow as many existing and newly emerging cultures and even principles of authority as possible to live and prosper together. This too is part of our patriotic heritage. Absent a prominent place for such a democratic vision, we fear that cultural civil wars within many "nation-states"—maybe even our own—will intensify.

A World of Immigrants

Besides the obvious horror of it, one reason September 11 was so upsetting is that the terrorists managed to blend easily into American life. There are good reasons for this. American life is less culturally homogeneous than ever. Some new Americans now easily imitate or even embrace the outward consumer trappings of our society while speaking different languages and holding different cultural and religious ideals. The complex adjustment of most immigrants to America can be a source of anxiety for those long settled here, but it need not be.

Still, when some visitors engage in criminal violence, our response can easily be, "Let's find and expel the foreigners living here in our midst." Especially when these "intruders" are here illegally, our government need not observe the nuances of law in dealing with them. Even some liberals have supported this kind of logic. *New York Times* columnist Nicholas Kristof wrote about FBI failures regarding 9/11: "One reason aggressive agents were restrained as they tried to go after Zacarias Moussaoui is that liberals like myself have regularly excoriated law enforcement authorities for taking shortcuts and engaging in racial profiling." This impels him to advocate racial profiling as a necessary trade-off for security.[10] Racial profiling, however, remains suspicion of guilt by association. Although its short-term efficacy is debatable, it makes our domestic world a more divided place and undermines our patriotic heritage of liberty for all.

Though the world is dangerous, there are other ways to combat the danger. Kristof points out that Moussaoui aroused suspicion because he was a poor pilot but wanted to learn how to fly jumbo jets. Prudent background checks for those who want to fly such aircraft might have stopped him, among others. When we read about Moussaoui, we also wonder why one would even need to focus on his ancestry. The man paid for his lessons with $8,000 in cash, an act Kristof labels as merely mildly suspicious. In an era of checks, credit and debit cards, walking around with thousands of dollars in cash is not merely imprudent, it clearly suggests one wants to avoid leaving a paper trail.

Kristof also argues that racial profiling has made Israel's airlines the safest in the world. However, it can also propel the evolution of terror into new forms. Israel has already suffered from suicide bombing by young women, who had not been suspect before, a phenomenon that also should give profilers pause.

When intentional human actions turn our technologies against us, those who have already been coded as enemies of our values and lifestyles are immediately singled out for blame. Before September 11, the worst instance of terrorism on our soil was the Oklahoma City bombing. We have quickly forgotten the woeful performance of the U.S. media in its immediate aftermath. Myriad network experts painstakingly identified the various "Arab" terrorist organizations that were the likely perpetrators.

While even some liberals now contemplate giving government more rights to spy on dissidents in political and religious settings, almost no one talks about the fiasco of the white Midwestern pipe bomber. *Boston Globe* columnist Derrick Jackson has been virtually alone in reminding us of the hypocrisies implicit in the case of Lucas Helder: "Helder was stopped not once, not twice, but three times for traffic violations during his terrorist rampage and let go all three times. During one of the encounters, Helder said, 'I didn't mean to hurt anybody.' During another he was cited for having an expired driver license, and that still did not raise any alarms. The police chose to see a tired, apologetic figure worthy of sympathy. One officer let him go because it was Helder's birthday."[11]

Again, here at home, copious circumstantial evidence suggests that the anthrax perpetrator could only have been one of a small number of our bioterrorism experts.[12] A better case probably could be made for preventive detention of all U.S. bioterrorism experts than for the thousands of Arab visitors who have been rounded up and jailed without charge.

Whatever one thinks of the legal merits of profiling, it hinges on a highly questionable dichotomy between host and guest, of inside and outside. While the Justice Department officially turns a hostile eye toward noncitizens it deems potentially dangerous, Congress, lobbied by high-technology corporations, devises visa provisions that make it easier to bring highly trained foreign technicians to our shores. Even less esoteric occupations such as gardeners, waiters, maids, and busboys often must be filled by immigrants, legal or not.

Much of the dynamic of the modern world revolves around the supply and demand side for immigrant labor. On the demand side, paragons of our culture, including world-class hotels, restaurants, meat packing and food-processing firms, widely employ "illegal aliens" but seldom press for their legalization. Having the ability to turn these workers in to the Immigration and Naturalization Service ensures that workers will work cheap and without complaints, no matter how fast the line runs or however long the hours. An INS that enforces its mandates selectively serves business purposes well.

On the supply side, most of these workers come from nations where the myth of nationality is pervasive and destructive. Modern nations are composed of many so-called ethnic groups, and even these groups are hardly pure and easily demarcated from one another. The quest for national unity leads to rampant discrimination on ethnic, religious, economic, and ideological grounds. Minorities are often compelled either by force of arms or economic circumstance to relocate. The rapid flow of financial capital, information, and goods exacerbates the urge to reestablish a mythical national purity and makes human flight more necessary all the time.

To point out that the agents of terrorism may emerge from these diasporas or be due to other societal ills can be misunderstood as an excuse for or even a defense of terrorism. Yet unless we think of terrorism as a random aberration—in which case moral revulsion and consistent policy response hardly seem appropriate or effective—or unless we really do believe it is the work of The Devil, we need to identify the conditions under which terrorism thrives *and* capture, punish, or kill the terrorists themselves.

Terrorists often inhabit or have inhabited nation-states that claim in one way or another that political society can be held together only by common religion, ethnicity, and cultural practice. They respond to the implicit or explicit demands for conformity or subservience not with a critique of a hard national ideal fixed in intolerance, but by attempting to become the new center of power and belief—even by annihilating those who once discriminated against or subjugated them. Paradoxically, terrorists sometimes ape or even intensify the worst aspects of the oppressive regimes in which terrorists most often emerge.

The notion that a functioning state must rely upon pure ethnicity or on one highly specified set of cultural and religious beliefs widely and deeply shared by those within its boundaries may be one of the most destructive ideals of past millennia. Europeans once believed that the demise of Catholicism as a universal and binding ideal was essential to the preservation of order and civilization. Many of the Protestant rebels shared the conviction that until their faith became the universal imperative, all would be lost. It took the tragedy of continuing wars and the solvent of politics to broaden horizons at least to the point where the ideals of the secular state could take hold. Even in the ostensibly secular state of today, however, dogma remains a danger, and getting beyond the politics of demonization is a way to higher moral purpose.[13]

Culture Wars and the Clash of Intellectuals

Even well before September 11, Samuel Huntington famously warned of a "clash of civilizations," in which the new fault lines in international affairs would become "civilizational" rather than ideological. Benjamin Barber, on the other hand, was concerned about a clash of a different kind. As the world embraced (or was forced to adopt) modern fully internationalized capitalism, Barber warned, the tendency for this "McWorld" to clash with jihad, a fundamentalist reaction to the economic and cultural domination of modern capitalism, would intensify. In Barber's view, a kind of jihad can occur anywhere in the world, including the United States, where modernization provokes a reactionary movement in defense of "traditional" principles. Where Barber seeks answers in more democracy from the bottom up to change power relations, Huntington seeks more power and wiser use of it. Yet there is one important similarity between the two views. Each claims problems will result when profound cultural differences run up against each other. Barber believes these differences can be negotiated through a deepened democracy. Huntington thinks they should be kept apart.[14]

Huntington's view is predicated on the claim he makes that the United States, indeed the West, has been losing power relative to certain other parts of the world. In order to protect itself materially and culturally (Huntington views the West's culture as superior), it must do two things at once. First, maintain economic and military superiority. Second, do so without chasing the fool's gold of trying to universalize its values, although he lionizes them because they are based on what putatively are universal principles. Thus Huntington at once produces a framework that is western-centric, calls for a kind of "imperial" self-defense, but still rejects dangerous uses of the very power he implores us to create. He has been consistent over time in his views. He opposed the war in Iraq.

Barber's solution is quite different. While he is fully aware of cultural differences between and within nations, he argues that more democracy everywhere, taming corporate intrusions into community life, is the way to avoid the clash represented by jihad's reaction to McWorld.

Each author's argument has been referred to as a plausible explanation for 9/11. For some who use Barber's argument as a general theory, 9/11 was evidence of the effects of irresponsible globalization. Western cultural and political penetration provoked a fundamentalist reaction. For some who used Huntington's argument, the attack on the World Trade Center and the Pentagon was definitive proof that there was indeed a clash of civilizations that was no longer latent and is essential to understand for the sake of our future.

While these uses of Huntington and Barber's ideas fit some preconceived postures within the culture wars, and their broad sweep is instinctively appealing, we doubt either helps much in explaining 9/11 itself. It would take a longer discussion to assess the general theories offered by Barber and Huntington, each of which has some merit.

Understanding the reasons for 9/11 involves a specific inquiry into a range of issues. To prevent future Al Qaedas, indeed to eliminate this one, we need to know why they did what they did. Sweeping theories can set parameters for possible reasons, and most of us have one overarching framework in our heads in any case, but they cannot give us the answers we need to make us safer. We were not attacked by Hamas terrorists, or Hindi militants, or Basque separatists. We have important relationships with all of the countries these groups inhabit. We were attacked by Al Qaeda, which is led by bin Laden and which, tragically, as Barber knows, selectively adopted aspects of McWorld (cell phones, jets, oil money) to plot and carry out its crimes.[15]

Questions can also be asked regarding the two authors' overall theories. Is Huntington's celebration of universally superior but not universalizable western values based on an identity-securing faith as much as on enlightened rationality? In turn, is he reinforcing his theory or his faith by pointing to societies he claims are incapable of practicing western values? Does he fail to see the role a faith similar to his can play as others try to export western values in ways he considers dangerous?

Barber understands that the globalization juggernaut has undesirable effects and that blindness to these effects only heightens their seriousness. However, he underplays the political and social fallout from the paradoxical need to have both faith-grounded identity and to unsettle that identity. Each of these is not only part of the clash between jihad and McWorld, but one within democracy itself. While Huntington would intuitively understand these dangers, our own argument is not to withdraw from promoting democracy abroad. But we would approach the situation with the understanding that while democracy allows participation that "disturbs and denaturalizes" aspects of the "cultural unconscious," under conditions of deprivation and inequality it also "can intensify the reactive demand to redogmatize conventional identities." Such deprivation, we would add, can be relative, and also need not be material.[16] This seems buttressed by the evidence that many terrorists are not, in fact, materially deprived.

September 11 provoked a variety of responses from intellectuals across the spectrum. Noam Chomsky opposed the Afghanistan invasion because of the harm it would do to innocents. He argued that while bin Laden was the murderer, U.S. Middle East policy, which he detailed, remained the major cause of the attacks. As to the McWorld thesis, he had this to say: "As for the bin Laden network, they have as little concern for globalization and cultural hegemony as they do for the poor and oppressed people of the Middle East who they have been severely harming for years."[17]

Richard Falk reluctantly and somewhat surprisingly supported the invasion. Given the magnitude of the attack and continuing American vulnerability, he concluded, "There were no credible alternatives to war, neither proceeding by way of the UN, nor through reliance on the past responses of retaliatory missile strikes and law enforcement efforts, nor by way of diplomacy reinforced by sanctions."[18] As for bin Laden, he was a genocidal murderer who had targeted Jews, Christians, Americans, and anyone else who could be considered a "crusader." Still, Falk argued for the need to develop a reconstitution of international law in a postmodern framework, or, failing that or until such time, applying a just-war framework with careful limits.[19] He talked especially about the need to rethink international law and institutions in the postmodern face of terrorism, a "megaterrorism" that does large-scale harm through an international network of nonstate actors. He worried that the Bush administration had defined the war so broadly (while mirroring bin Laden's Manicheanism) that it runs the risk of becoming a war without end. Instead, he argued, "the war can be won only by a narrowing process that refocuses the defensive undertaking of the U.S. government on al-Qaeda."[20]

Political theorist Jean Elshtain saw things rather differently. For her, as for President Bush and others, "they loathe us because of who we are and what our society represents."[21] Yet are we really that exceptional? There is little doubt Islamic fundamentalists also hated the Soviet Union, indeed, worked with us to fight it. Did they hate the communists because of *their* freedoms?

According to Elshtain, they hate us because of our commitment to freedom, so changes in policy are irrelevant: "We could do everything demanded of us by those who are critical of America, both inside and outside our boundaries, but Islamist fundamentalism and the threat it poses would not be deterred."[22] Here she pushes her first claim about why fundamentalists *hate* us over the Manichean rhetoric ledge, now surmising why Al Qaeda *attacked* us. She does this without regard for evidence that our Middle East *policies* motivated our attackers (this fact is irrelevant to the virtue of those policies), most importantly the stationing of troops in the Muslim holy land of Saudi Arabia during and after the first Gulf War.

In this world of terrorist threat, Elshtain believes America has a special burden to carry. It must use its power to do good in a violent world, and in particular to prosecute a "just war against terror." Indeed, she implores us, "international civic peace vitally depends on America's ability to stay true to its own principles for without American power and resolve, the international civic stability necessary to forestall the spread of terrorism can be neither attained nor sustained."[23] Her conclusion is worth repeating at length:

> We recognize that all war is terrible, representative finally of human political failure. We also know that the line separating good and evil does not run between one society and another, much less between one religion and another; ultimately, that line runs through the middle of every human heart. Finally, those of us—Jews, Christians, Muslims, and others-who are people of faith recognize our responsibility, stated in our holy scriptures, to love mercy and to do all in our power to prevent war and live in peace.
>
> Yet reason and careful moral reflection also teach us that there are times when the first and most important reply to evil is to stop it. There

are times when waging war is not only morally permitted, but also morally necessary, as a response to calamitous acts of violence, hatred, and injustice. This is one of those times.[24]

If, as Elshtain correctly argues, war is terrible and it represents political failure, and yet there are a limited number of circumstances in which it may be necessary, don't several considerations gain added relevance? Since the line between good and evil does "run through the middle of every human heart," once a grievance is felt deeply and a path toward war is embarked upon valid claims of justice may escalate into lumbering claims of righteousness. Those with the military or other capacities to strike back hard, indeed to curb world violence, may be inordinately inclined to see their very power in the world as proof of their virtue. This, after all, is the teaching of Calvin. To point to these implications of Elshtain's discussion of human vulnerabilities is not to say that claims for justice or preemptive acts to protect one's security lack merit. It simply reminds us to be cautious, to examine the claims, the facts, and the history. And also to review the track-record of those seeking war. When powerful governments make claims of righteousness in their cause, they deepen their responsibility to tolerate dissent both through vigilant maintenance of civil liberties and refusal to demonize opponents of war as unpatriotic, as if the fact of opposition was relevant to making *that* case. It is not enough to gesture toward human frailties and then, when we are aggrieved, proceed as if they have been overcome.

Where Is *the Outrage?*

Each of these views plays a role in the ways the culture wars roil our nation vis-à-vis the war on terror and the invasion of Iraq. Chomsky is the radical critic who always seems to see the root of all problems in things the U.S. government does, yet his account is clear on bin Laden's culpability and the utter moral degeneracy of the bin Laden network. Falk is the international lawyer and liberal thinker who articulates an internationalist solution that looks to the future. Yet he supported the invasion of Afghanistan, feeling that 9/11 demonstrated that current international practices and institutions are not yet up to the task of providing an adequate defense, especially in facing the stateless-actor terrorist threat. Elshtain articulates again her notion of the central place individual responsibility must have in our scheme of values, warns again against excusing bad or evil behavior through a cant that emphasizes prior victimization of the perpetrators of evil. Her faith in America's gifts to the world is strengthened by 9/11. The world needs both our values and us. But evil, she reminds us, can lurk in *any* heart.

Not so with William Bennett. His post-9/11 book, *Why We Fight: Moral Clarity and the War on Terrorism,* provides few surprises, nor would he want it to. He has always had moral clarity. America and western civilization are simply superior. Israel is, too. Islam has not been hijacked. It really is intolerant in ways that cause violence. There is good and evil in the world. He is proud to be on the side of good. "They hate us," he agrees with Elshtain, because of who we are, answering the question George Bush posed in his address to Congress on September 20, 2001:

> Americans are asking, Why do they hate us? They hate what we see right here in this chamber—a democratically elected government. Their leaders are self-appointed. They hate our freedoms—our freedom of religion, our freedom of speech, our freedom to vote and assemble and disagree with each other.[25]

Unlike "sophisticates," liberals, leftists, and especially postmodernists, Bennett, like Bush, knows evil when he sees it, and he's against it.

As the war in Iraq approached, Bennett added a new preface to his book, called (without acknowledging Jeanne Kilpatrick's famous speech to a past Republican convention) "Blaming America First":

> There is a name for this attitude, and the name, once again, is anti-Americanism. In today's circumstances, in the face of an evil that only the United States can defeat, to hold this attitude is worse than irresponsible; it is a species of deep perversity. From the rest of us it requires a renewed response, one based on a true knowledge of our enemies and, especially, on a true knowledge of ourselves. This book is intended as a contribution to such knowledge.[26]

Unless we utterly fail to grasp what the words "a true knowledge of ourselves" mean, his book fails to contribute anything to his or our self-knowledge. For all 9/11 seems to have taught Bennett is that the "true knowledge" he always had is even truer today than when he set us straight before. Consider Bennett's earlier book *The Death of Outrage: Bill Clinton and the Assault on American Ideals* as he was driven to the edge by a public seemingly indifferent to Clinton's moral failure. It might please Bennett to know he has helped us find our outrage by suggesting that those who opposed the Iraq war, as we did, are "anti-American." Indeed, his book is mostly a diatribe designed to demonstrate that people who are unwilling to face the truth, which he knows with absolute certainty (e.g., that Iraq has stockpiled WMDs to attack America), suffer from perversity. It might please him more to know that we have no postmodernist hesitation in judging his overall argument to be wrong, manipulatively structured, based on very selective if not distorted history and, well, to be bad. In fact, Bennett is a case study in what we have called the politics of moral personae. People who disagree with him are in turn wrong, evil, and perverse, an intellectualized/moralistic/pop-psych trifecta.

Bennett's harshest words are reserved for postmodernists, relativists, intellectual sophisticates, and a variety of leftists and liberals. They either hate America directly, or they are studiously neutral about all ideas, actions, moral postures, or people, whether good or bad, which for him comes to the same thing:

> Subtly or crudely, nonjudgmentalism often serves as a mask for what can only be called judgmentalism of another and much worse kind. Summoning us to some all-embracing indulgence of the views of others, however wrong or evil, it encourages us, subtly or crudely, to deprecate the good when it happens to be ours—our own values, our own instincts, our own convictions, our own civilization. To put it another way, the refusal to distinguish good from evil is often joined with the doctrine that one society—namely the United States, or the West—is evil, or at the very least that it is to be presumed evil until proved otherwise.[27]

Unfortunately for Bennett, he ignores an obvious implication of this general point. "All-embracing indulgence" in *his own views* masks injustice done by politicians and states *he* endorses, and obscures and distorts the views of his opponents. He also writes as if the most common danger in human nature is too much tolerance, rather than self-love welded to power of the kind he advocates. He rightly asks: "Where was the peace movement [in the 1990s] while all this was going on, and was known to be going on? How could it sit idly by as a dictator acquired the means of mass destruction, the means to hold the whole world at bay?"[28] Putting aside the hyperbole and inaccuracy (he wrote before the Kay report stating Iraq had no such weapons), how dare he make this charge and not even mention that the Reagan administration, in whose cabinet he sat, materially and deliberately supported Saddam Hussein and helped enable his depredations? The chemical weapons attack killing five thousand Iraqi Kurds in Halabja, Iraq, which Bennett himself cites and both presidents Bush adopted as a mantra—"he gassed his own people"—took place in *1988*. Bennett is right that Hussein's regime and the man himself were simply barbarous, but they were the most barbarous when we supported them and looked the other way at their war crimes. With relativist aplomb, he has nothing to say on his own complicity with Saddam.

Bennett is not wrong about all he surveys. Some Americans on the left do have an instinctive dislike not just for policies of the American government, but also for American people and culture. Some postmodernists forget their debt to the modern commitments to dig deeply and to be rational, in ways that lead to moral dead ends, even as they remain harsh moral critics of people who don't agree with their point. Nor is Bennett alone. There are fundamentalisms, left, right, and center that adopt demonizing stances with structural similarities akin to Bennett's. Each of these postures inflames and thereby enables support for the others. They engage each other in a neurotic dialectic in which not just synthesis but respect is impossible.

After reading *Why We Fight*, we went to the Human Rights Watch Website. The horrors are there for all to see about Saddam Hussein; the facts are appalling. Did our own opposition to the war and the way it was unethically promoted make *us* insensitive to his evil, not wanting to know? Were we simply *unwilling* to give the administration the benefit of the doubt as to the reasons for war because of *who* the main advocate of war was? We always said had the Bush administration told us plainly that this was a war to *liberate* Iraqis, without the dissembling about WMDs and Al Qaeda, we would have given that view a fair hearing. But would we?

Each Bennett of the world, whether on the left, right, or in the middle; modernist, postmodernist, or religious fundamentalist, instigates a process of closing down discussion, averting already polarized eyes from inconvenient facts. Each sounds a retreat into the sanctity of purified identity in the gear-up for total culture war. President Bush's rush to war under false pretenses made us angry. The worst offenders of the *culture wars*, however, are the clever intellectuals who ask, "Where is the outrage?" and then selectively deploy the question. Where *is* the outrage? For Bennett, it's where he feels like placing it. And not just in the terror war, but as warrior extraordinaire in the war for the soul of American culture.

8

Preserve the Environment! Become an Environmental Sport

The war on terrorism, the invasion of Iraq, and the Israeli-Palestinian conflict keep oil close to our hearts and minds. Reaching record highs in 2004–2005, prices at the pump bring it into our wallets. Questions surrounding oil not only raise foreign policy and economic issues, but those of the environment as well. Why do we use so much? Will we run out? What do we destroy in our search for more? How can we break the habit? Sometimes foreign and environmental policies come together: Must we break the habit to disentangle ourselves from the Middle East?

Too often, however, our questions about the environment are framed rather like the one that asks: "Do you believe in God?" Do you believe in a clean and healthy environment? No one wonders whether the environment exists, and even most of those with the most horrendous environmental policies believe it should be clean and healthy, too. Almost all believe in that, but what should we do to bring it about? How can those of us who think environmental protection should be vigorously pursued through (but not only through) democratically inspired governmental action devise the best policies and create an atmosphere in which tough environmental protection becomes *politically* sustainable?

First we need consider *who* can answer this question, rather than *how* to answer it. Our sense is that it is the environmentalists who may oppose or seek to limit SUVs, jet skis, or Hummers—but who still might allow themselves to enjoy a ride. Environmentalists, in other words, who know themselves well enough to resist the temptation to caricature and demonize those with whom they disagree. We need activists who also look carefully into their opponents' eyes, thoughts, needs, and desires, to the place where the emotional life hits the road and the heat of policy clashes rises. We need committed advocated who are ready to give the initial benefit of the doubt about character and purpose, although not policy, to others with whom they disagree. Let's begin looking now into *how* we can develop politically sustainable environmental policies, in part by breaking through polarization.

Roger and Me, and My SUV

Mainstream environmental organizations like the Natural Resources Defense Council by now have a familiar take on issues such as air pollution and the greenhouse effect. Since hydrocarbon emissions play so basic a role in the CO_2 accumulation in the atmosphere and in smog, these emissions must be checked. Under the polluter-pays principle, gas-guzzling vehicles should be discouraged. Fuel economy standards are one way to discourage guzzler production and marketing, and incentives such as "feebates" can be used to encourage purchase of appropriate vehicles. The problem, of course, is to generate the political will for this transformation. If it were true that most of us are selfish most of the time, the prospects for further significant environmental reform remain clouded.

We would like to suggest that this view of the problem badly misconstrues the historical, cultural, and political origins of modern consumerism. Tax policy by itself is not going to defeat the sport utility vehicle, but not primarily because of our reputed selfishness. Sport utility vehicles have much more to do with the assertion of individual identity in our modern corporate economy. That identity is asserted in the context of particular understandings of nature, democracy, and the individual.

We have begun by implying there may be limits to the familiar, neoclassical, view of the consumer. He or she always wants more goods and services. We would also like to challenge a familiar left-wing view of this —call it the Roger and Me school of political economy.

We are referring of course to the movie *Roger and Me,* a film that fifteen years ago attributed the decline of working-class communities such as Flint, Michigan, to the singular greed of Roger Smith, the CEO of General Motors, and his corporate cronies. Though the film did not directly address transit systems, it might well have added to its litany of complaints the findings of a 1974 Senate Anti-Trust Subcommittee investigation regarding GM's purported role in the decline of mass transit in this nation. The contention, for which there is considerable documentation, is that a joint subsidiary of GM, Standard Oil, and Firestone Tire company bought up many urban mass transit systems in the 1930s, mostly electrified rail, and converted the systems to diesel buses, the popularity of which declined. The process led to the decimation of mass transit and the triumph of the automobile.

There is no doubt in our minds that this scenario unfolded pretty much as the Senate subcommittee would have us believe: that it was a conscious business strategy and that it did expand the market for autos, and in time for sport utility vehicles. But as a broad-gauge historical theory, it has some major inadequacies. Even in the thirties, the automobile was already something a large majority of the American population already hoped to acquire. General Motors was a leader, but surely not alone, in establishing three practices that became staples of our consumer culture: the annual model change, a segmented product (different divisions and autos targeted to different levels of the society), and consumer credit.

To balance this scenario, we need to consider how the public received this story. Though the findings of the Senate subcommittee did not gain the kind of currency that other startling revelations of the era, such as Watergate, received, the conclusions were hardly buried—and they produced something well short of outrage.

Americans of the 1970s, just like those of the 1930s, wanted cheap cars. And as children of Progressive-era and New Deal reforms, they felt ambivalence toward the large corporation. They often feared and distrusted it, but they also valued its productive efficiencies and when push came to shove, they weren't ready to really break it up. This reluctance made sense in the absence of any alternative model of corporate governance besides the proprietary model or the nationalized version of European and Soviet socialists, both justifiably nonstarters for U.S. citizens.

Beyond the normal business strategies, consolidation, advertising, and market creation, if we are going to understand the culture of sport utilities it is important to take a look at consumers and their day-to-day lives in neighborhoods and workplaces over the last half century. We do not accept the contention that it is natural to want an SUV, but nor do we conclude that a narrow and single-minded corporate elite imposed these on the rest of us.

That SUVs are purchased primarily for utilitarian reasons is on the face of it a hard argument to sustain. Industry research shows that only a quarter of the purchasers of these vehicles use them for off-road adventure or for towing heavy loads. Something more subtle is going on for most purchasers. Jerry Hirschberg, Nissan's president of North American design, once said: "There's a feeling, when I am in my car, I am in command of my future. Home and work have not been symbols of stability."[1] Hirschberg is implying an understanding of consumer behavior here that is subtler than either the neoclassical view or the simplistic leftist notion of corporate consolidation and brainwashing. In this regard, we think the recent discussions of worklife, working hours, consumer culture, and the evolution of the corporate political economy developed by Juliet Schor provide a more fertile way into our understanding of this phenomenon.[2]

Schor's fundamental premise is that we are social beings. We are lost without some set of socially constructed norms to guide us. In a society where some version of the Protestant work ethic has always valorized work and material success as its just rewards, getting and spending have added meaning to life. Consumer goods, especially the ones that are visible, are statements about ourselves. More to the point, they have often also been an expression of one's individuality, something very powerful in the American context.

But if social and personal identity are necessary for us, must these identities be regarded as forever unalterable, subject neither to contestation nor change? By implication, Schor's argument suggests that an identity of getting and spending has taken a social toll at least as severe as its consequent environmental toll, and that challenges to this identity are possible.

Keeping up with the Joneses is more American than apple pie. In the fifties and sixties, it may have occasioned the kind of bland and occasionally oppressive conformity symbolized by Levittown, but the standards were often set as much by neighbors as by distant authority. And in neighborhoods where income ranges were relatively small, the standards could be met by many.

Today's consumerism is qualitatively far more problematic, and it is this form of consumerism that lies at the heart of the sport utility vehicle phenomenon. The role of the neighborhood in our lives is less substantial. Even in two-parent families, mom is ever less likely to be at home. Mom and dad are both working and the Joneses with whom they strive to keep pace are increasingly coworkers and supervisors. And for almost everyone, television with its ads and opulent on-screen lifestyles, is the new neighborhood.

In the modern workplace, the power and income spread has reached unprecedented levels. Keeping up appearances is thus a daunting task. Schor demonstrates, through studies of purchasing patterns for such highly visible consumer goods as cosmetics and branded clothing and through consumer surveys, that much consumer spending is designed for positioning ourselves in this increasingly stratified and competitive universe. Similarly, purchase of a sport utility vehicle makes a very conspicuous statement. It isn't merely the fact that the vehicle is large and expensive. It suggests a certain kind of life—independence, access to the country, to the leisure and camping activities that the most affluent and successful professionals and families of wealth have always enjoyed.

The obsession to spend more on consumer goods denudes the public sector. In language reminiscent of Rousseau, Schor portrays a world where extreme individualism and massive inequalities eviscerate political life. As taxes are cut and individuals put more resources into private solutions to their problems, public functions are performed less well, and people turn farther away from public goods, turning to private pursuits like acquiring an SUV, for utility, identity, and recreation.

The decline of the public sphere takes on great significance in terms of the kinds of private goods we buy. As Barry Bluestone and the late Bennett Harrison have pointed out, there has been a decline in public infrastructure spending for such items as roads and bridges.[3] In addition, ever more crowded and trafficked urban areas cause many traffic accidents. People feel safer in SUVs. Such utilitarian defense of these vehicles makes some sense (actual safety depends on the specific car), but it sits within a larger context of social policy and social evolution.

Nonetheless, far from breeding a sense of satisfaction, this new consumerism often disappoints. Much of what we buy we hardly use and, unsurprisingly, get rid of fairly quickly. Keeping up with the higher-ups at work requires perpetually new consumption. American consumers are often characterized as materialistic, but in an interesting twist our consumer patterns demonstrate little intrinsic interest in the material good. Goods are continually discarded as their social value is spent. And even as some of us gradually gain the material level to which we aspire, so do many others, and the bar is then raised.

The sport utility vehicle is a perfect illustration of this phenomenon as well. The first purchasers did enjoy some safety advantage and bragging rights. But 14 percent of all vehicles sold now are SUVs, and not only does status suffer but safety does as well. As one Sierra Club official remarked, "You can't see over the traffic any more, you just see the SUV in front of you."[4]

Not to be outdone, some corporations are now making even larger versions. An obsession to spend ever more often surfaces even as people fret about the direction of their lives. More than a quarter of those earning over $100,000 per year report that they would need very large increases in income just to continue to meet their "needs."

Hirschberg implicitly and Schor explicitly acknowledge another vital aspect of this story. If keeping up in the consumption game is ever harder to do, so too have the costs of not keeping up increased for many. The insecurities that have marked blue-collar work for a generation now increasingly infect middle- and upper-management levels as well. In *Fear of Falling*, Barbara Ehrenreich comments that for a frightened and squeezed middle class, "securing a place means going upscale." How one is perceived may well have a bearing as to whether one is a victim of the next downsizing. In workplaces employing people of different classes, showing that one identifies with the values of the corporation and its owners is just as vital as one's immediate work performance. What better way to demonstrate those values than through one's upscale consumer choices? "The penalties of dropping down are perhaps the most powerful psychological hooks that keep us keeping up, even as the heights get dizzying."[5]

Schor's analysis of consumerism suggests an approach to the sport utility phenomenon that goes well beyond taxing the vehicles as an environmental strategy. Along with mainstream environmental economists, she advocates changes in the tax code, but her approach is more subtle. She advocates higher proportional taxes on luxury autos and expensive homes. To those who object to such "interference" with markets, she correctly notes the ways the current tax code now subsidizes the consumer culture. Why not, she asks, use the code to encourage sufficiency and discourage invidious and self-defeating forms of competition? Even luxury taxes on SUVs, unless the taxes are very high, are unlikely to accomplish all that Schor might desire. These vehicles will remain items of positional consumption for many.

To address this problem, we also need to get at positional consumption with respect to work: the desire to hold on to or advance one's position within an occupational hierarchy. Here, Schor's approach is prescient and makes important theoretical gains on Marx. The latter of course is notorious for his eschatological and utopian reading of history, wherein all political and distributional conflict is eventually transcended. But one part of his eschatology that seldom receives the attention it is due is the question of leisure. Leisuretime remains an important goal of Marx's, but it is achieved only with and through ever-increasing material growth. In Marxism, leisure is always at the end of the rainbow.

Schor is clearly aware, instead, that the issue of leisure must be part of an ongoing political and social process. She suggests that as individuals we take a step back when we feel we must have a particular consumer item that does not serve some clear and obvious need. We should ponder closely the hidden messages in the commercials. Will the new car or the new dress really help us get the mate or the promotion? And toward what other purchases will such new goods likely lead us? She suggests that individuals who feel burdened by the psychic demands of working long hours in order to spend more consider negotiating hour reductions or becoming self-employed if possible, and consequently reduce their spending and free up their time.

Schor has provided one more reason why workplace reform should be a priority not only for most workers but for environmentalists, children's advocates, and women stuck also with the second shift at home. Reducing the massive inequalities in reward and the disparities in power between front-line workers and top-level management and owners would not end all the emulative consumption but it might moderate it. Moreover, it would create better conditions to discuss its causes and effects. When workers enjoy more equitable pay, more input in day-to-day affairs, and a voice in the selection of their own supervisors, the criteria for advancement might even become more related to ability to perform and work with others than to one's choice of power suits or Rolex watches. Certainly to the extent workers felt less burdened by these conspicuous consumption demands, they would be in a better position to advance their concerns.

In an era when individuals are asked to solve too much and democratic governance is too easily deemed helpless, cooperative strategies can help us recognize and implement alternative ideals and ways of life no longer centered on individual consumption. At the level of neighborhoods and small communities, concerned citizens can negotiate voluntary nonaggression pacts: parents can agree on limits to be spent for children's birthday parties or for their own social occasions. Nor need each of us purchase items such as power tools or riding lawnmowers. We can find ways to facilitate sharing and perhaps even community loans. Might we even consider finding ways to limit auto purchases by sharing vehicles for certain purposes?

Ultimately, of course, one major implication of Schor's work is the need to reassert some sort of a common good lying in the public provision of a range of goods and services that would reduce the need for individual consumption. Schor recognizes this need, but fortunately understands the paradoxical nature of such public goods in a way that escaped Rousseau. While necessary to a thriving individuality, social goods, and the push for equality, can go so far as to occlude and suppress individuality. Contrary to Marx, she suggests that just because much of current consumption is positional and can become a form of commodity fetishism, we cannot thereby conclude that all personal consumption must take this form.

To her great credit, nothing in Schor's compelling book is hostile to personal consumption across the board, nor is she dedicated to forcing us to spend less or live one particular lifestyle. Indeed, she quotes with obvious approval a reformed shopaholic who acknowledges that new and distinctive clothing choices will remain some part of her life: "I think it's fun to dress . . . , [b]ut I like to do it on my own terms, not because of pressure to look a certain way."[6]

Schor's discussion of consumerism invites one last question: What kind of society are we seeking to build? A corporate-dominated political economy and an emulative consumer culture are flawed ideals in our eyes, but their flaws can be understood on two levels. As corporate political economy has evolved, consumerism has moved increasingly from a widely shared goal to an imperative whose demands occasion increasing dissatisfaction, a discontent whose source is not always recognized.

But the goals and ideals of the consumer society also arise within the larger project of modernity. By modernity, we refer to an era in which faith in an orderly hierarchy of being, in which both human society and the nonhuman world were seen as embodiments or expressions, had broken down. Modernity, even as defined by its greatest theorist and defender, Max Weber, is an era in which "life is stamped with the imprint of meaninglessness," a time during which there are no mysterious, incalculable forces that come into play but rather one can in principle master all things by calculation.

One question a serious reexamination of issues such as the use of sport utilities poses is this: if environmentalists cannot adequately curb the voracious public appetite for environmentally harmful items such as SUVs, need we revert to some form of a resacralized nature to win the battle? This is a tempting course and some have adopted it. We submit this stance is counterproductive, unnecessary, and possibly dangerous.[7]

Nature, Surprise, and Democracy

Some in the environmental movement, like Rousseau, see nature as a realm of harmony and sustenance in which human beings can take an appropriate part if only they will adopt the appropriate political forms and personal and political mores. Rousseau argues in the opening lines of *Emile* that "everything is good as it leaves the hands of God." Man cannot go back to this innocent state, but Rousseau famously posits the possibility of a politics of the general will which, under a set of highly restrictive moral and political assumptions and prerequisites, allows each to retain the freedom of nature within the framework of law and community. Participatory community and appropriate or sustainable technology are seen as growing together and reinforcing each other.

We need to avoid counterposing to our modern realities idylls of romanticized premodern or intentional communities where conflict and exploitation supposedly did not exist. General Motors did not simply impose a new mode of life and corporate governance on passive and unwitting workers and citizens. Nor did it disrupt essentially satisfied and harmonious neighborhood communities. The triumph of the large corporation is owed in part to internal problems, inadequacies, and tensions within an older proprietary capitalism. Proprietary capitalists both feared the large corporation and longed for the stability and job opportunities it offered.[8] And while they denounced the wealth and power of corporate owners and managers, many longed for these same things. For many women, corporate workplaces and big-city life led to new forms of oppression, but also to ways out of the confines of the narrow rural mores.

Finally, even those who found the new corporate life unbearable also worried about the consequences of the intrusive, public utility model of corporate reform being propounded by Theodore Roosevelt, the most "progressive" of the major corporate reformers of his day. The emergence of corporate capitalism must thus be seen as something more than the corporate class imposition that some of the socialist critics in the 1960s, such as James Weinstein, made it out to be.

The social values and practices of the older communities themselves took their toll. Consider Andrew Ross's portrait of Polynesia in this regard. Many premodern societies did place substantial restraints on the use of the natural environment. We find these restraints admirable today, but we often fail to recognize the subtle forms of human exploitation that went hand in hand with particular resource management practices:

In socially stratified Hawaii, use of the natural environment was regulated and constrained by chiefly *kapu* (taboo), a sacred system of consumption laws which applied to all aspects of the food, labor, and general material economy. It is likely that the sacred function of *kapu* often functioned ecologically for the communal good, either to guard against overfishing or to conserve species during breeding seasons. But they also served as a means whereby nobility could reserve certain species—sea turtles, for example—for their own consumption at particular times of the year, or to exact labor and tributes from commoners for their chiefly comfort. . . . Indeed, the uses made of *kapu* were virtually indistinguishable from the exercise of power. If ecological conservation was an effect of the kapu system, then it was as much a selective byproduct as a community minded aim of the chiefly control of resources. Consequently, the effect could be reversed if and when the structure of power was redefined, either from above or below.[9]

This brings us back to the politics of consumption. Environmentalists often seek higher taxes on SUVs and an outright ban on jet skis, another symbol of consumerism and environmental degradation to many. Is this another *kapu*? For such posture allows affluent suburbanites to continue to buy and drive their vehicles to wilderness areas while putting an inequitable regressive tax on the vehicles of working-class persons who might also want such a long-prized form of recreation.

If, as Schor suggests, we need individual and collective values and even narratives that suggest alternatives to a consumption-oriented lifestyle, to what degree must we impose our narratives on others, and how single-mindedly do we impose these even on ourselves? We could, in good Marxist fashion, view codes like the *kapu* as merely a rationalization of the position of an economic elite and suggest that once economic power was equalized, any code would express the full synthesis of the individual and the social being. But this may be another and quite repressive way to resacralize nature, in this case human nature and the human community.

Modernity's own quest for absolute epistemic and moral certainty may be seen as reflecting both its anxiety in the face of the breakdown of the feudal order, and its unacknowledged inheritance from monotheistic religions, under which truth is unitary. From God as the pinnacle of a great chain of being, we move toward the notion of God as omnipotent creator who can make and reshape the world at will. From there we move to a notion of humans as beings able to reshape the world. But there is a green and communitarian version of this theological journey as well, one that suggests a direction within the human community toward perfect harmony of person with person and of persons with nature, especially within the small-scale and low- or appropriate-technology community.

A genuinely radical approach to the politics of the SUV and the jet ski would explore the possibility and suggest the presumption that nature, both animate and inanimate, while not possessed of final purpose or unitary direction, does contain instances of action and agency that exceed our reckonings and predictions and can evoke wonder. Nature can, in the words of political theorist Jane Bennett, become a source of enchantment. Rather than revert to Aquinas or Aristotle in order to counter the rampages of industrial growth, Bennett draws on Lucretius. Though recognizing, unlike Lucretius, that human beings do not form a picture of nature unmediated by their concepts, she sees ecological and ethical merit in articulating his naïve portrait of nature. This picture suggests that nature is constituted by infinitely small "primordia," but the atomism of Lucretius is not the mechanistic atomism of Newtonian physics. Invisible matter bits travel downward through a void, but, in the words of Lucretius's poem the *De Rerum Natura,* "at times quite undetermined and at undetermined spots they push a little from their path, yet only so much as you would call a change of trend."[10] As Bennett puts it, the swerve is not a moral flaw or design because the nature in which the primordial moves about is not designed. Nature is not chaotic, because the texture and shape of the primordial set limits on their combinations, but these are full of surprises.[11]

This Lucretian perspective is mirrored and further developed in some contemporary work in both physics and ecology. Developments in ecology are most relevant to our story here. Since the nineteenth century, evolution has been understood in at least two disparate ways. The very phrase "survival of the fittest" has been subject to contrasting interpretations. Natural selection can be understood in teleological terms to suggest that the emergence of certain species with specific characteristics is the working out of a grand master plan implicit in nature. A species survives because it fits the plan. Ecological theory based on such teleology has assumed the existence of stable and organized communities of natural organisms that are consistent over time and space and maintain a general homeostasis. To explain apparent inconsistencies at particular times and locations, notions of succession and climax are developed.

But natural selection has also been understood as suggesting that whatever survives is "fit" merely by virtue of its survival. There is no grand plan. Today's survivors may well fail as changing circumstances, defined not only by competitors but climatic and geologic change, dictate. In the words of William Drury, one of the most perceptive and eloquent critics of teleological ecology, "A 'plant association' or 'plant community' consists of a 'collection of strangers' whose membership is defined by recent historical accidents, chance effects in seedling dispersal, and the ways in which colonists match the characteristics of the place."[12] From this perspective, there still are patterns, but these are local and always subject to unexpected disruptions. There is a clear element of mystery and unpredictability at the core of nature.

In more recent work, Jane Bennett has gone on to develop a broad understanding of materialism that stands at the intersection of ecology and ethics. She argues for a view of matter that treats it as neither inert, dead, nor governed by or expressive of a providential design. She calls her perspective "thing-power materialism," which "figures materiality as a protean flow of matter-energy and figures the thing as a relatively composed form of that flow."[13] She cites a variety of literary and scientific texts in support of a notion that all matter has moments of life in some form.

Bennett is exemplary in acknowledging the speculative nature of her conception of materiality. But she is equally strong in articulating the ethical and political case for presenting her speculative and at times playful portrait of physical nature. She

> hazards an account of materiality even though materiality is both too alien and too close for humans to see clearly. It seeks to promote acknowledgment, respect, and sometimes fear of the materiality of the thing and to articulate ways in which human being and thinghood overlap. . . . I pursue this project in the hope of fostering greater recognition of the agential of natural and artifactual things, greater awareness of the dense web of their connections with each other and with human bodies, and, finally, a more cautious, intelligent approach to our interventions in that ecology.[14]

We have suggested that human beings are driven, on the one hand, by an insistence on closing the gap between their finite concepts and a world not amenable to conceptual control, and, on the other hand, as having the potential to appreciate novelty and surprise in themselves and their surroundings. Bennett's playful nature picture encourages this potential and acceptance of or even delight in a politics that seeks to find more space for inevitable expressions of difference. If human beings are especially complex assemblages of physical "stuff," in interdependent relations with organic and inorganic worlds, perhaps any of our narratives won't fit even ourselves all the time, let alone others.

Materialism construed in Bennett's terms would not repudiate an appreciation of consumer goods per se, nor of their role in a life well lived. It does, paradoxically, lend support to more measured forms of consumption, to appreciation of the material good and thus, as Bennett puts it, to less thoughtless waste. It could foster the form of measured consumption as a genuine expression of individuality, to which Schor has alluded.

We would add that the relationship we articulate in this chapter between work life, consumption, and conceptions of materiality is reciprocal. Materialism properly understood can foster new attitudes toward work and consumption, but by the same token a revised materialism is more likely to emerge when pressures for conspicuous consumption and long hours of work have been eased within the culture and political economy. These revised understandings of work and materiality together may also serve in tandem to reduce pressures toward demonization in our politics. The "community of strangers" in the world of plants may prefigure a more light-handed approach to forming the new local, national, and international communities we will need to resolve many contemporary problems.

Every code, even those that spring from relatively egalitarian and participatory communities, is to some degree a *kapu*, an instrument of power over some of us all of the time, and perhaps even over most of us some of the time. If this is the case, maybe we would do well to celebrate those forms of order that allow real diversity.

This isn't an easy task. Environmental constraints are real, and society does need a set of rules and common understandings to endure. Orders that build slack into their norms and structures will therefore require a willingness to continually adjust the rules needed to sustain social peace and environmental integrity as technology and social conditions change. Bonnie Honig argues that it also requires a different understanding of democratic politics. Politics is celebrated as a good in itself. It is not simply a procedural vehicle toward a final consensus and thus for its eventual withering away, but a realm to be valued for the challenges it helps un-earth.[15]

Jet Skiers, Tree Huggers, and Other Forms of Life

We would like to now suggest that jet skis in moderation may be far from the abomination many make them out to be. More important, at least some of the opposition to this recreational pursuit springs from other concerns besides noise, safety, and environmental pollution. Some may rest in the deep conviction of some environmentalists that there is only one way to enjoy nature, their way. Or it may reflect an envy for a kind of lifestyle they crave but dare not acknowledge, even to themselves. In our pursuit of sustainability, have we as environmentalists hidden some inner doubts about our own values and lifestyles, marked by hiking, sipping water, and quiet contemplation of nature? There is probably a class component here, just as with the *kapu*. Jet skiers are probably from less elite backgrounds than are the leaders of mainstream environmental organizations.

Perhaps it would be more reasonable, even as we seek to ban jet skis from areas where their noise is a disturbance, to suggest other areas and times where they might be allowed. And rather than banning sales, perhaps we should encourage collective forms of consumption of this consumer toy also. Such proposals are not intended as a perfect or final resolution of such contentious dilemmas. Even if adopted, they would doubtless produce further issues that would then need to be addressed. Nonetheless, we think they could be a useful suggestion. At the very least, environmentalists need to acknowledge that even if these products pose either environmentally or socially unacceptable costs, banning them focuses on a portion of the population whose consumerism really doesn't differ much in kind or damage from that of others.

Such intervention would be pragmatic environmental politics as well. Just as some environmentalists who have been denied a place at the political table have become defensive and dogmatic about their politics, their own dogmatism and aggression stimulates resistance to many facets of the environmental agenda, especially from those whose economic circumstances and political voice are limited.

The only enduring answer to the social, economic, and ecological dilemmas SUVs and jet skis and other items of consumption pose is a world characterized by a higher degree of real political, economic, and cultural freedom. Individuals would have far more choice as to how much they work and spend and what public policies to countenance. They could have the opportunity to carve out personal and social visions that gripped them but did not overwhelm and dominate every aspect of their waking lives. If the evolution of consumerism teaches a cautionary lesson, it is that even the noblest social goals or visions can become annoying, obsessive, and even oppressive.

People need space for an individuality that is not colonized by the demands of consumer culture, the workplace, the neighbors, or even their own ideals. The institutions of our consumer society, while providing the goods for many, have also added burdens of questionable value. It is time to adjust the balance. Democracy grounded in a respect for individuality and openness to nature's surprise is our best hope for a scientifically sound and politically viable answer to the environmental problems we are encountering. But we cannot wait for that day as if it were sometime in the future. That ethos is needed today to avoid the divisive rancor that prevents strong environmentalism from being more fully sustainable politically.

Conclusion
A New Democratic Covenant

American politics has a tendency toward demonization, which is not the exclusive province of conservatives, moderates, or liberals. Demonization has deleterious consequences for democracy because it closes off dialogue, reinforces polarization, and deepens partisanship. We think that there are common sources of the practices of demonization—the psychological and political processes that lead to the demonization of opponents—whether engaged in by the powerful or the powerless, by religious fanatics, or radical secularists. While these practices differ in style and sophistication, to an insufficiently appreciated degree they have some common roots in our society and, indeed, perhaps reflect common temptations in human nature.

Demonization by the powerful, however, has distinctive political consequences. It denies to excluded and denigrated groups the economic and political power they need if they are to survive and thrive. Furthermore, it has occasioned forms of political surveillance that are the enemy of effective dissent. Nonetheless, counterdemonization by those with less power carries its own price.

Take the example of demonization by progressives of conservatives in power. When progressives are demonized by their opponents on the right, their political prospects may be harmed. When they reply in kind, they often suffer negative consequences for their own points of view that are rarely acknowledged and which often remain misunderstood.

The practical problem is that demonizing attacks often work, and progressives do not yet have the media structure to effectively compete in this game. However effective moveon.org, Michael Moore, and Al Franken's fledgling radio network *Air America* may prove to be, notwithstanding the contribution each makes in bringing alternative views to the public, these venues are currently no match for the right wing's Fox TV and its numerous talk radio shows and mobilizing engines, including Michael Savage, Rush Limbaugh, Sean Hannity, Bill O'Reilly, and Laura Ingraham. Whatever biases conservatives may fairly discern in the major networks or CNN, none of these corporations plays the mobilizing role that Fox News does in clearly promoting and proselytizing certain issues, opinions, and political attacks, and often in leading the charge with demonizing rhetoric. Consider Fox News's inexcusable behavior in consistently and willfully confusing the war in Iraq with the war on terrorism *in their news coverage* as if it were self-evident that the two were the same. Instead of probing this controversial and critical public debate, they flack for the Bush administration's view, setting and resetting the stage for demonizing opponents of the Iraq war as if they are opposed to fighting terrorism.[1]

In spite of this institutional weakness, progressives do face a political dilemma. Ronald Reagan and George W. Bush have shown them that the best way to push a political agenda is to win political power even before you have majority popular support for your program. Then make your program the norm to which others must reply, effectively shifting the overall political debate in your favor. The stakes therefore are programmatically very high as to *who* wins power, and this fact puts a premium on winning power at any cost. Thus, not to reply in kind is to invite electoral defeat with severe consequences. That's one reason so many in the progressive media like to attack President Bush, for example, as greedy, unfeeling, lazy, and stupid. Their hope in 2004 was to mobilize their base and cast doubt in the minds of those who were undecided.

Even if these attacks are effective in the short run, they have long-term consequences both for the quality of public discourse as well as for the development of a progressive political agenda that can ease the very economic and social anxieties that allow demonization to thrive. For example, the rhetoric can often lead to facile conclusions that replacing one set of leaders with another will redress the problems that progressives claim to be committed to solving. We fully understand the place of humor, the temptations of ridicule and exaggeration, and the need to break through to a public too often preoccupied or otherwise indifferent. Michael Moore's ridicule of the president's character, brains, and work habits, for example, is entertaining to many, sometimes including us. But it ill prepares both his own constituency and the public at large as to what its expectations should be should Moore's preferred candidates win. The unintended effect can be to disempower the public by distracting it from *structural* sources of problems, at once making it too beholden to a new set of leaders and prone to being disappointed when the leaders don't deliver and the problems don't ease. The public then becomes receptive to a new round of demonization based on the character of the new failed leaders, or to deepened political apathy. In this regard we find the deft touch of Jon Stewart and his *Daily Show* colleagues to be more effective (and more fun), as they sharply and wittily make their points without quite demonizing their opponents.

Demonizing responses (or indeed forays) by the disadvantaged, or perhaps more accurately by their leaders, however emotionally satisfying or useful for political mobilization, can thus run the risk of bringing additional harm to them. A film like *Roger and Me* cannot harm "the rich" in the way that demonizing welfare recipients has harmed the poor. Such works can still do harm, however, to the extent they undermine unwittingly the long-term ability to develop coherent programs and alliances that would more effectively redress power imbalances and lessen vulnerability to demonization. If for no other reason than this, it is therefore essential to understand why patterns of demonization and counterdemonization exist and often grip us. A politics that is circumscribed by demonizing rhetoric on all sides facilitates acceptance of such rhetoric by closing off other possibilities, limiting exploration of a full range of policy options, and inviting retaliation, heightening anxieties, and reigniting the entire process.

The disadvantaged in our society are often victims but they are not *merely* victims. Precisely because they are relatively powerless—but not entirely so—they are the ones who need to be most vigilant about being backed into corners from which there is no exit. We think engaging in demonization is one of those corners.

This process can lead to facile theories of political change, as if by merely toppling one leader, noxious policies and exclusions will stop. In addition, modes of analysis that focus on the evils of a particular leader distract one from understanding the systemic pressures that constrict the parameters of the policy agendas of both parties. And worst of all, counterdemonization by the weak can encourage even more vindictive policy responses by the strong.

We recognize that demonization-free discourse is likely an impossible ideal—there are ontological reasons the temptation exists—or at least an ideal impossible to fully realize. There will always be political leaders or followers who will have a need to demonize others. There will always be political leaders or individuals who will use demonizing tactics to advance their own goals. The distances between tough criticism and demonization, psychological need and accurate perception, and manipulative tactic and sincere belief are also not easy to behold, and claims of right and wrong, while not relative, are sometimes contestable.

Although we should always resist "demonizing" others in the sense of striving to attribute, or allowing others to attribute, to them unwarranted characteristics of evil or deviance, there are enough examples of evil in the world—such as genocide and efforts to exterminate all political dissent— that call for the strongest possible condemnation. Proper condemnation requires appropriate distinctions. "Evil" and "deviant" are extremely strong terms, and most bad behavior is neither evil nor even deviant. Nefarious private actions, while they are revealing about a political leader's character, usually tell us nothing at all about the character of his or her political agenda.

We need to oppose the casual proliferation of demons while redressing those actions and policies that deny personal and political space to others. Understanding these things, our goal has been to find and analyze some important sources of tendencies toward degradation of the democratic process.

Moving away from demonization in politics toward a shared notion of citizenship and obligation requires both an accurate assessment of responsibility for problems, and the freedom to act democratically. Chastising the weaker among us for their (and our) social ills, or indeed attacking the inherent malfeasance of government for failing to solve them, without at least considering systemic tendencies toward such results, moves us exactly in the wrong direction. Is there a new "covenant" that allows greater individual empowerment, inspiring our sense of justice, and also allowing us to hold each more fairly accountable? Is there a covenant through which the binds of popular governance can be relaxed, and governing itself be made more democratic, adding to the authority of democracy while weakening its legitimacy problems? We now turn to a proposal for change.

The New Political Covenant

Political participation must be increased at all levels and in all modes of activity, but in some ways most critically at the national level and in national elections. As President Reagan ably demonstrated, it is national elections that set the tone, and national policy that sets the future agenda. Changes will be difficult. Here are some suggestions. First, we need to recognize the problem of nonparticipation in elections as a fundamental political issue. Then we need to consider ways that raise our low participation levels and also neutralize the severe class bias that now exists.

Some examples follow. To lower the "cost" of and thereby increase voting, we should adopt universal automatic voter registration of the kind our European allies have. We should also hold elections over the course of a "Democracy Weekend," or at least declare Election Day a holiday both to free up time for voting and underscore the importance of the act. Recognition of a need for more time for civic duties in general, and the possibility of more people gaining a voice within the political system, may even help tone down demonization in American politics.

To allow greater choice and thereby increase the benefits of participation, we should consider reasonable forms of proportional representation and must create much fairer campaign finance and electoral rules for "third" parties. Political parties need to be reinvigorated as real participatory institutions, or other informational and mobilizing institutions or networks founded. Groups like moveon.org have become a model, but we need other models to help organize those with less computer ability and access. Once again the goal is to lower the "cost" of involvement and facilitate participation down the socioeconomic and educational ladder.

Simple equity and the need to open the political agenda to the needs of those now abstaining from participating require that we entirely eliminate the role of money as an inequitable resource in politics. In 1976 the Supreme Court decided in *Buckley v. Valeo* that Congress may regulate contributions, on the theory it had the authority under the Constitution to stop the corruption that may flow from large contributors currying favor. It may not, however, regulate expenditures, which it viewed as tantamount to constitutionally protected free speech. The 2003 Supreme Court decision *McConnell v. Federal Communications Commission* upheld the McCain-Feingold law that weakened the role of "soft money" in politics. It did so by broadening Congress's constitutional authority to regulate campaign-relevant contributions and certain types of spending by supporting the "corruption" rationale it had moved close to in several recent decisions: while Congress still may not regulate "speech" by limiting expenditures, it may create policies to prevent, not just quid pro quo corruption, but corruption of the democratic process itself. Still, this decision does not go far enough. Congress and state and municipal legislatures are still prevented by *Buckley* from regulating expenditures, thereby allowing wealthy candidates or individuals to have, from a democratic point of view, grossly unfair abilities to influence politics. Moreover, McCain-Feingold doubled individual limits on contributions in presidential elections from $1,000 to $2,000, a sum way out of reach for many citizens. This sum is also large enough to augment the political power of those who can afford it because many of them are also in a position to "bundle" numerous top-end contributions and, in effect, present a very large sum of money to a campaign. The proliferation of so-called "527" organizations, "independent" groups that can accept unlimited donations and that set up campaigns parallel to those of their preferred candidate and party, deepens this problem. The rewards are favors, access, and an ability to have undemocratic influence on the political agenda: if you want my money, shape your policies according to my tastes.

Other reforms that make the process more intelligible and less confusing will also help, such as developing media formats that make issues comprehensible and streamlining layers of government and elections at all levels. For example, we support the idea formerly raised by Jesse Ventura when he called for unicameral state legislatures. In general, simplification for the sake of intelligibility is a good principle to follow.

Because education is so closely correlated with nonparticipation and the ability to navigate the political world, it should become a fundamental right under the Constitution. In 1971, in *San Antonio Independent School District v. Rodriquez,* the Supreme Court decided that no such right existed. It did so upholding the constitutionality of an inequitable Texas school financing system in which each school district's funding, rich or poor, was dependent on its ability to raise money through the property tax. Some state courts have begun to address this issue through their construal of state constitutional provisions. Still, *San Antonio* should be overturned, or rendered void through amendment.

The president should also appoint a National Commission on Nonvoting with two objectives. First, presidential action would put on the political agenda the seriousness of nonvoting as a problem for a democratic polity, and underscore its structural nature. Second, the commission should study recommendations such as those we have offered and come up with a plan of action to raise voting participation in national elections to the 70 percent range while reducing political inequality below its 1964 levels.[2]

One of the most important issues that such a commission must consider is the disenfranchisement of ex-felons. Various states have different laws with respect to the impact of incarceration on the right to vote. But with the number of Americans who have been implicated in the criminal justice system now so historically and comparatively large, and so heavily skewed by race, this is no trivial issue. Obviously, demonization through the politics of moral personae has played a major role. Demonization of felons, especially when they have a particular racial cast, is all too easy and leads to easy arguments for their political exclusion. But bringing them back to political life may increase their commitment to the larger society and can lessen misperceptions about them. We harbor no illusion that progress on this issue would be easy. Nonetheless, the way in which the exclusion of felons had an impact in Florida on the results of the 2000 presidential election has opened up some space for considering this proposal.

The purpose of all of these reforms is simple. It is to put into action a principle of fairness in American politics that does not yet exist, but one to which we *can* come closer: one person, one person's worth of political access and opportunity to exercise political power.[3] We call this principle *real* political equality.

Real political equality is an important step toward citizen power, efficacy, and self-esteem, but by itself remains insufficient. Other tasks are needed. To mitigate future legitimacy problems and their manipulation and consequent citizen disenchantment, over the long term we need both a renewed social covenant and an invigorated democratic ethos. Each needs to be conceivable within our political culture and be capable of lending support to and being defended by greater political equality. In order to achieve these ends, political debate needs to be shifted, in the near term, away from divisive wedge issues to the critical issue of quality of life—what kind of society do we as individuals and we as a nation want to live in?—a balance of self-interest and society's interests. It is through such discussion, we believe, that a renewed covenant and ethos are most likely to emerge.

However, before we can settle in on the shape of that debate or the nature of the covenant or ethos, we need to recall the theoretical underpinnings we have pointed to in this work. We think these help explain why there has been so much disaffection from politics and government. Jürgen Habermas focuses on structural and ideological constraints on modern people, and Jean Elshtain and some other advocates of "civic republicanism" on their failures of responsibility and will. Let's remember, however, who modern people are and what they face.

Modern individuals have multiple sources of resentment that feed disaffection. They are conscious of their mortality and face the rigors of finding life's purpose. They believe they are responsible for defining their identities and how they fit into society. Meritocracy brings with it the notion that they are responsible for where they and their loved ones wind up. They are pulled back and forth between the poles of puritan discipline and hedonist consumerism within America's moral paradox. They believe they have the right to control their own destinies, yet they live in a world of impersonal, powerful forces over which they have insufficient knowledge and little control. Their democratic representatives seem continually to fail them. No one helps them, they think, yet people who apparently reject the standard of self-responsibility to which they subscribe, from junk bond dealers to welfare recipients, seem to live off the system quite effortlessly.[4]

Those who historically have endured the greatest inequities have also most often been the targets of these resentments, especially racial and ethnic minorities, the poor, and women. As the role of government in the economy and society grew in the 1960s, a variety of groups pressed separately against government in the form of rights or entitlement claims to remedy their perceived oppression or promotion of their own interests, which they saw as primary. Affirmative action or minority set-asides, for example, have been justifiable as public policy interventions at specific points in our history. Such policies and agendas may also, as we shall see, play a key role in fostering universal rights. Nonetheless, when calls for these compensatory and redistributive policies are elevated into becoming rights claims themselves, there is an irony—and a flaw with consequences. In such cases, rights talk becomes too specific, even too narrow and self- or group-interested to be *rights* talk. Thought of as a right or entitlement, the policy seems to become the end in itself, increasing rancor over disagreements regarding it and closing off possibilities of genuine alliances over actual rights that may be promoted through diverse policy options. At the same time, the state becomes the focus of the appeal, discounting the fears of earlier generations of populists and radicals of the state's corrupting influence, while weakening the legitimacy of the state to enforce rights by making it the target of opponents of specific policies.

One essential function of politics, especially in democracy, is for people and groups to meet their needs, wants, and desires. These are perfectly valid assertions of interests, and all people should have a *right* to the kind of political equality and economic opportunity that allow them to do so fairly. Interest claims may be perfectly valid, smart, worthwhile, beneficial, and even fair, but they should not be inappropriately inflated into rights, even though the line between rights and interests is itself a subject of discussion, even of political contestation. One important example of such a contest is criticism by many feminists of the idea of the abstract universal citizen of liberal political philosophy as, in fact, an interest-laden masculinized figure that promotes male power and therefore sexual oppression.

The civil rights movement of the fifties and sixties, unlike groups pressing for some of the targeted interventions of more recent times, employed a paradigm of rights in their broadest sense. That movement aimed to make the putatively universal rights Americans enjoy as citizens and as consumers genuinely universal. What distinguishes the idea of rights from policies or interests is that they codify fundamental and universally applicable principles. Their objective is to establish a just and equitable place for all within a society. Their contours are contestable, but that contest is constrained by these parameters. Persons of different races or gender or class backgrounds may have different interests that they seek to satisfy, but their fundamental rights should be the same.

In fact, exorbitant use of the language of rights may grow out of or even inflate patterns of demonization. I have a right to a certain claim by virtue of who I am. Should others try to prevent me from cashing in on my right, I am a virtuous victim of their perfidy. When political discourse becomes only rights claims, conflicts of interest become translated into denials of rights, with rancorous consequences. Someone who blocks your self-interest is guilty of one kind of transgression; someone who denies you your rights, quite another.

Because claims of rights have greater moral weight than those of interests, there is an inherent tendency in modern liberal or social democratic polities for rhetoric to escalate from one to the other.[5] This should be resisted. Nevertheless, we should never forget that the "rights talk" that is often criticized stems from a 1960s awakening regarding the distance between ideals and practices. That gap is narrowed and reconfigured, but remains.

When rights claims are inflated, three things of consequence happen. First, the claim cannot carry the moral weight placed upon it, weakening the status of other, more appropriate assertions of rights. Second, when the claim is both inflated and for a finite resource, material or moral, rights discourse especially loses its essential universal aspect. It becomes a zero sum game, a competition over "rights" as if they were opportunities, goods, or services, especially weakening the power, in general, of rights claims. Appropriate rights claims nevertheless will often at the same time involve conflicts over power and resources. The winning of the vote by African Americans, for example, lessened the political power of white Americans, although it was based on realizing the universal principle of one person, one vote. Third, civic virtue erodes, and the kind of coalition politics that might empower the group to achieve its objectives becomes less likely. A balkanization of political spirit sets in, which divides constituencies, further depletes legitimacy from the idea of active, democratic governance, and adds to the decline of civic life.

An American Universalism

The understanding of demonization we have developed in this book makes it incumbent upon us to consider an expansive conception of rights that strives not to become another part of the problem. We need to articulate a set of rights whose goal is to allow as full a panoply of individuals as possible not only to live together but to flourish.

But a perspective attuned to the temptations of demonization also recognizes the ways in which any articulation of rights can freeze out of modes of difference we find threatening. Therefore, the most inclusive rights are those whose content enables to the degree possible the means by which other claims can be specified and given a hearing. In addition, for a set of rights to contribute to the goal of delimiting demonization, they must be supported *and* limited by an ethos of care and concern for the potential limits and damages of any agenda.

This perspective on rights rejects classical teleology in this sense: there is no guarantee that the list of rights is complete or even that potential future rights should be understood as necessarily implicit in the current set.

Nor can we be sure that our attempt to recast politics through the set of rights we suggest, with an eye toward minimizing demonization, can successfully redress the alienation and anger so prevalent in current American politics. Nonetheless, we think this set is worth the gamble. We believe that if a few thoughtful liberal, moderate, and conservative thinkers and political practitioners become attuned to some of these concerns, the content and direction of American political life may begin to change.

From this line of analysis, we believe that five related rights are as basic to effective democracy in today's world as the right to vote was in an earlier era. And like the right to vote they would be potential building blocks to more expansive freedoms.

Rights of Opportunity

Here we would suggest considering the following five proposals as universal American rights of opportunity. We believe they meet the broad criteria for rights that emerge from our discussion. First, they apply in principle to all people. Their universal applicability has the additional virtue of moving the debate about them some distance from the normal wedge-issue debate and more onto the broad terrain of the question of quality of life. Second, their achievement provides a basis in power and security upon which, should they choose, people can challenge our society to become more democratic and inclusive, indeed even to challenge the "covenant" *we* endorse.

Our proposals appeal to goals or ideals many of us already hold. We suggest them to prompt us to narrow the gap between goal and reality by rethinking and enhancing the opportunity structure in America. Some of these proposals redress power and security imbalances and enliven the democratic political process. Others try to lessen anxieties and mitigate stresses of living in modern times. We commend them, therefore, not only because a society that adopted them would become fairer and more decent, but also because they just might mitigate—but not eliminate—some of the pressures toward uncivil discourse we have identified. Even more will be required, including old fashioned Tocquevillian "habits of the heart," to which we shall soon turn.

Real Political Equality

We have already discussed the first right as an opportunity to have *real* political equality: the ideal not just of one person, one vote, but of one person, one person's worth of political influence, if that person chooses to be involved. We suggested a number of ways to achieve this right, most particularly by dramatically raising electoral turnout to limit the class and educational bias of contemporary elections, and eliminating the role of private wealth in public politics.

Effective Citizenship

The second is the right to a real opportunity to be an effective citizen. This right is essential to allow full participation, should one choose, in the life of the nation. Education and information are central. While all Americans have a constitutional right to a public education of some sort, the public financing of that education can vary greatly. Thus, the right is not fundamental in the parlance of constitutional rights. That is why *San Antonio* needs to be overturned, and Congress and state legislatures should develop a more equitable educational system. Furthermore, because the inequity also involves disparity between private and public education, policies to redress inequities throughout the entire school system need to be addressed.

A right to an equitable education and to access to information is essential for several reasons. Educational skills and information are needed for full participation in politics, economics, and culture. Furthermore, a rich public discourse on how best to achieve a decent society with a high quality of life will require an "educated" and informed public in at least two senses. The public needs to be skilled in seeking and demanding information and thoughtful analysis from leaders and institutions, and it needs to have both the resources and the self-confidence to engage in debate over complex issues, and to know when things aren't all that complex, expert opinion notwithstanding.

Critical information is needed in specific areas and creative solutions should be sought out. For example, purchasers of goods who wish to advance environmental and health goals need accessible, clear, and straightforward product information in all of these regards. In this context we suggest there is still a need, notwithstanding all the good work of present-day consumer groups, to establish a very high profile and nonpartisan

National Consumers Union to act as a clearinghouse for information, which could provide a catalyst for consumers to organize themselves better at the point of consumption.

Information in general must be easily accessible. Citizens, therefore, need a broad "right to know" as a supplement to quality education. For example, people who wish to influence our trade policies need greater access to treaty negotiations (they need to be held in public) and to facts about their implementation.

Because citizens also need modern tools, computer and Internet technology need to be even more widely available. At the same time, "information" needs to be sifted—there is simply too much, and much of it, even when "correct," is unimportant—and rendered intelligibly useful. Democratic societies today face an especially daunting challenge of refining and developing institutions that can make important information accessible and comprehensible to a broad public. Otherwise, celebrations of the triumph of the "information age" really are tributes to a new style of hierarchy.

Today, education is ritualistically appealed to as the path to the future, by enhancing our economic competitiveness as a society and the competitiveness of each individual within our society. These are important goals, but the one we are advancing is more old-fashioned, more fundamental. Education is needed for the citizen to fully participate, and for the democracy, through educated citizens, to best determine the nature of the competition, indeed, the nature of the society. Whichever goal one subscribes to, however, we need to make it a top national priority and take it seriously enough to provide a good and equitable one to all living in the United States.

Basic Social Security

The third right is to basic social security that all citizens within an affluent society such as ours should be able to enjoy. This includes basic security in childhood and old age, and for those who otherwise cannot support themselves in between through no failure of effort of their own. It also includes health-care security for all Americans throughout their lives, both physical and mental, and remedial and preventive, including adequate nutrition and opportunities and facilities for exercise. Social security of this kind broadens our covenant to include the weakest among us at a minimum level of physical well-being, the hallmark of a generous nation that takes pride in acting as a community.

Community Well-Being

The fourth is the right to real opportunity to live in healthy, safe, and secure communities. Here we have in mind an array of issues, from environmentally sound communities and places of business, safe streets, efficient and clean transportation, public parks, and athletic facilities, to reasonable commuting. Hopefully such a goal will spark greater thoughtfulness as to how we need to design our communities and places of business and leisure to achieve objectives such as these. Life is already full of stresses, some of which we can't eliminate, some of which we may even secretly enjoy. No one enjoys feeling unsafe on the street, or "road rage" while mired in "freeway" traffic or breathing in smog. Is there doubt that a more habitable, pleasant, and secure living and working environment would contribute in important ways to more generosity of spirit, and less need to flee from a life really lived in the community?

Opportunity for Work and Leisure

The last right we endorse is especially important in order to create a decent life. It is the opportunity to sufficiently satisfying, meaningful, reasonably remunerative and secure work, and for time for family, leisure, and community.

Corporations need to become more responsible and accountable to their employees and the public. We endorse neither an absolute right to a job, nor the idea that everyone is on his or her own. Money must be earned and work, for most of us, is rarely play. Jobs remain determined by economic need, and qualifications. The goals are a less alienated work life and a greater attention to family, friends, and community, now paid lip service by politicians across the spectrum.

One aspect of this right suggests the importance of time, and what we do with it. In a highly technological and affluent society, we need to give greater thought to how and why we spend the considerable time we do at work, and how much time and of what quality is left over for the rest of life. The centrality of reinvigorating leisure cannot be stressed enough. It could be viewed as a micropolitical change with the potential to affect political sensibility and macropolitics as well. In particular, it might enable us to better mitigate resentments spawned by America's moral paradox involving the pushes and pulls of consumerism and puritanism.

In moments that are not structured and monitored by the demands of schools or workplaces, one can potentially appreciate the diverse and speculative thoughts, moods, and instincts that too often must be shuttled out of consciousness. In the midst of such experience, there also lies the possibility that we can become aware of the ways our demands and expectations of others unduly constrain their possibilities. This right will elicit and be elicited by forthright consideration of the extent to which our economic culture is leading us to a higher quality of life.

In this context, we endorse the kind of idea embodied in the notion of spiritual retreats from the rigors of everyday life. Instead of limiting sabbaticals, periodic leaves from one's workplace, within the academy, they should be broadened beyond it. A range of corporate practices should be scrutinized, and at least in the case of forced overtime eliminated. The objective is to empower people to fashion their working and private lives in ways beneficial to their happiness and helpful to having a more decent society. A right such as this will likely require a full-employment economy as a national political priority and enhancement of the right that now exists to organize at one's place of work. One goal, related to this overall right, is to enhance the opportunity to earn a living and live a reasonable life for those who opt out of the competitive cycle of work and consumption.

Some will reject not just the specifics but the vast scope of these suggestions and what appears to be an enlarged role of government and a very hefty price tag. They will say in the guise of claiming to raise a number of carefully specified and limited rights that we have actually advanced a broad political agenda, and a social-democratic one at that. What we propose, of course, has clear political implications. Yet we are not advocating that these become constitutional or legal rights, although that question might itself be part of the debate over them. We are here proposing them as rights of principle, rights as ideals to pursue, rights that will require other laws and constitutional principles. We recognize a broader right to equality in our society than exists in the Constitution. Putting economic equality to one side, for example, *real* political equality as a constitutional principle could be clearer in our Constitution. Moreover, we have no preconceived idea as to how these goals should be achieved.

One of our aspirations is for people as employees, voters, and consumers to empower themselves by changing the balance of forces between people and our large private and public institutions in ways that give more power back to individuals to shape their lives.

Our belief is that discussions about changes of the kind these rights embody will open up possibilities for their achievement, not just through government, but also through the market and through public interest organizations and others within civil society. However, we choose not to closely stipulate here a detailed public policy program. Discussion of them as broad goals for consideration regardless of ideological predisposition is our most important objective. Our hope is that focusing debate on quality of political, social, and private life issues such as these will move us away from demonization and toward more frank and open discussion; that it will call to a new pragmatism in American politics, one inspired and challenged by America's most cherished democratic ideals.

Are we being wildly idealistic to think we can achieve all these goals? Yes, of course we are. And yet, although these goals are in tension with important trends in contemporary American politics and economics, they resonate with several enduring aspects of our reform traditions. Here now is a brief sketch of what might be called a "social democratic" contribution to the dialogue to advance some of these rights that we as a society need to have.

The United States is often portrayed as the preeminent liberal society in which the market is king. But as Theda Skocpol, former president of the American Political Science Association, has powerfully demonstrated, a range of interventions in the market in the form of such "social welfare" programs as Civil War pensions and Social Security have been popular when they are broad based and in accord with widely accepted moral ideals.[6] The concept of a minimal government-guaranteed pension as a reward for (Union) military veterans of the Civil War during the nineteenth century, and that of Social Security at the culmination of a life of work in the twentieth century, became firmly established.

The experience with Social Security especially demonstrates to her that programs that eventually help those most in need have the best chance for political support—and success—if they become developed within and after universal programs that benefit a wide range of citizens. Although such programs might in the beginning help those "less needy than the most desperately poor," "before long such measures could create new opportunities for more targeted efforts." In contrast to policies that start small but target the poor or other groups, such an approach is less likely to become conceived in ways that stigmatize the disadvantaged, and much more likely to be politically sustainable. She calls this process "targeting within universalism."[7]

Skocpol believes Social Security proves her point: "Today Social Security is not only the most politically unassailable part of U.S. public social provision, but also America's most effective antipoverty program." Considering needs in today's world, while keeping these principles in mind she proposes that in addition to Social Security for the elderly,

> [t]he United States could develop what might be called a family security program available to all children and working-age citizens. The new policies would include child support assurance for all single custodial parents, parental leave and child-care assistance for working families, job training and relocation assistance for displaced workers and new entrants to the labor market, and universal health benefits.[8]

Yet we would add that many Americans could also be receptive to democratic government taking more responsibility in giving citizens an opportunity for self-development and economic advancement. In a world increasingly dominated by corporate employers and changing job structures, this might translate into a serious commitment by the federal and state governments to retraining, and should that be inadequate, even some mode of guaranteeing minimal employment opportunities. Within the context of our decentralized polity and public-private partnerships, such a guarantee could be designed in ways that would avoid the political dead end of make-work schemes. A jobs program, for example, could address community needs not now met by government or the market. It would include federal grants to meet those needs especially in communities where unemployment remains persistently high, perhaps from the effects of international trade and changing labor and capital markets. It could also be fostered and promoted by giving citizens tax credits (which are more egalitarian than tax deductions) for contributions to local nonprofits active in areas of priority needs. Private employers could also be recipients of grants.

To assure the broad rights we outline, we suggest the possibility of democratizing workplaces in ways that might foster greater equity within them. Secure jobs, child allowances, and adequate care for children and the elderly also underscore the social importance of nurturing. More democratic workplaces and more time for family and self-development could lead to the emergence of diverse perspectives on consumerism and the sanctity of endless material growth for growth's sake. The growth and scarcity spiral has played a crucial role in fostering the zero sum character of contemporary competitiveness, which itself breeds resentments and moral paradoxes.

Such intervention would provide more time and opportunity to fashion a politically effective citizenry that could make the state itself more democratic. The achievement of such policies would be a means to as well as an effect of political movements that might choose to embody some of these ideas in their own organizations. In any case, this is our contribution to the debate that we would like all of us to engage in more fully than today.

We realize, of course, that our *policy* orientation would require greater infusions of tax money than the policy goals we articulate currently receive. While it is certainly true that money does not solve all problems, money is essential to solving some of them. Concern at the state level about serious federal underfunding of President Bush's "no child left behind" program is a case in point. More broadly, does anyone doubt that public schools in wealthier areas and wealthy private prep schools, all other things being equal, provide a better education than public schools in general? Does anyone doubt that this disparity makes a large contribution to denying full equal opportunity of earning a good living when children become adults? It is impossible to have equality of opportunity while we have unequal educational opportunity. This is a fact. The question is what to do about it.

Proposals such as these will require thinking through our present governmental priorities. This will include our current levels of military spending but, even more importantly, the kind of role we think we should play in the world in order to best improve our national security and our quality of life. It also requires rethinking current tax policy, especially with regard to equity in the tax code, President Bush's rounds of tax cuts, and his weak-dollar policy. Finally, somewhat ironically, it also requires more fiscal prudence, to stop the current federal deficit spiral, or at least more care about what we go into debt to achieve. Good businesses often take on debt in order to reap the reward of a better business in the future. They invest. Too much of the government debt we have been taking on lately does no such thing. Some of it can even be harmful in surprising ways.

It is clear that President Bush's plan to privatize part of Social Security, allowing diversion of a portion of Social Security taxes into private accounts *while* continuing to pay off contemporary obligations, will require large-scale government borrowing. Doing so has all sorts of economic consequences that are easy to see, but it also has national security implications as we become more in debt to nations like Japan and China who buy many of our bonds but with whom we must deal on a range of other economic and international-relations issues.

It is reasonable to oppose the policy orientation we lay out here as a poor way to achieve the rights we endorse. It is also reasonable to oppose use of government tax monies in these ways. It is less reasonable simply to claim that the money doesn't exist. Important priorities are being set right now on how to expend our nation's resources, whether in budget allocations or in fiscal and tax policy. Right now we are going into massive debt. In our view, it is debt that does little to achieve the rights of opportunity that we have outlined. These budget and fiscal priorities are not inscribed in nature. They are political decisions, and they can be changed.

While we have suggested a set of priorities that we endorse, we do *not* believe these to be the only ways the rights we outlined can be achieved. For if we did, we would be elevating our policy commitments into rights, the very kind of escalation of rhetoric that we have warned against. Our major commitment is to having a higher-quality debate and higher-quality democratic process of decision making over what rights we think essential and how best to achieve them. Then, let the chips fall where they may.

An International Dimension

If these rights, and especially these policies, might well encourage challenges to the sanctity of the market, they would also require changes in our understanding of the state, and not merely along the dimensions of its internal democracy.

We have suggested a set of rights. Our policy specifications suggest they can be assured through markets when possible and through tax and regulatory policy when necessary. Our focus has been on the United States, but in a world where ideas and even workers and capital are increasingly mobile, we must also address the parameters of the national state. In this regard, western European experience suggests some possibilities and limits.

As we have seen recently, even traditionally liberal and tolerant European nations face serious threats from an antiforeign far right. In Europe, the welfare state itself was premised on the ability of national states to moderate the course of capital markets and to frame satisfying social identities for their citizens by aggregating the will of those living within their boundaries. These states were assumed to represent a full synthesis of geography and history. The idea of state and nation, however social democratic it may be, was frozen with regard to the "nature" of "its people." On this model, even if the nation-state is able to respond to many of the problems caused by the mobility of capital, it runs the risk of doing so through exclusion or limitation of those not seen as original partners in that state and nation. Some Europeans now acknowledge the limits of the nation-state. Still, it is worth noting but hardly surprising that historic nationalism still plays an important role in European Union discussions, for example, over equity, growth and stabilization policies, and the European constitution. That nationalism remains important in Europe, with its more developed social-democratic traditions, suggests the limits of social democracy alone in achieving fully inclusive societies.

People in post-traditional societies, such as the western industrial democracies, have their own distinctive problem of identity. Because modern ideas like science, technology, administration, and free enterprise are not as normatively formidable as religion and tradition, children of the Enlightenment have a special need for identities based on conventions that are more self-consciously the creation of people, and not based unreflectively on tradition, religion, and other standards. Yet, the very fashioning of these identities has a fundamentalist moment. In order to repress the self-consciously conventional character of such identities, differences with then that emerge are sometimes characterized as hostile or irrational. Citizens in what we might call traditional societies, for instance the Islamic Republic of Iran, also face analogous anxieties. Many have eased doubts about the demands and tensions in their lives by retrenching into various forms of theocratic fundamentalism.

The tendency to see one's identity in terms of fully grounded, natural, national, and even racialized superiority is especially pronounced in times of economic uncertainty. How does a working class, whether in Europe, Canada, the United States, or in other democracies, justify to itself sacrifices on behalf of an identity that feels under threat, especially when democratic governance seems powerless to solve problems? The naturalization or even racialization of identity stills doubts about both the failure of policy and the nature of that identity itself.[9] Often a politics of moral personae takes hold that focuses on the defects of individuals while still trading on group stereotypes and racism.

Democracy is not immune to normalizing pressures and the creation of pools of others who are then resented. Thus, even in a global market regime composed of democratic participants, there will remain temptations to define other national groups as threatening, especially those whose political and economic practices differ from ours. In the process, the hostility that develops from economic competition and pure ethnic animosity alone is intensified.

Those who advocate free trade, markets, economic growth, and progress as presently defined as "natural" may unleash forces they cannot fully control. For these notions as unproblematic theoretical ideals must still enlist human beings who in reality have never been bound by the abstract philosophical liberal ideal of "economic man" upon which these notions depend. The consequences are not always good. Should the world economy becomes more tenuous and if economic troubles grip people, we can expect a new economic/social fundamentalism to assume more political salience. People sometimes refuse to see themselves as fungible economic units, and the consequences are not always benign. We doubt we have heard the last gasp of protectionism.

Even a more democratic state, therefore, needs to be supplemented and contested, among other things, by a transnational collaboration of interest groups and grassroots organizations within the state over the role the state should play. Labor internationalism, for example, is itself an important development. Kim Moody has documented the rise of a new social movement unionism, pointing out that the current pattern of economic internationalism does give workers some leverage as well as problems.[10] U.S. jobs can be outsourced to low-wage states, but the increasingly complex dependence of manufacturing plants on each other makes disruptions at one or a few plants very dangerous for the corporation as a whole. The new unionism has sought to take advantage of these trends by building bridges between workers and unions in the industrial North with workers in less developed societies.

There are other limits to the efficacy of the nation-state that need to be considered. What environmental political theorist Thom Kuehls has pointed out with respect to ecopolitics also applies to the problem of international trade: "The problem of ecopolitics is not just that the effects of decisions in one territorial space have impacts on other sovereign territorial spaces; the problem also involves how these sovereign territorial spaces are constructed."[11] Looked at historically, U.S. sovereignty was constructed through an ideologically driven process of treating lands inhabited and used by Native Americans as not rightfully theirs because these lands were not subject to division, appropriation, and exploitation. From the middle of the nineteenth century, consolidation of U.S. identity has involved acculturating into their roles in society former slaves and immigrants first from western Europe, then southern and eastern Europe and China and Japan, then Puerto Rico, the Caribbean, Central and South America, and more recently from other Third World countries. Moreover, each of these people in one way or another was displaced by larger social, economic, and market forces, especially over the last sixty years, fostered in good part by U.S. economic and free trade policies and pressures.

There is nothing new about how dislocations foster cross-fertilization among cultures. International unionism has reopened questions of both domestic and international identity. It has broadened its negotiating stance to include questions of decision making in the workplace and how the use of long overtime hours not only burdens workers and families but also deprives other community members of jobs. In the late nineteenth century, however, efforts by such organizations as the Knights of Labor to reduce working hours were deeply indebted to the role of immigrants in seeking to free time for traditional religious rituals and family life. European socialism brought here by some immigrants also played a role in American thought.

The Keynesian agenda itself can be broadened and deepened not to vitiate trade but to reconstitute it by including international guarantees of minimum wage standards pegged to each member's mean level of productivity. And an international development bank of the kind Keynes envisioned the International Monetary Fund to be, funded by major players in the international economy, could prevent currency manipulation, encourage a growth-oriented model of trade, and fund development loans aimed toward modern, ecologically based infrastructure development throughout the less developed states.[12]

Trade treaties themselves could include minimum wage standards pegged to each member's mean productivity level. Without such standards, capital mobility and flight cheapens labor worldwide, intensifies resentments, and may even lessen demand for goods and services and cause international recession or worse. But many Third World governments regard any such standards as another form of failed protectionism advanced by more privileged workers in the First World. How is this impasse to be bridged? One way would be to insist that new trade treaties guarantee the rights of workers everywhere to organize. Any state not willing to guarantee agreement could not be a full player in the trade regime. Under this right to organize, Third World workers would be in a better position to determine for themselves their own needs and wage demands in the real economic world as it is. These are a few elements of an economic package that could help expanded trade meet its promise as a vehicle of prosperity, equity, and democracy freer of demonization.

But if states without even minimal standards of labor rights should not be granted full partnership, including especially what has variously been called "Most Favored Nation" (MFN) trading status and then "normal trade relations," or entry into the World Trade Organization, should they be denied any form of assistance? In this regard, we might consider drawing a far more nuanced set of distinctions than most on the left or right have been accustomed to.

We would be inclined to argue that forms of technical assistance, for example advice on new energy systems and loans and grants for their purchase, and most especially debt forgiveness, could still be considered. Such assistance would make these states better environmental neighbors and perhaps better consumers of western goods without dragging down workers in the West or the world economy in general. And such technical assistance would also increase cultural contacts and exposure to democratic values on the part of some members of these states. Negotiation and contact of one sort or another would still be open even as the denial of full trade rights continued to act as a sanction against their denial of basic labor rights. Such technical assistance should not be given, however, without appropriate safeguards if it is likely to worsen the plight of those trying to earn a living in those societies.

Expanded international trade can and may in fact be necessary to democracy, mutual understanding, and world peace. We believe these goals will be most likely achieved by, first, recognizing that "free trade" as presently understood is not inscribed by nature; it is a political choice. Second, by giving priority to democracy. Third, by recognizing that affluence, however important, is only one goal of domestic and international development. Finally, we need to extend our notions of democracy to include not only politics within states but broader collaboration between states and between activist and citizen groups across traditional borders. Movement in each of these areas is necessary to the others.

Overall, there is a need to think through carefully what we mean by the ideas of free trade, markets, economic growth, progress, and democracy itself in order to have the kind of full discussion we need about quality of contemporary life. It is our contention that such reflection and discussion give us the best chance to loosen rather than further entrench positions we adopted in earlier, less successful efforts to negotiate modern paradoxes.

Focus on issues of quality of life can even help us navigate several of the paradoxical situations in which free trade implicates itself and democracy. The very quest for a stable free-trade regime may engender political resentments among those left behind that undermine the stability that is necessary for free trade itself. Moreover, free-trade regimes require democratic nation-states *and* need to undermine them in order to become politically viable and economically successful. They require national democracy because they need democratic legitimation for enforcement and acceptance of a range of domestic and international legal standards and agreements. But they undermine democracy because they must limit the power of the territorial democratic state and real input from its citizens, substituting for it private and quasi-public, and largely unaccountable, international economic and political actors.

There is no guarantee that focusing on quality of life in international or domestic economics will "solve" any of these problems. Focusing on it does not eliminate the need for identity, self-interest, corporate interest, or national interest. But it can freshly shape some of their parameters. It can, in other words, ease and perhaps even avoid some of the resentments identified in this book, thereby lessening temptations toward culture— even shooting—wars and the lure of demonization. Otherwise, as we reach for economic integration, greater "efficiency," more economic growth, and freer trade, we run the risk of dividing the world more, both between and within nations, repoliticizing economic relations in dangerous ways, and thereby ending up with greater instability. And those who promote the unbridled market as an article of religious faith will find it all so surprising and condemn those who rebel against the social and economic dislocations they suffer as heretics to the cause.

Free trade can promote international understanding, stability, and peace. However, to best achieve these ends, we have to deepen our commitment to democratic practices that prize individuality, feature the issue of quality of life, and question the normalization of personal identity and the naturalization of discourse. Through such practices we may be able to formulate policies to temper the deeply felt resentments such identities and discourse engender. If we don't do so—in the reach for free trade—ironically, we may find ourselves solving the economic and political crises we find ourselves in through the ultimate Keynesian remedy—wars large and small.[13]

Universals and Identity Politics

Finally, any quest for universals in politics must address the question: Does the invocation of universals inevitably serve to diminish or exclude traditionally devalued members of the community? Iris Marion Young has argued that there is a tension in political theory between the universal as the standpoint of generality or the common good, and the full participation of all.[14] The general standpoint is inevitably defined in such a way as to exclude some segments of the population.

Young's caution is valuable, but it is drawn too starkly. It is hard to see how widespread participation can be achieved apart from certain widely shared and socially assured substantive commitments to quality education, voting rights, information access, and economic opportunities.[15]

But a politics of the common good is just that—it is an explicit affirmation of a political position. It claims to be an effort to articulate a set of rights that would benefit all, but it is an effort to articulate such a vision from the here and now and is clearly not neutral. Because it is explicitly political and because its stated goal is to achieve greater universality, such a claim invites and invokes the participation of those who feel excluded either by the principles or by their implementation.

The rise of identity politics reflects major exclusions and injustices even though, as Skocpol points out, it may create problems of its own regarding coalition and community. Some identity politics may be, as political theorist Wendy Brown[16] and others cogently argue, too closely tied to standard contemporary terms of discourse. Nonetheless, any problems they cause may be as much a symptom of liberal and left failures as their cause. These movements, however haltingly, sometimes point us to a nuanced understanding of the nature of subordinated identities.

Some identity politics is also both broad based and extraordinarily significant in its implications for universal rights. Michael Omi and Howard Winant wish to avoid the perils of suggesting that racism is either an easily discarded anachronism of American politics or a deeply embedded and virtually irreversible attribute of some human beings.[17] In their view, race is instantiated in American life through both cultural symbols and institutional practices, which interact with each other. Racial practices in turn evolve over time, and take more or less virulent forms. Today, for example, formal legal segregation in education and real estate practices have ended, all to the good. Nevertheless, because of extralegal discrimination, African Americans remain underrepresented in good housing or jobs. That fact is then used by some to "prove" the innate inferiority of specific individuals "who happen to be black." Colin Powell and Condoleezza Rice, in telling their own stories, remind us that even their considerable talents would not have landed them in their present jobs without ongoing political efforts to counter the legacy of race and gender.

To see the overall impact of race and gender in American life it is worth reviewing a little history. From the earliest days on our shores, the racialization of differences has played a role in sustaining our social order. Race, gender, and class have always been complexly interwoven in the continuous and ever porous process of identity formation. A group of refugees from Europe's religious wars wished to see themselves as God's chosen people. Fearful of death and living in a turbulent world, they sought to establish their distinctiveness both from the native peoples and medieval traditions. They regarded their ability to transform nature as proof of their excellence in God's eyes. To buttress their claim and to ease their anxieties about the truth of their goals and their purposes, men strove to distinguish themselves from women, viewed as limited by the exigencies of child rearing, and men and women from the more collectivist and "steady state" societies upon whom they in fact depended for many goods. Men placed women and natives in a "natural" hierarchy of race and gender, regarding them as not simply different but as other. They grounded this hierarchy on perceived physical differences, which were then sketched and catalogued to buttress the scheme. Though even this process proved to be problematic, it was used to lend legitimacy to the whole social ontology. The very hostilities produced through such encounters further encouraged efforts to treat difference as otherness to be reformed or eliminated.

Fast-forward to the New Deal, where the politics of race and gender played a crucial and deleterious role in the evolution of the original Social Security legislation. As Linda Gordon has pointed out,[18] Franklin D. Roosevelt's decision to exclude seasonal and domestic workers from the old age program and his devolution of so many responsibilities to the states for unemployment insurance and welfare reflected his unwillingness to challenge the highly racialized southern labor system and the southern Democrats on whom he relied. The existence of welfare as a means-tested program and the inadequate, state-run unemployment compensation system are consequences of political decisions based on race and gender politics and limited the universality of the programs adopted. A high social and political price was paid for Roosevelt's unwillingness to take on the southern conservatives, a task which Gordon feels might have been possible in the 1930s. Broad and truly universal rights could not be achieved without understanding and addressing the origins and legacy of race and gender inequalities.

Naturalized categories of race and gender also must not be reinscribed through seemingly liberal reform. Programs to aid the dispossessed are more likely to survive if they are aspects of programs designed and defended in terms of their ability to address universal needs and concerns. That is a very important political consideration. Nonetheless, achieving genuine universality itself may still require confrontation with historic conceptions of, and oppressions based upon race, gender, and sexual orientation. For example, if stereotypes of African American families as more lazy or dissolute than white families and therefore worthy of more police scrutiny are not challenged, those stereotypes become entrenched and grow—in part from the effects of the disproportionate police scrutiny itself.

In order to combat such practices, one must often gather data along racial lines, thereby lending at least temporary legitimacy to the concept of race itself. Yet to lend temporary legitimacy to race in an effort to move toward genuine universality is an instance of what Gayatri Spivak calls "strategic essentialism,"[19] and the case for such a strategy seems compelling as long as we remain attuned to its risks.

Considerations regarding universality neither rule in nor rule out, in principle, targeted programs to help those who have suffered and still suffer discrimination. To take one example, focus on affirmative action as the solution to racism and sexism inevitably places inordinate economic and psychic burden for social change on poor and working-class white males. The message to them, often given by liberals, is that white working-class distress is not really as important a problem as extending a helping hand to deserving minorities. This subtext to these white males that they've earned their fate is a recipe for resentments and entrenchment of racialized identities. While identity-based rights claims should be seriously considered and respected, so should the discontents of others. Those who advance or benefit from them are not inherently more virtuous, nor are they natural victims permanently in need of help.

In this context Joanne Barkan argues that progressives should

> drop the defensiveness about scrutinizing individual programs. Affirmative action begs for democratic management—for careful design and monitoring by the people who live with it. When a fair evaluation shows a program to be ineffective, fraud-ridden, wasteful, or unjust, the left should endorse revamping or dropping it.[20]

A similar sensibility can be applied in other arenas, such as voting rights. It has become a commonplace to argue that although African Americans may not have achieved economic justice, at least they enjoy political equality. This assertion needs to be questioned because the ultimate manifestation and instrument of demonization is the denial of effective political voice through historical and contemporary electoral arrangements. After too many instances of illegal disenfranchisement in 2000 in Florida, we cannot even take for granted the formal right to cast the ballot.

Lani Guinier has famously argued that white electoral privilege is entrenched through formally race-neutral districting and, more basically, through the winner-take-all system. She suggests that procedural norms are just as vital as substantive politics because procedure helps to shape substantive outcomes. She argues for a system of cumulative voting in which voters are allowed the same number of votes as there are seats to vote for, but they are not limited to voting for representatives within their geographic district. Joel Olson points out that her system provides citizens with an incentive "to organize alliances to vote as a single block or to form strategic coalitions with other groups to gain mutual benefits." Olson correctly observes that "Guinier's contribution to democratic theory is not her specific proposals . . . but her theoretical orientation. She demonstrates that the tyranny of the white majority remains a central problem of American democracy and shows how it is a problem of privilege and participation as well as one of exclusion and inclusion."[21]

A great strength of both Guinier's and Olson's analyses is that they directly address important and underappreciated burdens of race. Nonetheless, they do so in ways that are politically infeasible and, if successful, would in their way further inscribe racial categories.

The overall challenge is to recognize the contemporary remnants of past exclusions and to present remediation of them as one part of a general program for improvement. There are no easy ways out of the politics of demonization. Yet the enduring commitment of most of our population to democratic dialogue and decision making offers an opening.

A New Democratic Covenant of Becoming

The kind of covenant needed in America today is one that places the burden of change neither solely on structures or laws, nor on individuals, leaders, or parties. We should not absolve individuals of responsibility, nor abstract them out of social, economic, and political context. To do one or the other is a strategy for misunderstanding important reasons for demonization, thereby failing to ease it and perhaps even contributing to it. The essential question as we see it is this. How do we need to change in order to engage in vital public, democratic politics of the kind that is both a good in itself and that best helps us freely prepare for ourselves happy, fulfilling, private lives? How, in other words, can we achieve what seem to be the contradictory goals of seeking consensus and seeking change, what we call a *covenant* of *becoming*?

Our analysis indicates that four commitments are necessary to a new covenant of the kind needed in today's world to fulfill earlier republican aspirations of citizenship. We do not presume these to be the only constituents, but we do think them to be very important.

Commitment to Opportunity

The first commitment is to the Rights of Opportunity that we outlined earlier. Perhaps premier among these is the *real* political equality that forms the democratic basis and encourages political self-respect and mutual respect for all citizens. A covenant without the real participation of most of its citizens in its "founding" and continuous refounding is left wanting in legitimacy. Greater equity, security, freedom, and empowerment of individuals also greatly add to the confidence that decisions taken are done so with greater democratic legitimacy, because more individuals would have a more secure foothold in society.

This overall commitment indicates that we see our society not just as an opportunity society, although we wish it to be that, but as a society that respects far more than one's ability to position oneself to take advantage of opportunities. A more generous notion of what we respect about people allows further pursuit of opportunity with less compromise of self-esteem. Pursuit of opportunity in a context of mutual respect is itself a powerful resource against demonization.

Commitment to Quality of Life

The second commitment is a determined effort by citizens to concentrate political debate on quality-of-life issues, with special emphasis on the relationship between our views and measures of progress to the kind of quality of life we want for ourselves. Regarding demonization specifically, we will want to consider how the pressures of modern work, consumption, and even much "leisure" may find an unfortunate outlet in political resentments. These would be eased, we think, if we commit ourselves to asking questions such as: How can we marshal our material, cultural, and intellectual resources in a way to enhance our well-being as individuals and as society?[22] A polity most clearly focused on how to live well, in its fullest meaning, will be a polity less susceptible to efforts to demonize.

As in Walt Whitman's wish for humanity in *Leaves of Grass,* healthy democracies strive to "contain multitudes," while war, even political wars of words, seeks to obliterate all that departs from its sterile mold. We suggest two additional commitments to help achieve Whitman's wish.

Commitment to Teaching Respect

Third, therefore, we need to deepen our commitment further to a social ethos that teaches self-respect as well as respect for others, regardless of who one is or what one has become. Competition has many positive rewards, both for individuals who succeed and for building the overall economic base of a society. However, it also takes a toll, and not only one in inequity and injustice. This is recognized in myriad self-help books reassuring those of us in the middle class why, in spite of some of our feelings, we're really OK, or explaining why we're afraid to succeed, or pushing us, as TV personality and author Suze Orman does, to "have the courage to be rich."

Jesse Jackson used to engage African American audiences in incantations of "I am Somebody!" to bolster self-esteem damaged by racism. He should not have stopped there. All Americans need to consider how our own esteem is shaped, sometimes prospers, but also is damaged in the vicissitudes of modern life. Too many are already brash, even arrogant one might say, and the real need is old-fashioned respect for others. We don't disagree. Those who really respect themselves, however, we think are the quiet citizen activists working for mutual respect.

We need to give serious thinking, therefore, to the impact on individuals, to the injuries, if you will, of the competitive nature of society, especially as globalization takes a stronger hold. We also need to consider the political and micropolitical fallout from this impact, not restricted to but certainly including the resources it provides for strategies of demonization.

Commitment to Respect for Individualism

Fourth, individualism has always been prized in our society. Respecting individuality in others, and in ourselves, takes more courage than it might seem. The broadest privacy protection from government, corporations, or others remains vital for individual personal and political freedom, especially during times of fear of terrorism. Tolerance of dissent is still the critical constitutional goal. However, an ethos of democracy can broaden beyond this into one in which our first impulse is to give the respect of the benefit of the initial doubt to different ideas and ways of doing things, within reason.[23] We neither celebrate nor demonize that which is different from us. We allow ourselves to be open and take in. Then we decide.

This overall democratic covenant implies a specific stance with regard to itself. Greater individual empowerment will help ensure that even this apparently fine compact does not become oppressive in the eyes of others or look too rusty in the future. Citizens who endorse it, therefore, also need to sign on to the right and responsibility of others to try to unsettle, challenge, or change it, and their own obligation at least to listen.

. . .

These four commitments are interrelated in important ways. Political equality forms the covenant's basis of legitimacy and encourages respect. Equity, security, and empowerment lessen social and economic anxieties and pressures. Together with an ethic respectful of people as people, they can help generate greater mutual respect and self-respect. Centering debate on the quality of life allows us to imagine lives with less anxiety and pressure and to detach our images of self and others from the marketplace of self-worth. A democratic ethic of greater openness strengthens tolerance, mutual respect, and self-respect. Individuals, more secure in themselves, grounded in strong values of human worth, inhabiting less alienating institutions, discussing issues they know really matter, believing they can really do something about problems through democratic institutions they control, will have more self-respect and regard for others and less need to demonize, either to enhance self-worth or to gain political advantage. That is the diagnosis, the ideal, and the hope.

Democracy without Demons

And there is hope, we think, to move away from the politics of resentment and demonization. It begins with the American commitment to political equality as an ideal of political respect: one person, one person's worth of political influence. It is this ideal, more than any other, which provided hope for disenfranchised populations throughout our history that they too could some day become full participants, that peaceful change was possible through democratic participation. That America would prove to be different.

Some argue that a new covenant requires greater commitment to civic engagement and more civil discourse, a renewed faith in republican principles. We agree, with a caveat. The republican practices (not the democratic principles) that we have inherited are an incomplete work, perhaps incomplete in principle. Unfortunately, as things stand now, the political rules are simply unfair. They block fuller participation, encourage too many debates unrepresentative of many citizens' needs, and undermine democratic impulses.

The deficiencies are partly responsible for the reason our present covenant is frayed in the first place, one reason our "democracy" is "on trial," to use Jean Elshtain's phrase.[24] Scolding the weakest among us as the cause of that trial as she sometimes does, however, deflects attention from this essential political fact. While eloquent on the responsibility of citizens, therefore, advocates of a new covenant such as Elshtain also need to be outspoken in advancing the right of those who by any reasonable measure do not yet have real political equality to fully and effectively participate as citizens. Since accountability is appropriate precisely in those circumstances where people do enjoy equitable power, political equality becomes the moral adhesive, the sine qua non, for a new democratic covenant, one that can more fully hold its citizens responsible.

Others on the left argue that our politics can't be reformed until we have achieved a more egalitarian society. That would seem to leave us trapped within the terms of a vicious circle. We believe, however, that reform can be sufficiently protected from social and economic inequalities to be achieved. There is no reason political and social reform cannot proceed apace, indeed there is some reason to believe that trying to advance either alone will fail.

Still others, on the right, fear that an egalitarian society would signal the end of liberty. In politics, however, freedom is already inequitable, with too many people having virtually no chance to influence crucial political decisions that affect their lives. Some, on the left, might fear that an empowered majority could unleash disrespect for difference now buried in powerlessness. Real political equality, however, embedded in a strong constitutional framework that protects rights, within an equitable culture that respects persons as such, can empower individuals to take into their own hands a greater measure of protection of their own liberty, and thereby generate greater respect.

Greater empowerment breeds enhanced self-respect and commands greater respect from others. Recognition of existing inequities breeds greater respect for the powerless, and a more measured self-respect, better guarded against *hubris,* for those with power. Enhanced respect for each encourages greater respect for all, for the community, and for American society. Such respect provides a firm psychological basis for a freshened covenant of democratic possibility based on an old political ideal, while tempering the need to demonize, to single out as deviant or evil. Thus it further protects liberty.

Respect for ourselves and others emboldens the democratic spirit, allowing us to think more clearly, listen more carefully, be more willing to expand the debate and thus debate more fully. It makes us more willing, in turn, to respect decisions because they are more likely to be fair. Respect strengthens our character, which refuses to be defiled, and rejects the temptation to defile others. It eases us from the degraded politics fueled by the politics of resentment toward greater realism and easier generosity. It points toward a democracy without demons, in which all are finally included, and where more want to get involved.

Notes

NOTES TO THE INTRODUCTION

1. Indeed, see "U.S. Attitudes Altered Little by Sept. 11, Pollsters Say," *New York Times,* May 20, 2002, A12.

2. For left-wing paranoia, see, for example, Cheryl Seal, "Do Not Let the Murder of Paul Wellstone Be the Murder of America," November 1, 2002, newsinsider.org/seal/paul_wellstone.html.

3. George F. Will, "Vulgarity at Home," *Washington Post,* February 3, 1998, A17.

4. Robert Scheer, "Media Fall for a Sorry Tale of Leaks and Lies," *Los Angeles Times,* February 3, 1998, 7.

5. We distinguish this sharply from the plausible view that certain agendas should be supported or opposed because of the kinds of "character" they purportedly enable in people who live under their regime.

6. In mythology they are tutelary spirits or immaterial beings "holding a middle place between men and the celestial deities." See, for example, *Webster's Universal Dictionary of the English Language,* vol. 1 (Cleveland and New York: The World Syndicate Publishing Company, 1936), 448, and *The American Heritage Dictionary,* 4th ed. (New York: Houghton-Mifflin, 2001), 232.

7. Symbolic rituals in the past have helped societies understand, indeed, recognize themselves. Sobered by the horrors of the twentieth century, we don't wish to dismiss ancient rites and rituals, even demonology, too cavalierly. Still, demonization both then and now "helps" understanding by too rigidly fixing identities.

8. Thomas L. Friedman, "Wanted: Fanatical Moderates," *New York Times,* November 16, 2003.

9. At the level of political philosophy, this perspective has taken the form of John Rawls's "original position" or the German philosopher Jürgen Habermas's "ideal speech situation." Their work has been subject to wide-ranging critique regarding the inherently contestable nature of their attempts to postulate intersubjective rational standards.

10. For a brief review of the authors' position on some of these issues, see

Tom De Luca, "Introduction," in *The Two Faces of Political Apathy* (Philadelphia: Temple University Press, 1995).

1. James Morone, "Presidential Trystory," *Asbury Park Press,* February 6, 1998, A19.

2. In the eighteenth century, the *Wilkes* case established the sacred nature of personal papers maintained in one's own possession, a protection Jeffrey Rosen claimed, even before 9/11 and the USA Patriot Act, had been watered down, weakening privacy protections. Rosen remarks: "To avoid triggering the onerous warrant requirement for every search, the Court's ill conceived solution was to pretend that lots of obviously unreasonable invasions of personal privacy weren't really searches and seizures in the first place"; Jeffery Rosen, "The End of Privacy," *New Republic,* February 16, 1998, and "Annals of the Law," *New Yorker,* June 1, 1998.

3. Scott McNealy, the chairman, president, and chief executive officer of Sun Microsystems, famously has made similar comments many times. See, for example, "On the Record: Scott McNealy," *San Francisco Chronicle,* September 14, 2003, at http://www.sfgate.com/cgi-bin/article.cgi?file=/chronicle/archive/2003/09/14/BU141353.DTL&type=business.

4. See, for example, Paul M. Sniderman and Thomas Piazza, *The Scar of Race* (Cambridge Mass.: Harvard University Press, 1993); Howard Shuman, Charlotte Steeh, Lawrence Bobo, Maria Krysar, *Racial Attitudes in America: Trends and Interpretations,* rev. ed. (Cambridge Mass.: Harvard University Press, 1998); and Alan Wolfe, *One Nation, After All: What Americans Really Think about God, Country, Family, Racism, Welfare, Immigration, Homosexuality, Work, The Right, The Left and Each Other* (New York: Penguin Books, 1999).

In *Reaching Beyond Race* (Cambridge Mass.: Harvard University Press, 1997), Paul M. Sniderman and Edward G. Carmines find decreases in bigotry and greater tolerance among whites as well as strong opposition to race-based policies. They conclude these can be explained as perceived violation of American ideals of fairness and justice. David O. Sears et al. suggest, however, that current white opposition to racially targeted policies cannot be explained as a product of non–racially motivated political conservatism. They suggest that a new form of "symbolic racism" has taken hold. It has origins both in older-style antiblack attitudes and nonracial conservative attitudes, and mediates the effects of each. But it also constitutes a *new* form of racism. David O. Sears, Collette van Laar, Mary Carrillo, Rick Kosterman, "Is It Really Racism? The Origins of White Americans' Opposition to Race-Targeted Policies," *Public Opinion Quarterly* 26 (February 10, 1997), or at http://www.sscnet.ucla.edu/issr/crisp/april16.pdf.

5. For discussion of some differences between "baby boomers" and "generation X," see Kevin A. Hill, "Generations and Tolerance: Is Youth Really a Liberalizing Factor?" in *After the Boom,* ed. Stephen Bennett and Steven Craig (Lanham, Md.: Rowman and Littlefield, 1997), 107–126. Thomas C. Wilson also reports that racial prejudice toward blacks, Hispanics, Jews, and Asians declined in the post–World War II cohorts. However, "most-recent cohorts" show no additional gains in tolerance and, outside the South, show an increase in prejudice over the post–World War II cohorts. See Thomas C. Wilson, "Cohorts and Prejudice: Whites' Attitudes toward Blacks, Hispanics, Jews and Asians," *Public Opinion Quarterly* 60, no. 2 (Summer 1996), 253–274.

6. See, for example, Richard Fleisher and Jon R. Bond, "Evidence of Increasing Polarization among Ordinary Citizens," in *American Political Parties,* ed. Jeffrey Cohen, Richard Fleisher, and Paul Kantor (Washington, D.C.: CQ Press, 2001), 55–77. They see citizen polarization, although now with a life of its own, as caused and nurtured by efforts of polarized elites to maximize votes in order to prevail in elections; see pp. 72–76.

7. Robert Shogan, *War without End: Cultural Conflict and the Struggle for America's Political Future* (Boulder, Colo.: Westview, 2002), 283.

8. Interview with Robert De Luca, September 21, 2004. See also Barry Newman, "Lords of the Dance: Off to Cooperstown—with Bells On," *Wall Street Journal,* May 17, 2004, A1.

9. We discuss this in chapter 3 on pp. 57–61.

10. For an excellent discussion of this history, see Thomas Byrne and Mary D. Edsall, *Chain Reaction: The Impact of Race, Rights, and Taxes on American Politics* (New York: Norton, 1991). See chapter 10 for their discussion of race-coded language.

11. For two different views on this topic, see Thomas Ferguson and Joel Rogers, *Right Turn: The Decline of the Democrats and the Future of American Politics* (New York: Hill and Wang, 1986); and Byrne and Edsall, *Chain Reaction.*

12. See the work of Robert Putnam for the twentieth-century decline of institutions of civil society that have relevance for political culture and, therefore, the decline of what he calls "social capital." Robert Putnam, *Bowling Alone: The Collapse and Revival of American Community* (New York: Simon and Schuster, 2001).

13. We agree that personal empowerment is impossible without a structure of action that insists on responsibility. However, we reject the demonization of welfare recipients and welfare bureaucrats as if the defect of character of one and the self-interest (and therefore character) of the other created the problem of poverty and are perpetuating it.

14. These works are classics: Thorstein Veblen, *The Theory of the Leisure Class: An Economic Study of Institutions* (New York: New American Library,

1953; originally published in 1899); C. Wright Mills, *White Collar: The American Middle Classes* (New York: Oxford University Press, 1951); Vance Packard, *The Status Seekers: An Exploration of Class Behavior in America and the Hidden Barriers That Affect You, Your Community, Your Future* (New York: D. McKay, 1959). For more recent work, see Juliet Schor, *The Overspent American: Upscaling, Downshifting, and the New Consumer* (New York: Basic Books, 1998); and *Born to Buy: The Commercialized Child and the New Consumer Culture* (New York: Scribner, 2004).

NOTES TO CHAPTER 2

1. When supporters of Vice President George H. W. Bush were accused of racism for using this ad, they countered that Horton, an African American, was a rapist who had been let out on parole under Dukakis and then committed murder. There is little doubt, however, that the ad would have been less politically appealing had Horton been white.

2. For the classic example, see Arthur M. Schlesinger, Jr., *The Imperial Presidency* (Boston: Houghton Mifflin, 1973).

3. Michael Rogin, *Ronald Reagan, the Movie: And Other Episodes in Political Demonology* (Berkeley and Los Angeles: University of California Press, 1987), xiii–xviii.

4. Our emphasis. David Brooks, "The Presidency Wars," *New York Times,* September 30, 2003.

5. James A. Morone, *Hellfire Nation: The Politics of Sin in American History* (New Haven: Yale University Press, 2003), 4.

6. Ibid., 3–4.

7. Ibid., 13–14.

8. Ibid., 7.

9. Ibid., 13–14.

10. Ibid., 33.

11. Ibid., 380–381.

12. Ibid., 407–408.

13. The film uses and breaks with stereotypes. Young women are attracted to older men and are sources of inspiration, of rejuvenation, for those men. Music is the vehicle for articulating the grievances Nina and other victims feel, but it is white, middle-aged Beatty who does the rapping. Nina's African American family appears strong and committed to the welfare of its children in spite of white victimization. There is no "culture of poverty" in her family.

14. Texas law professor Julius Getman's study of a 1980s strike, *The Betrayal of Local 14,* shows much community resentment of irresponsible corporate behavior. It also points to a union leadership and membership badly divided over such questions as owners' prerogatives and how much to cooperate with

management. Such divisions prevented the union from fully implementing the broad corporate campaigns that on some occasions have deterred the worst corporate practices. Many workers feel that business is too big and powerful, but they don't always support political efforts to balance that power. Are they as brainwashed as leftist critique often imagines? A hard claim to maintain in bold face. See Julius Getman, *The Betrayal of Local 14* (Ithaca, N.Y.: ILR Press, 1998.) For a critique of the explanatory power of "false-consciousness," see Tom De Luca, *The Two Faces of Political Apathy* (Philadelphia: Temple University Press, 1995), chaps. 12 and 10.

15. In today's world of political advertising, spin, and multimedia image management, in which politics must compete for attention in the media with all sorts of diversions and with advertising, political language and conventional film language may be coming closer together.

16. Our knowledge of genre allows us to understand when the character is doing something conventional for the genre, even if heroic, or something exceptional, something of importance, even if cowardly.

17. However, it is a world whose constructed nature, artifice, and arbitrariness are usually hidden in order to appear neutral. Some critics think this loss of distancing between audience and film is itself an ideological danger of the medium precisely because it creates a simultaneous illusion of neutrality and reality. See Jacques Aumont, Alain Bergala, Michel Marie, Marc Vernet, *Aesthetics of Film* (Austin: University of Texas Press, 1992), translated and revised by Richard Neupert, 123.

18. This is what Jean-Pierre Oudart called *l'effet de réel* (the real effect) and distinguished from the reality effect, *l'effet de réalité*.

NOTES TO CHAPTER 3

1. We fully understand, of course, that much demonizing rhetoric has to do with the "game of politics." Exposing manipulative uses of demonizing tactics is important, but it can also divert our eyes from broader cultural and political sources of demonization. George Lakoff thinks that important differences between liberal and conservative thinking lie in the way each "frames" issues, reflecting different moral perspectives and outlooks on life. In general, conservative framing is more conducive to articulating values and liberal framing to policy positions. See for example, *Moral Politics: How Liberals and Conservatives Think* (Chicago: University of Chicago Press, 2002).

2. Some defenders of Clinton regarding sexual harassment charges were on offense when it came to Anita Hill's accusations against Clarence Thomas.

3. Daniel Bell, *The Cultural Contradictions of Capitalism* (New York: Basic Books, 1978), xx. The pagination with Roman numerals refers to the foreword to this printing, in which he explains this work, originally published in 1976, es-

pecially reacting to the charge that "those whose work decries those aspects of contemporary culture which make cheap claims to 'liberation,' often find themselves labeled as 'neo-conservative,'" xi.

4. Ibid., 84.

5. Ibid.

6. Ibid., 250fn. One can't help but wonder if his cultural critique is not more fundamental than his economic critique. He thinks it is culture, after all, that now takes the initiative in change; the economy is too bureaucratic and now follows culture; and modernist culture has replaced religion as the prime legitimation for social behavior.

7. Fifteen years ago the United States became a debtor nation and to date has accumulated $3 trillion in debt to foreign creditors; last year alone, American businesses, households, and the federal government borrowed $540 billion from abroad. See William Greider, "The Serpent That Ate America's Lunch," *The Nation*, May 10, 2004, 13.

8. See, for example, David G. Blanchflower and Andrew Oswald, "Well-Being over Time in Britain and the USA," *Journal of Public Economics* 88, nos. 7–8 (July 2004): 1359–1386. Also see Paul Wachtel, *The Poverty of Affluence: A Psychological Portrait of the American Way of Life* (Philadelphia: New Society Publishers, 1989).

9. Good as they were, GNP growth, productivity growth, and to some degree unemployment rates, recorded at the *height* of the Clinton boom, only equaled the averages of the post–World War II period.

10. Stanley Aronowitz, *Just around the Corner: The Paradox of the Jobless Recovery* (Philadelphia: Temple University Press, 2005), chap. 4. The references are taken from Aronowitz's manuscript prior to publication.

11. Lester Thurow, *The Future of Capitalism* (New York: W. Morrow, 1996).

12. According to Aronowitz, when "missing workers" are added, the percentage leaps to 13.5. *Just around the Corner,* chap. 4.

13. In 2004 the poverty level was closer to $20,000, and even in rural areas and the Deep South, few households could make ends meet at the official poverty-level income. According to a United Way survey, for example, in 2002 the minimum comfort income for a Queens, New York, household of four was $43,000.

14. Theda Skocpol, *Boomerang: Clinton's Health Security Effort and the Turn against Government in U.S. Politics* (New York: Norton, 1997), 184.

15. Ron Pollack in a speech, "Health Care," at "What We Stand For: Ideas and Values to Take Back America," May 15, 2004, New York University.

16. David Himmelstein, ibid.

17. Alan Elsner, *Gates of Injustice: The Crisis in America's Prisons* (Upper

Saddle River, N.J.: Financial Times, Prentice Hall, 2004), 12, 27–28. As Elsner points out, this figure is "more than the combined worldwide workforces of General Motors, Ford and Wal-Mart, the three biggest corporate employers in the country." Although education is seen as a major way to avoid running afoul of the law, even blue-state California spends more on prisons than on its entire higher-education budget.

18. Juliet B. Schor, *The Overworked American: The Unexpected Decline of Leisure* (New York: Basic Books, 1993), chap. 2.

19. "U.S. Economy Grows 4.2%; War Spending Provides Push," *New York Times,* April 30, 2004, C1. Without increased war spending during this quarter, the increase would be 3.5 percent. Although economists now often refer to Gross Domestic Product (GDP), GNP is still in popular usage.

20. Herman E. Daly and John B. Cobb, Jr., *For the Common Good: Redirecting the Economy toward Community, the Environment, and a Sustainable Future* (Boston: Beacon Press, 1989), 418–420.

21. Ibid., 372.

22. Marc Breslow, "Is the U.S. Making Progress?" *Dollars and Sense,* March/April 1996, 16–21.

23. Ibid.

24. Juliet B. Schor, *The Overspent American: Upscaling, Downshifting, and the New Consumer* (New York: Basic Books, 1998), chap. 5.

25. The idea of equal opportunity, as John Schaar shows, is not inconsistent with the idea of hierarchy. In fact, it seeks to create hierarchy based on merit, hence the term "aristocracy of merit." See also Michael Young's *The Rise of the Meritocracy* (London: Thames and Hudson, 1958), a work that explores the consequences for society of such an aristocracy. The theoretical and practical issues surrounding equal opportunity are profound. To take one example, does it require an end to inheritance and all other advantages of birth, thereby requiring equality of (nongenetic) condition (whatever that means), the idea with which it is most often contrasted in order to prove its worth? Does it require genetic equality, whatever that could mean?

26. John H. Schaar, "Equal Opportunity and Beyond," in *Equality: Selected Readings,* ed. Louis P. Pojman and Robert Westmoreland (New York: Oxford University Press, 1997), 139–141. This essay was originally published in *Nomos IX: Equality,* ed. J. Chapman and R. Pennock (New York: Atherton Press, 1967). For Schaar, "equal opportunity" accepts the current rules of the race, including definitions of which talents are meritorious. Therefore it legitimizes existing inequality and promotes inequality based on meritocracy in which 'the natural' and social aristocracies would be identical." Ibid., 139.

27. Ibid., 140–141. For Schaar, the equal-opportunity principle is inherently undemocratic: "The democrat rejects in principle the thesis that oligarchy of

merit (special competence) is in some way different in kind from oligarchy of any other sort. . . . The democrat who understands his commitments holds oligarchy itself to be obnoxious, not merely oligarchy of this or that kind." Ibid., 142–143. As we argue in the conclusion, however, there can be equality to "rights of opportunity" that mitigate rather than deepen excesses of competition and their material and psychological burdens.

28. In Schaar's words, the equal-opportunity principle "certainly leaves the losers with no external justification for their failures, and no amount of trying can erase the large element of cruelty from any social doctrine which does that." Ibid., 140.

29. Ibid., 144–145.

30. Ibid., 140.

NOTES TO CHAPTER 4

1. Stanley B. Greenberg, *The Two Americas: Our Current Political Deadlock and How to Break It* (New York: St. Martin's Press, 2004), 21. This discussion is largely taken from chapter one of this text.

2. Jeffrey M. Jones, "Bush Ratings Show Historical Levels of Polarization: Six in 10 Republicans strongly approve; 6 in 10 Democrats strongly disapprove," The Gallup Organization, June 4, 2004.

3. David G. Lawrence, "On the Resurgence of Party Identification in the 1990s," in *American Political Parties: Decline or Resurgence?* ed. Jeffrey E. Cohen, Richard Fleisher, and Paul Kantor (Washington, D.C.: CQ Press, 2001), 52.

4. Richard Fleisher and Jon R. Bond, "Evidence of Increasing Polarization among Ordinary Citizens," in *American Political Parties*; see pp. 57, 64–65. See also Jon R. Bond and Richard Fleisher, *Polarized Politics: Congress and the President in a Polarized Era* (Washington, D.C.: Congressional Quarterly Books, 2000). Also see Paul DiMaggio, John Evans, and Bethany Bryson, "Have Americans' Social Attitudes Become More Polarized?" *American Journal of Sociology* 102, no. 3 (November 1996): 690–755.

5. Ibid., 71–73. Even those who were part of the post–New Deal cohort (those born after 1947) and entered politics less partisan because of the effects of Vietnam and Watergate became more partisan beginning in the Reagan years.

6. Greenberg, *Two Americas*, 21.

7. It should be noted, however, that independents vote at significantly lower rates than either Republican or Democratic identifiers. See, for example, *National Election Survey Guide to Public Opinion and Electoral Behavior, 1948–2002*, table 6A.2.2, "Voter Turnout 1948–2002: Percent among Demographic Groups Who Responded—'Yes, voted,'" which can be found at http://www .umich.edu/~nes/nesguide/2ndtable/t6a_2_2.htm.

8. Greenberg, *Two Americas*, 25.

9. Donald Green, Bradley Palmquist and Eric Schickler, *Partisan Hearts and Minds* (New Haven: Yale University Press, 2004). Reviewing this literature was inspired by David Brooks's thoughtful piece, "Circling the Wagons," *New York Times*, June 5, 2004. The classic on this subject, Angus Campbell et al.'s 1960 *The American Voter* (repr., Chicago: University of Chicago Press, 1980).

10. This discussion of Damasio is taken from William E. Connolly, *Neuropolitics: Thinking, Culture, Speed* (Minneapolis: University of Minnesota Press, 2002), chap. 1, and especially 32–36.

11. Ibid., 28.

12. Ibid., 20.

13. Edward N. Wolff, *Top Heavy: A Study of the Increasing Inequality of Wealth in America* (New York: Twentieth Century Fund Report, 1995). Wolff's study effectively challenges such defenses of inequality as those advanced by Michael Novak, "What Wealth Gap?" *Wall Street Journal*, July 11, 1995, A16.

14. Edward Wolff, "Changes in Household Wealth in the 1980s and 1990s in the U.S.," Levy Institute Working Paper No. 407, May 2004.

15. The international comparisons were compiled by International Institute for Democracy and Electoral Assistance and can be found at http://www.fairvote.org/turnout/intturnout.htm. Comparison of U.S. turnout over time was done by Curtis Gans of the Center the Study of the American Electorate. See his report "President Bush, Mobilization Drives Propel Turnout to Post-1968 Highs; Kerry, Democratic Weakness Shown" at http://www.fairvote.org/reports/CSAE2004electionreport.pdf. See also Mark N. Franklin, "Electoral Participation," in Comparing Democracies, ed. L. LeDuc, R. Niemi, and P. Norris (Thousand Oaks, Calif.: Sage Publications, 1996), 218.

16. Franklin, "Comparing Democracies," 230.

17. Frances Fox Piven and Richard A. Cloward, *Why Americans Don't Vote* (New York: Pantheon, 1988), 119. Our emphasis.

18. Margaret Conway reports that when other social characteristics are controlled for, "voter turnout increases with age." See *Political Participation in the United States,* 2d ed. (Washington, D.C.: C.Q. Press, 1991), 17. According to the census, in 2000 turnout increased with age until age seventy-five, when it started to slip.

19. According to National Election Survey (NES) data using voting-age population, the gap in percentage turnout between whites and blacks was 12% in 1992 and 1994, 11% in 1996, 1% in 1998, 2% in 2000, and 8% in 2002. For the year 2000 the Census Bureau reports that, among citizens, blacks were 5% less likely, Hispanics 16.7% less likely, and Asian-Pacific Islanders 18.5% less likely to votes than whites. In 2000, according to the census, women voted at a rate of 2.6% more than men, while the NES has men voting 4% more than women. The gender gap has largely disappeared for some time, but according to

NES data in 2002 men voted at a rate of 10% more than women. NES data is at http://www.umich.edu/~nes/nesguide/2ndtable/t6a_2_2.htm. For the Census Bureau's data, see Amie Jamieson, Hyon B. Shin, and Jennifer Day, *Current Population Reports*, "Voting and Registration in the Election of 2000: Population Characteristics" at http://www.census.gov/prod/2002/pubs/p20-542.pdf. For an argument that failure to mobilize black turnout in the 1970s and 1980s led to an erosion of the gains made in the 1960s, see Steven J. Rosenstone and Mark John Hansen, *Mobilization, Participation and Democracy in America* (New York: Macmillan, 1993), 219–224.

20. Jamieson et al., "Voting and Registration." Census turnout figures are still based upon self-reports of respondents and tend to inflate turnout. Since here we are interested in ratios and measures of change (difference with a base year), inflated turnout figures should not affect our results very much. Since the census does not divide respondents into income quintiles, we estimated turnout for the top and bottom quintiles. We did so by adding or subtracting respondents from adjacent income categories until we reached the right number for a quintile. To find the percentage of voter turnout within a quintile we did the following: (a) In quintiles for which we had to borrow respondents, we added the number of reported voters for each income category within the quintile to our estimate of the number of voters from the borrowed income category and divided by the number of respondents constituting a quintile in that year. We arrived at an estimate of the number of voters we needed to borrow by multiplying the average percentage turnout for the category from which we borrowed by the number of respondents we borrowed to complete the quintile. For example, in 2000, to create the low-income quintile we first used income categories of $15,000–24,999 and below. We then borrowed enough respondents from the $25,000–$34,999 category to complete the quintile and multiplied that number by the rate of turnout for that income category. (b) Where we had to "subtract" respondents (for example, in 2000 the over-$75,000 category constitutes more than a quintile), we simply calculated or used the turnout rate for the upper/lower income category as the estimate for the quintile rate. For every year, we used voting-age population rather than citizen population to calculate turnout, consistent with the census data reporting format for presidential years prior to 2000. In 2000 the census began reporting turnout based on the citizen population, and we used the data it provided to calculate turnout for the voting-age population. In all years, we excluded those who didn't report income. In 2000, for example, this comprised approximately 14% of the voting-age population. The reported turnout of this category was lower than that of the average turnout for the general population; for example, in 2000 it was 48%, compared to the average turnout of 57%. Because we are interested here in ratios, using voting-age population, estimating the turnout of those borrowed or "subtracted," and excluding those who didn't report income should not affect the

value of the ratios as a guide to voting equality. If anything, the assumptions we make in estimating the turnout of those we borrow or "subtract" and our exclusion of the relatively low turnout nonreporters of income would tend to have a slightly conservative influence on our estimates of inequality.

21. The census data are for all voting-age persons.

22. In their analysis of class bias in turnout, Leighley and Nagler conclude that income-based voting inequality, while large and fluctuating, has shown no marked increase in presidential elections from 1964 to 1988. They believe only statistics such as the Gini coefficient, which analyze turnout among all percentile groups relative to one another, should be used. Such measures, however, show significantly increased inequality only if turnout inequality increases all along the income ladder and may underplay trends that occur primarily within the very bottom and/or top income categories. In any case, they nevertheless show large inequalities in voting participation. See Jan E. Leighley and Jonathan Nagler, "Socioeconomic Class Bias in Turnout, 1964–1988: The Voters Remain the Same," *American Political Science Review* 86, no. 3 (September 1992): 729.

23. For off-year elections, the ratio is generally lower, indicating greater inequality.

24. Please note that the differences in the declines in participation over time between top and bottom quintiles from the baseline are often not great. Yet inequality still increases. Instead of an artifact of this methodology, we think this reflects diminished *voting strength* at the bottom. Deducting relatively equal percentages from already unequal turnouts means that *the lowest income quintile is losing a larger amount of its smaller share of the vote.* Joe the Bookie once explained it to us this way: "Look Doc[s], suppose I've got a gang of fifty guys and you've got a gang of fifty guys. Now let's say I knock off thirty of your guys and you knock off ten of mine. I'm in good shape, I've got 80 percent left. You've only got 40 percent. I've got *twice* as much muscle. Now let's suppose we each knock off another 20 percent of each other's men from where we started, so you've got 20 percent left. But I've got 60 percent. So I wind up with three times your muscle even though we both just lost 20 percent. It's the same with voting." Tom De Luca, "Joe the Bookie and the Voting Class Gap," *American Demographics,* November 1998, 28.

25. Rosenstone and Hansen, *Mobilization,* 135, 136.

26. Ruy Teixeira, *Why Americans Don't Vote: Turnout Decline in the United States, 1960–1984* (New York: Greenwood Press, 1987), 34, 36, 9. Failure to engage in analysis of the changing meaning of educational categories over time may be a weakness here. For a discussion of Teixeira's work, see Tom De Luca, *The Two Faces of Political Apathy* (Philadelphia: Temple University Press, 1995), 203–210.

27. Sidney Verba and Gary R. Orren, *Equality in America: The View from the Top* (Cambridge, Mass.: Harvard University Press, 1985), 9–17.

28. Rosenstone and Hansen, *Mobilization,* 43–45.

29. Rosenstone and Hansen report that "Blacks and women encounter an 'ascriptive barrier' to communication with predominantly white, male, public officials," psychologically doubting white male politicians will be sympathetic. "African-Americans are less likely to be central to the electoral coalitions of white politicians, and office holders are therefore less likely to mobilize them to express their opinions." Rosenstone and Hansen, *Mobilization,* 75–79. For Latinos the problem is compounded by language and/or recent immigration.

30. Teixeira, *Why Americans Don't Vote,* 3–4.

31. Rosenstone and Hansen, *Mobilization,* our emphasis, 248.

32. Ibid., 241.

33. These claims, however, must always be understood within historical context. Claims are relative to some notion of what is appropriately to be considered political within a given era. Thus, broader economic justice claims can be made today than in the nineteenth century, when overall turnout of eligible voters was far higher.

34. Rosenstone and Hansen, *Mobilization,* 248.

35. Bureau of Labor Statistics, 2001.

36. John B. Judis, "The Contrast with K Street," *New Republic,* December 4, 1995, 22.

37. Ibid.

38. Theda Skocpol, *Boomerang: Clinton's Health Security Effort and the Turn against Government in U.S. Politics* (New York: Norton, 1996), 86–87.

39. Theda Skocpol, *Diminished Democracy: From Membership to Management in American Civic Life* (Norman: University of Oklahoma Press, 2003), 12.

40. Ibid., 13.

41. Quoted in ibid., 232.

42. Ibid., 233–234.

43. See Thomas Edsall, *Chain Reaction: The Impact of Race, Rights, and Taxes on American Politics* (New York: Norton, 1991), and E. J. Dionne, *Why Americans Hate Politics* (New York: Simon and Schuster, 1991), for discussions of these effects.

44. See Theda Skocpol, *Social Policy in the United States* (Princeton, N.J.: Princeton University Press, 1995), and *The Missing Middle: Working Families and the Future of American Social Policy* (Princeton, N.J.: Princeton University Press, 1995). Less well known about the American state is that well before the New Deal it did provide provision for various needs, for example, post–Civil War pensions for Union (but not Confederate) soldiers, and Shepard Towner provision of health services for young mothers.

45. Frances Fox Piven and Richard A. Cloward, *Regulating the Poor: The Functions of Public Welfare,* 2d ed. (New York: Vintage, 1993).

46. See Elsner, *Gates of Injustice,* especially chaps. 3–7.

47. Ibid., 21.

48. Ibid.

49. Ibid.

50. Alabama, Florida, Iowa, Kentucky, Mississippi, Nevada, Virginia, Wyoming, Arizona (second felony), Maryland (second violent felony), Washington (convicted before 1984), and Tennessee (some old convictions). See The Brennan Center, Editorial Memorandum: "An Unhealthy Democracy," July 2, 2003, at http://www.brennancenter.org/programs/downloads/ed_memo_johnso _v_bush.pdf.

51. A 2002 Harris survey revealed that 80 percent of the public approves of restoring voting rights to ex-felons, although that rate drops depending on how severe the crime was. Nevertheless, the only category in the survey that received less than majority support was restoration of the vote to people still in prison, with roughly only one-third supporting that proposition. The results are summarized at http://www.sentencingproject.org/pdfs/ManzaBrooksUggenSummary .pdf.

52. All Kennedy references are to Elsner, *Gates of Injustice,* 216–218.

53. Bonnie Honig, *Democracy and the Foreigner* (Princeton, N.J.: Princeton University Press, 2001), 76.

54. David Cole, *Enemy Aliens: Double Standards and Constitutional Freedoms in the War on Terrorism* (New York: New Press, 2003), 26.

55. Ibid., 5–6.

56. Ibid., 6–7.

57. Ibid., 91–92.

58. Ibid., 7–8, and chaps. 8–11.

NOTES TO CHAPTER 5

1. For one of the most powerful arguments in this vein, see Michael Sandel, *Democracy's Discontent: America in Search of a Public Philosophy* (Cambridge, Mass.: Belknap Press, 1996). Sandel attributes the rise of divisive identity politics, desertion of the political process, and the sense that things are out of control to a change in the conception of freedom—to demanding and having choices rather than responsibly participating in the shaping of a common vision, as in the older civic republican tradition. Sandel identifies the key moment in the transition in the late New Deal's advocacy of government job creation and economic growth as the key goal of public policy. However, Sandel underplays the social divisions during the pre–New Deal civic republican era he celebrates. Today's cultural wars, even identity politics, are hardly new, and the New Deal was less a break from the past than he realizes. Moreover, important aspects of the changes, for example, away from small-town life and small businesses, were ig-

nited by contradictions and discontent with those older "republican" forms. Although Sandel suggests that communities can become unduly repressive, the pluralism he offers is somewhat static, as pieces from a unitary pie, as though all of the injustices involved in earlier renditions of the common good have now been resolved, and that the new alignment of people and power has not produced other subterranean discontents.

2. Jean Elshtain uses this idea to refer to efforts by gay groups to have their lifestyle validated through the political process. We see no reason this can't be applied to all groups, including those that revalidate themselves by denying legitimacy to others. See Jean Elshtain, *Democracy on Trial* (New York: Basic Books, 1995).

3. Sometimes such rhetoric may indicate major clashes of interest that defy compromise. That such contests surface may be a sign of democratic vitality; that they cannot be resolved may point to a future source of democratic dissolution.

4. Michael Sherry, *In the Shadow of War: The United States since the 1930s* (New Haven: Yale University Press, 1995).

5. There is, of course, a broad range of "otherness" from "domestic" to "foreign." One of the goals of constructing "others" is to make those who were participants of a society into a kind of foreigner and, at worst, a traitor.

6. American members of the Communist Party were easy targets because they were domestic, "natural" Americans, but seemingly allied themselves to a foreign power and what many perceived as a foreign ideology.

7. A May 20–23, 2004, CBS poll reported that 70 percent of registered voters responded "no" to the question "Do you think the issue of gay marriage should be part of this year's election campaign, or not?" For a listing of the results of numerous polls on these issues going back several years, see PollingReport.com: Law and Civil Rights at http://www.pollingreport.com/civil.htm.

8. Often lost in the framing and heat of the debate over gay marriage are other issues that flow from the question of whether the state should "endorse" gay marriage. Should the state be in the business of sanctioning private relationships at all? Should public sanctioning properly be left to religious or other organizations within civil society? Should the state sponsor legal and tax disadvantages that single people bear, especially those without children, whether gay or straight?

9. "Among Wealthy Nations . . . U.S. Stands Alone in Its Embrace of Religion," Pew Research Center for the People and the Press, December 19, 2002, at http://people-press.org/reports/display.php3?ReportID=167.

10. "Origins of Human Life," Gallup Poll, August 24–26, 1999. N = 1,028 adults nationwide. MoE = ±3. The question was: "Which of the following statements come closest to your views on the origin and development of human beings? [Rotate:] (1) Human beings have developed over millions of years from less

advanced forms of life, but God guided this process. (2) Human beings have developed over millions of years from less advanced forms of life, but God had no part in this process. (3) God created human beings pretty much in their present form at one time within the last 10,000 years or so." 47 percent agreed with (3); 40 percent agreed with (1); 9 percent agreed with (2); 4 percent had no opinion. Gallup found similar results in 1997, 1993, and 1982.

11. Fox News/Opinion Dynamics Poll, August 25–26, 1999. N = 902 registered voters nationwide. MoE ±3. "Which do you think is more likely to actually be the explanation for the origin of human life on Earth: the theory of evolution as outlined by Darwin and other scientists, the biblical account of creation as told in the Bible, or are both true?" 26 percent said both, while 9 percent were not sure.

12. William E. Connolly, *Political Theory and Modernity* (Oxford, U.K.: Basil Blackwell, 1988), 138.

13. Ibid.

14. Connolly, *Political Theory and Modernity,* 146.

15. Julius Kovesi, *Moral Notions* (London: Routledge, Kegan and Paul, 1967).

16. To say demonization always inhibits discovery is to overstate the case by modernizing it. First, we are using the term in the way we defined it in chapter 1. Beyond this more restricted definition, note that demonology may have been and may be part of important symbolic rituals that help societies understand, indeed, recognize themselves. A kind of discovery may even occur when new demons are recognized. Being modern writers yet sobered by the horrors of the twentieth century, we don't wish to dismiss ancient rites and rituals too cavalierly.

17. We sharply distinguish such a strategy of demonization from proper criticism of communism and, it goes without saying, terrorism.

18. Bonnie Honig, *Democracy and the Foreigner* (Princeton, N.J.: Princeton University Press, 2001), 73–74.

19. Ibid., 76.

20. Ibid., 12.

21. Ibid., 7.

22. Ibid., 4.

23. Ibid., 97. She continues: "That is, nativist ideologies may shape, direct, and accelerate the xenophobia in question. But contra Rogers Smith, it is misleading to see them as the external corrupters of an otherwise fundamentally egalitarian and tolerant liberal tradition whose only weakness is its failure to inspire in communitarian terms. Indeed . . . Smith's characterization of the problem as one of liberalism's corruption at the hands of an outside agitator itself replays the xenophobic script that Smith is out to criticize."

24. Ibid., 76.

25. Ibid., 94.
26. Ibid., 76.
27. Ibid., 120—121.
28. Ibid., 114.

NOTES TO CHAPTER 6

1. See, for example, Margaret Crenshaw, "The Logic of Terrorism: Terrorist Behavior as a Product of Strategic Choice," in *Origins of Terrorism: Psychologies, Ideologies, Theologies, States of Mind,* ed. Walter Laqueur (Washington, D.C.: The Woodrow Wilson Center Press, 1998). For other perspectives, see in *Origins of Terrorism:* Jerold Post, "Terrorist Psycho-Logic: Terrorist Behavior as a Product of Psychological Forces"; Albert Bandura, "Mechanisms of Moral Disengagement"; and Ariel Merari, "The Readiness to Kill and Die and Suicidal Terrorism in the Middle East."

2. Quoted in Bruce Hoffman, *Inside Terrorism* (New York: Columbia University Press, 1998), 161.

3. Ibid., 163.

4. Ibid., 94–95.

5. The definitions of terrorism on the following pages are taken from Jonathan R. White, *Terrorism: An Introduction, 2002 Update,* 4th ed. (Belmont, Calif.: Wadsworth, 2003), 12.

6. Ibid., 8.

7. Ibid., 7, 8.

8. Ibid., 9. See also Martha Crenshaw, ed., *Terrorism, Legitimacy, and Power: The Consequences of Political Violence,* reprint ed. (Middletown, Conn.: Wesleyan University Press, 1986).

9. White, *Terrorism,* 8–9.

10. To those on the left who were especially concerned about the death of immigrant wait-staffs in Windows on the World, because, unlike business persons, they are not "agents of global capitalism," Noam Chomsky sets the record straight: "As for the bin Laden network, they have as little concern for globalization and cultural hegemony as they do for the poor and oppressed people of the Middle East who they have been severely harming for years. They tell us what their concerns are loud and clear: they are fighting a Holy War against the corrupt, repressive, and 'un-Islamist' regimes of the region, and their supporters, just as they fought a Holy War against the Russians in the 1980s and are now doing the same in Chechnya, western China, Egypt. . . . Bin Laden himself has probably never even heard of 'globalization.'" See *9-11* (New York: Seven Stories Press, 2001), 32.

11. Quoted in ibid., 16.

12. George Kateb, chap. 1, "On Political Evil," in *The Inner Ocean: Individual and Democratic Culture* (Ithaca, N.Y.: Cornell University Press, 1992), 204.

13. Ibid., 220.

14. Ibid., 205–206, 209–210, 215–216.

15. Ibid., 213.

16. Ibid., 212.

17. Ibid., 210.

18. William E. Connolly, "The Problem of Evil," in *Identity/Difference: Democratic Negotiations of Political Paradox* (Ithaca, N.Y.: Cornell University Press, 1991), 7.

19. Ibid., 8–9.

20. No doubt our efforts to integrate China into the world economic system, and China's growing economic importance, have also played a major role. Nevertheless, see "China: Human Rights Concerns in Xinjiang," *Human Rights Watch Backgrounder,* October 2001. http://www.hrw.org/backgrounder/asia/china-bck1017.htm. This report, produced by Human Rights Watch, explains: "Beijing has long claimed to be confronted with 'religious extremist forces' and 'violent terrorists' in Xinjiang, a vast region one-sixth of China's land area. Xinjiang has a population of 18 million and is home to numerous Turkic-speaking Muslim ethnic groups, of which the Uighurs, numbering eight million, are the largest." Because of the presence of approximately 22 Uighurs in Guantanamo it had been reported that Chinese interrogators were working with the American military and intelligence services at that base; Amnesty International had been very concerned that these men would be repatriated to China where they could face torture or execution, but in August 2004 Secretary of State Colin Powell said they would not be.

21. Edward Wong, "Iraq Is a Hub for Terrorism, However You Define It," *New York Times,* June 20, 2004.

22. Nancy Chang, *Silencing Political Dissent: How Post–September 11 Anti-Terrorism Measures Threaten Our Civil Liberties* (New York: Seven Stories Press, 2002), 44–45.

23. Peter Bergen, "This Link between Islamic Zealot and Secular Fascist Just Doesn't Add Up," *Guardian,* January 30, 2003.

24. For one thing, they believed conservative Republicans sometimes turned a blind eye toward repression in the Soviet bloc. According to Diggins, Anatoli Dobrinin, former Soviet ambassador to the United Nations, pointed out that United States military spending was far less important than the decision of Ronald Reagan in the later stages of his presidency to establish better relations with Russia, a move that allowed Gorbachev the internal political space to move toward reforms. And reform was surely needed because by the late 1980s Ronald Reagan's "Evil Empire" was a decrepit shell.

25. John Diggins, "The -Ism That Failed," *The American Prospect* 14, no. 11 (December 2003), at http://www.prospect.org/print/v14/11/diggins-j.html.

26. Philip Shenon and Christopher Marquis, "Panel Finds No Qaeda-Iraq Tie; Describes a Wider Plot for 9/11," *New York Times,* June 17, 2004. See Staff Statement 15 at http://www.9-11commission.gov/staff_statements/staff_statement_15.pdf.

27. David E. Sanger and Robin Toner, "Bush and Cheney Talk Strongly of Qaeda Links with Hussein," *New York Times,* June 18, 2004.

28. Philip Shenon and Richard W. Stevenson, "Leaders of 9/11 Panel Ask Cheney for Reports," *New York Times,* June 19, 2004.

29. Why did the United States go to war with Iraq? The question is especially perplexing since opposition to war extended beyond the usual suspects. Among America's elite ranks, war skeptics included former members of the national security establishment and even General H. Norman Schwarzkopf of Gulf War I fame. Once the last round of U.N. inspections was allowed to proceed, however, the reasons to rush to war sounded thinner and tinnier. The regime had indeed been contained. There was little reason not to wait to let the United Nations do its job.

30. Political pundits need not be steeped in history to remember that one of our major policy responses to the Iranian revolution and hostage crisis was to encourage Saddam Hussein in a long war against Iran. In those days, even while he was at his worst, Hussein was hardly seen as the world's most immediate source of evil.

31. The idea of wars between civilizations was popularized by Samuel Huntington, originally in his by now famous article, "Clash of Civilizations?" *Foreign Affairs,* Summer 1993. See our discussion of Huntington in chapter 7, pp. 140–142.

32. Roxanne Euben, *Enemy in the Mirror: Islamic Fundamentalism and the Limits of Modern Rationalism* (Princeton, N.J.: Princeton University Press, 1999).

33. He is particularly interested in the "symbiotic" connection between the countersubversive and the "subversive" and "the sources of that antagonistic connection in American history and in the countersubversive mind." Although he wrote in the 1980s, Rogin's analysis maybe applied to President George W. Bush. Rogin's own work here is on the presidencies of Lincoln, Wilson, Nixon, and Reagan. Michael Rogin, *Ronald Reagan the Movie: And Other Episodes in Political Demonology* (Berkeley and Los Angeles: University of California Press, 1987), xiii–xviii.

34. Christopher Hedges, *War Is a Force That Gives Us Meaning* (New York: Public Affairs, 2002).

NOTES TO CHAPTER 7

1. United Nations Office on Drugs and Crime, Global Illicit Drug Trends 2003 (New York: United Nations Publications, 2003), 15, at http://www.unodc .org/pdf/trends2003_www_E.pdf.

2. Office of National Drug Control Policy, Executive Office of the President of the United States, "Estimated Poppy Cultivation in Afghanistan," News and Public Affairs, at http://whitehousedrugpolicy.gov/news/press04/111904.html.

3. Geov Parrish, "Bush's Sickening Superbowl Propaganda," *AlterNet*, February 4, 2002, at http://www.alternet.org/story12335.

4. Note that the 9/11 Commission recently reported that there was no evidence of Saudi officials channeling money to Al Qaeda. Our claim here regards "private" money.

5. While bin Laden rails against the "Zionist-Crusaders" and lists places throughout the world where he claims Muslims have been brutally victimized, the mass murderer calls his *fatwa* "Declaration of War against the Americans Occupying the Land of the Two Holy Places." See the *Online News Hour* at http://www.pbs.org/newshour/terrorism/international/fatwa_1996.html.

6. Matthew Rothschild, "Mum's the Word," *The Progressive* 66, no. 7 (July 20002): 4.

7. This account is taken from Sebastian Mallaby, "Does Poverty Fuel Terror?" *Washington Post*, May 20, 2002, A21. The study, *Education, Poverty, Violence and Terrorism*, can be found at http://nber.org/papers/w9074.

8. Ibid.

9. In 2004 for the first time in history, a political party held a convention that went into September. And for the first time in its history the Republican Party held a convention in New York.

10. Nicholas Kristof, "Liberal Reality Check," *New York Times*, May 31, 2002, A23.

11. Derrick Z. Jackson, "Misplaced Suspicions in Our 'Crooked Looks,'" *Boston Globe*, May 31, 2002.

12. Deborah Makenzie, "The Insider," *New Scientist*, February 9, 2002.

13. A variation of this view is fully elaborated in William Connolly, *Why I Am Not a Secularist* (Minneapolis: University of Minnesota Press, 1995).

14. Benjamin R. Barber, *Jihad vs. McWorld: Terrorism's Challenge to Democracy* (New York: Ballantine Books, 1995, 2001); Samuel P. Huntington, *The Clash of Civilizations and the Remaking of World Order* (New York: Simon and Schuster, 1996).

15. Barber discusses fundamentalist uses of modern technology and even fashion. *Jihad vs. McWorld*, 17–20.

16. William E. Connolly, *Identity/Difference: Democratic Negotiations of Political Paradox* (Ithaca, N.Y.: Cornell University Press, 1991), 211. In an era

of globalization in which even in repressive countries there are aspects of greater information, often through commercial propagation, this alone can serve the project of dogmatization. This may help explain why terrorists are often not the most deprived in a society.

17. Noam Chomsky, *9-11* (New York: Seven Stories Press, 2001), 31.

18. Richard Falk, *The Great Terror War* (Brooklyn, N.Y.: Olive Branch Press, 2003), 64.

19. Ibid., 71.

20. Ibid., 10.

21. Jean Elshtain, *Just War against Terror: The Burden of American Power in a Violent World* (New York: Basic Books, 2003), 3.

22. Ibid.

23. Ibid., 6–7.

24. Ibid., 188–189.

25. Quoted in Falk, *Great Terror War*, 57.

26. William J. Bennett, *Why We Fight: Moral Clarity and the War on Terrorism* (Washington, D.C.: Regnery, 2003), 7.

27. Ibid., 64.

28. Ibid., 195.

NOTES TO CHAPTER 8

1. Keith Bradsher, "Domination, Submission, and the Chevy Suburban," *New York Times*, March 23, 1997, sec. 4.

2. Juliet Schor, *The Overspent American: Upscaling, Downshifting, and the New Consumer* (New York: Basic Books, 1998).

3. Barry Bluestone and Bennett Harrison, *Growing Prosperity* (Boston: Houghton Mifflin, 1999).

4. Bradsher, p. 2.

5. Schor, *Overspent America*, 97.

6. Ibid., 120.

7. In another work we argue that eco-fundamentalists (like fundamentalist believers in technology or markets) depend on a myth of origin. In the eco-fundamentalist case, we call it a myth of "paradise lost," which comports with what we here call the temptation to resacralize nature. For a general discussion of problems inherent in fundamentalist green stances, see John Buell and Tom De Luca *Sustainable Democracy: Individuality and the Politics of the Environment* (Thousand Oaks, Calif.: Sage Publications, 1996), chaps. 1, 3, 4, 7.

8. See Martin J. Sklar, *The Corporate Reconstruction of U.S. Capitalism, 1890–1916: The Market, the Law, and Politics* (Cambridge: Cambridge University Press, 1988).

9. Andrew Ross, *The Chicago Gangster Theory of Life* (London: Verso, 1994), 32.

10. Jane Bennett, *The Enchantment of Modern Life* (Princeton, N.J.: Princeton University Press, 2001), 100.

11. Ibid., 99–101.

12. William Drury, *Chance and Change: Ecology for Conservationists,* ed. John G. T. Anderson (Berkeley: University of California Press, 1998), 90.

13. Jane Bennett, "Steps toward an Ecology of Matter," *Political Theory,* June 2004, 349.

14. Ibid.

15. Bonnie Honig, *Political Theory and the Displacement of Politics* (Ithaca, N.Y.: Cornell University Press, 1993).

NOTES TO THE CONCLUSION

1. In addition to the actual coverage itself, Fox cable news still reports stories on the Iraq war with a banner on the screen reading "war on terror." Contrast Fox, for example, with the more liberal *New York Times,* which originally helped promote, wittingly or not, the belief that "weapons of mass destruction" existed in Iraq through stories on its news page by Judith Miller but opposed the war in Iraq on its editorial pages. For criticism of Michael Moore's work, see David Aaronovitch, "When Moore Is Less," *Guardian,* November 19, 2003, at http://www.guardian.co.uk/Columnists/Column/0,5673,1088297,00.html.

2. See chapter 4 p. 73 for our index of political equality for the years 1964–2000.

3. For a fuller discussion of these themes, see Tom De Luca, *The Two Faces of Political Apathy* (Philadelphia: Temple University Press, 1995), 236–241.

4. See the discussion of these themes in chapters 2–4.

5. Representative Jesse Jackson, Jr., from Chicago, is involved in a project now to articulate a broad range of rights that does just that.

6. This is the general theme of Theda Skocpol, *The Missing Middle: Working Families and the Future of American Social Policy* (New York: Norton, 2000). See especially 24–32.

7. Theda Skocpol, *Social Policy in the United States: Future Possibilities in Historical Perspective* (Princeton, N.J.: Princeton University Press, 1995), chap. 8.

8. Ibid., 267.

9. The different ways in which racial identities have been inscribed are discussed effectively in Howard Winant, *Racial Conditions* (Minneapolis: University of Minnesota Press, 1992).

10. Kim Moody, *Workers in a Lean World: Unions in the International Economy* (London: Verso, 1997).

11. Thom Kuehls, *Beyond Sovereign Territory* (Minneapolis: University of Minnesota Press, 1996), 127.

12. Several fully elaborated proposals along these lines have appeared in the last few years. Some are discussed in Jeremy Brecher and Timothy Costello, *Global Village or Global Pillage: Economic Reconstruction from the Bottom Up* (Cambridge, Mass.: South End Press, 1998). Another thoughtful treatment of such reforms is Ian Robinson, "Globalization and Democracy," *Dissent,* Summer 1995, 373–380.

13. By war we don't necessarily mean to imply massive global conflict. More likely are periodic disruptions that will nevertheless require the deployment of troops, sometimes under international auspices, and otherwise unnecessarily high levels of military spending.

14. See Iris Marion Young, *Inclusion and Democracy* (New York: Oxford University Press, 2002).

15. In addition, some conceptions of the universal seem more worthy of Young's critique than others. Those forms of universal values, such as the original position in Rawlsian liberalism, seem most likely to exclude while also precluding political contestation. At least in its early formulation, the original position is articulated as being above politics, as taking no political stance and implying no deployment of power.

16. See Wendy Brown, *States of Injury: Power and Freedom in Late Modernity* (Princeton, N.J.: Princeton University Press, 1995).

17. Michael Omi and Howard Winant, *Racial Formation in the United States: From the 1960s to the 1990s,* 2d ed. (New York: Routledge, 1994).

18. Linda Gordon, *Pitied but Not Entitled: Single Mothers and the History of Welfare* (Cambridge, Mass.: Harvard University Press, 1994).

19. See Gayatri Spivak, *The Post-colonial Critic: Interviews, Strategies, Dialogues,* ed. Sarah Harasym (New York: Routledge, 1990).

20. Joanne Barkan, "Symposium: Affirmative Action," *Dissent,* Fall 1995, 463.

21. Joel Olson, "Whiteness and the Participation-Inclusion Dilemma," *Political Theory* 30, no. 3 (June 2002): 384–409.

22. The term "quality of life" has often been used of late by politicians to refer to issues such as begging, prostitution, visible homelessness, and so forth. We use it in the much more global sense we describe in the text. For a broad discussion of this theme, see *The Quality of Life,* ed. Martha Nussbaum and Amartya Sen (Oxford, U.K.: Clarendon Press, 1993).

23. We are *not* suggesting that we can or should be open to everything. Just a greater degree of openness, mostly for our own sakes, to allow us greater understanding.

24. Jean Elshtain, *Democracy on Trial* (New York: Basic Books, 1995).

Index

Abortion, 66, 77; partial-birth abortion, 22
Adams, Jerry, 104
Adorno, Theodor, 13
Affirmative action, 22, 171, 190–191
Afghanistan, 106, 116, 117, 142, 144; Karzai
 government and drugs, 129
AFL-CIO, 41. *See also* Labor
African Americans, demonization of, 91; and
 voting turnout, 72
Air America, 164
Air pollution, environmentalist response, 150
al Zarqawi network, 122
Al Qaeda, 84, 115, 117, 118, 121, 122, 123,
 126, 130, 141, 142, 143, 144, 147
Alger, Horatio, 89
Alien (and Sedition) Acts of 1798, 83
Aliens, civil liberties, and war on terror, 84.
 See also Foreigners
American: attitudes to race-based policies and
 ideals of fairness and justice, 200n. 4; debt
 and economic growth, 204n. 7; de-
 monology, 127; patriotism, 135; political
 culture and foreignness, 99. *See also* Ameri-
 can exceptionalism; Americans; Patriotism
American Association for the Advancement of
 Retired People, 75
American exceptionalism, 78, 96–99
American Legion, 76
Americans: and decline of civic life, 75–77;
 and insularity, 134–135; and international
 influence on, 185; and ontological/psychic
 pressures on, 93–94; and religion, 47,
 93–94; and tolerance, 21, 32–33, 200n. 4,
 201n. 5. *See also* American; American ex-
 ceptionalism; Evolution; Individualism;
 Quality of life
America's moral paradox, 27–28, 47–52, 171,
 178. *See also* Hedonist liberalism, definition
 of; Puritan-Conservatism, definition of
"Another Hitler," 5–6; Adolph Hitler, 126
Anti-Americanism, 145–146
Aquinas, Thomas, 159
Aristotle, 159

Armey, Richard, 83
Augustine, 113
"Axis of Evil," definition and analysis of,
 125–127; President Bush's speech and criti-
 cism of, 119–123. *See also* Bush, George W.;
 Terrorism

Barber, Benjamin, 140–142
Barkan, Joanne, and affirmative action, 191
Bartlett, Dan, 122
Beatty, Warren, 40–43
Beer theology, 48
Bell, Daniel. *See* "Cultural contradictions of
 capitalism"
Bennett, Jane, 159–161; "thing-power materi-
 alism," 160
Bennett, William J., 50, 145–147; and anti-
 Americanism, 145; as culture warrior, 148;
 nonjudgmentalism, dangers of, 146
Bennis, Phyllis, 122
Berry, Halle, 40
bin Laden, Osama, 108, 112, 122, 131, 133,
 134, 141, 217n. 5; *fatwa* of, 130. *See also*
 Al Qaeda
Bluestone, Barry, 153
Bond, Jon R., 65–66
Bork, Robert, 22
Boston Tea Party, 106
Brooks, David, 34–35, 67–68
Brown, Wendy, 188
Bryan, William Jennings, 19
Brzezinski, Zbigniew, 106
Buckley v. Valeo, 168–169
Budweiser. *See* Beer theology
Bulworth (film), 40–43, 202n. 13; and moral
 personae, 40–43
Bunker, Archie, 27
Bush, George H. W., 5–6, 26, 202n. 1, and
 first Gulf War, 5, 123, 125. *See also* "An-
 other Hitler"
Bush, George W., 1, 2, 5–6, 19, 22, 61, 111,
 117–118, 125, 126, 147,165, 181; and
 "axis of evil" speech, 7, 118, 119–123;

Bush, George W. (*Continued*)
and Christian fundamentalism, 117; demonization of, 165; and gay marriage, 92; and GNP, 57; "no child left behind" program, 181; perceptions of, 65; and polarization of America, 1, 65; and privatization of social security, 182; and tax cuts, 57, 181; and terror alerts, 20; and terrorism, 108; and 2002 Super Bowl, 129; and war on terror, 115
Busing, 77

Calvinism, 48–49, 144; and work ethic, 48
Campaign financing, 74, 168–169; "527" organizations, 169
Campbell, Angus, 67
Candidate, The (film), 43
Capitalism, cultural contradictions within, 45
Carter, Jimmy, 34
Catholicism, 140; medieval Catholic thought, 22
Census turnout data, 208–9n. 20
Center for Constitutional Rights, 116
Chang, Nancy, 116–117
Chechnya, 121
Cheney, Richard, 122
China, 116, 121, 123, 182, 215n. 20; and incarceration, 55
Chomsky, Noam, 110, 142, 144; on bin Laden network, 214n. 10
Christ. *See* Jesus
Christianity, 23–24
Citizenship, effective, 175–176
Civic life. *See* Americans
Civic republicanism, 87, 98–99, 171, 211n. 1
Civic virtue, 87, 173
Civil disobedience, 107
Civil rights movements, 76, 172
Civil society, 201n. 12
Civil War pensions, 179
"Clash of civilizations," 140–142
Cleveland, Grover, 19
Clinton, Hillary, 22
Clinton, William, 2, 3, 8, 22, 87, 97; cycle of demonization, 25–27; demonization of, 19; economic record of, 54; impeachment of, 2, 44; and Monica Lewinsky scandal, 8, 20–21, 33; and military actions, 3, 20; personal character of, 2; and sexual harassment charges, 203n.2; social policy of, 55; and welfare reform, 78
Cloward, Richard, 72, 79
CNN, 165
Cobb, John, 59, 60, 61, 63
Coercive diplomacy, 110
Cold war, 41, 103, 118, 215n. 24; New Cold War, 131. *See also* Iran; Khomeini, Ayatollah; Reagan, Ronald
Cole, David, 82

Collins, Chuck, 71
Colombia, 129
Common Cause, 75
Communist Party, 212n. 6
Communitarianism, 24, 87, 211n. 1
Community, 11, 157; and democratic politics, 12; health and safety, 177; and individuality, need for, 12
Concerned Women for America, 75
Connolly, William, 69, 113–115; ontology of resistance, 93–94; ontopolitical extremism, 115. *See also* Evil, first and second problems of
Conrad, Joseph, 126
Conservatives, 61
Constitution, and real political equality, 178. See also *Buckley v. Valeo*; *Johnson v. Bush*; *Korematsu v. United States*; *Lawrence v. Texas*; *McConnell v. Federal Communications Commission*; *San Antonio Independent School District v. Rodriguez*
Consumerism, 28, 56, 150–156, 178; "keeping up with the Joneses," 56, 152
Consumption, 158; positional, 154
Counterculture, in 1960s, 46
Covenant of becoming, 192–195; definition of 192; and political participation, 192–193; and respect for individualism, 194; and teaching respect, 193–194
Creation, public beliefs about, 93
Crenshaw, Martha, 103, 109
Crime, 25
"Cultural contradictions of capitalism," 45–46
Culture war, 39; and drug war, 129–131; and intellectuals, 140–148; from 1960s, 44, 92, 115; and patriotism, 134–137. *See also* War
Culture warrior. *See* Bennett, William J.

Daily Show, The (TV Show), 166
Daly, Herman, 59, 60, 61, 63
Damasio, Antonio, 68–69
Death penalty, 25
Debt, 182
"Democracy Weekend," 168
Democracy without demons, 195, 197
Democratic Party, 19–20, 25–27, 66, 78, 190; and campaign fundraising, 26; and "Clinton Democrats," 25; and "Reagan Democrats," 25, 26
Demonic, definition of, 4–5
Demonization, 4–10, 91, 97, 203n. 1, 213n. 17; abnormalize, in 2004 election, 4–5, alternatives to, 193–197; bipartisan nature of, 2, 19; and certainty, need for, 94–95; as compensatory revenge by dissidents, 133; counterdemonization, 164, 166; definition of, 4–6, 213n. 16; and democratic politics,

About the Authors

TOM DE LUCA is Associate Professor of Political Science and Director of the Interdisciplinary Social Science Program at Fordham University. He is also the author of *The Two Faces of Political Apathy* (Philadelphia: Temple University Press, 1995).

JOHN BUELL is a columnist for the *Bangor Daily News* and a former Professor of Political Science at the College of the Atlantic. He is also a former editor at *The Progressive* and co-author of *The End of Homework: How Homework Disrupts Families, Overburdens Children, and Limits Learning* (Boston: Beacon Press, 2000).

TOM DE LUCA and JOHN BUELL are coauthors of *Sustainable Democracy: Individuality and the Politics of the Environment* (Thousand Oaks, Calif.: Sage Publications, 1996).